Alfred Billings Street

Woods and Waters, or, Summer in the Saranacs

Alfred Billings Street

Woods and Waters, or, Summer in the Saranacs

ISBN/EAN: 9783337140427

Printed in Europe, USA, Canada, Australia, Japan

Cover: Foto ©Andreas Hilbeck / pixelio.de

More available books at **www.hansebooks.com**

WOODS AND WATERS

OR

SUMMER IN THE SARANACS

WITH

TWO ILLUSTRATIONS ON WOOD

DESIGNED BY WILLIAM HART, AND ENGRAVED BY AVERY

By ALFRED B. STREET

AUTHOR OF "POEMS," "FRONTENAC, A NARRATIVE POEM," &C.

NEW YORK
PUBLISHED BY HURD AND HOUGHTON
BOSTON: E. P. DUTTON AND COMPANY
1865

Entered according to Act of Congress, in the year 1860, by
ALFRED B. STREET,
In the Clerk's Office of the District Court of the United States for the Southern District of New York.

CAMBRIDGE: PRINTED BY H. O. HOUGHTON AND COMPANY.

To JOHN A. GRISWOLD,

OF TROY, N. Y.

I dedicate this book to you, as a memento of friendship and of the happy hours we have enjoyed, with the other members of the Saranac Club, in the great wilderness of our native State.

THE AUTHOR.

ALBANY, N. Y., *August 1st,* 1860.

ILLUSTRATIONS.

MOOSE MOUNTAIN,... FRONTISPIECE.
DOE AND FAWNS, ... VIGNETTE TITLE-PAGE.
MOUNT SEWARD,.. PAGE 41

CONTENTS.

	PAGE
INTRODUCTION,	XV

CHAPTER I.
Camp of the Indian Carrying-Place.—The Saranac Club and Guides.—A Bear.—Seeking Deer and finding Musquitoes, ... 1

CHAPTER II.
The Start from Home.—The Yankee's Story of the taking of Ticonderoga.—The Ausable Valley.—The Driver's opinion of Deacon Brown.—Scenery on the road.—A quotation under difficulties.—Harvey Moody.—Scenery at Baker's, ... 13

CHAPTER III.
The Saranac Boats.—The Buckboard.—Harvey kills a Deer.—The Song of Glencoe, ... 25

CHAPTER IV.
The Lower Saranac Lake.—The Eagle.—Mount Tahawus.—The Loon.—The Gull.—Moose Mountain.—Cove Hill.—Mount Seward.—Whiteface, ... 31

CHAPTER V.
Lower Saranac Lake.—A Talk on Trapping.—A Moose Story.—Saranac River.—Moose Mountain.—Middle Falls.—Round Lake.—Umbrella Point.—Bartlett's.—Upper Saranac Lake, ... 43

CONTENTS.

CHAPTER VI.
Sunrise.—Indian Legend.—The Saranac Wizards.—Mode of Carrying the Boats.—The Beaver-Pond Hunt.—The Stony Ponds, ... 55

CHAPTER VII.
Stony Creek.—Origin of the Indian Plume.—The Racket River.—Moose Talk.—Panther Story.—Palmer Brook.—Racket-Falls Camp,.. 69

CHAPTER VIII.
Floating for Deer.—Night Scenery on the Racket.—Owls.—A Camp Scene, ... 82

CHAPTER IX.
Carry at Racket Falls.—Up the Racket.—Cold River.—Bowen's Camp.—Long Lake.—The River Driver.—Harvey's Woods. - Almanac, ... 97

CHAPTER X.
Camp Sketches in a Rain Storm.—Lumbering and River Driving, ... 104

CHAPTER XI.
Camp Sketches—Racket Falls Camp Left.—Down the Racket to Calkins.—An onslaught of Musquitoes upon the Saranac Club.—Mart's imitations, ... 118

CHAPTER XII.
A Rainy Day on the Racket.—Down to Folingsby's Brook.—Folingsby's Pond.—Bingham and the Ducks.—Captain Folingsby, ... 131

CHAPTER XIII.
Down the Racket.—Old Ramrod.—Trout Fishing at Half-Way Brook.—A Water-Maple.—Cloud Pictures.—Woods in the Wind.—The Great Oxbow.—Ramrod's Shanty; and Chase by Indians.—A Talk on Fishing, with the Opinion of the Guides about it.—A Night Scene on the River, ... 148

CHAPTER XIV.
Simon's Pond.—Harvey's Story of Old Sabele, the Indian.—Driving Deer.—The Simon's Pond Pirate.—Tupper's Lake.—Night Sail on Lake, ... 163

CONTENTS. xiii

CHAPTER XV.

Tupper's Lake.—Old Sabele continued.—The Devil's Pulpit.—Its Legend.—A Deer's Leap.—The Camp.—Trout Fishing,............ 177

CHAPTER XVI.

Bingham Kills a Deer in the Lake.—The Indian Park.—Leo, the Indian.—The Loon.—Showers on the Lake.—In Camp,........... 188

CHAPTER XVII.

Thunder-storms.—Lightning Island.—Thoughts at the Indian Pass.—A high Wind.—Captain Bill Snyder.—Night Sail in the Wind.—Cove at the Devil's Pulpit.—Mist on the Water.—Harvey's Indian Story,.. 202

CHAPTER XVIII.

The Sabbath.—Preaching at the Indian Park.—The Pool.—The Sky.—Politics.—The Constitution,..................................... 224

CHAPTER XIX.

Sail up Tupper's Lake.—Jenkins' Clearing.—The Shanty of the Spring.—Bog River Falls.—Head of the Lake.—Up Bog River.—Leo.—Track of the Moose.—Roar of the Moose.—Mud Lake.—Death of the Moose,.. 233

CHAPTER XX.

Back to Tupper's Lake.—Night Sail down the Lake.—The Echo.—Deserted Camp.—Message, woods fashion.—Tupper's Lake left.—Down the Racket.—Indian Camp.—The Water-lily.—Legend of its Origin.—The Mink.—News of the Party.—The Eagle-nest.—Through Racket Pond.—The Island.—The Irish Clearing.—Captain Peter's Rocks.—Camp at Setting-Pole Rapids,................................. 248

CHAPTER XXI.

Fish-Hawk Rapids.—Perciefield Falls.—Death of Sabele.—Beaver Trip agreed upon.—Floating.—The Dark Woods.—The Foot-Tread.—The Indian Jack-Light,.. 267

CHAPTER XXII.

Setting Pole Rapids behind.—Wolf Brook.—Little Wolf and Big Wolf Ponds.—Lumber-Road in the Rain.—Picture Pond.—Beaver Meadow.—Maine Shanty,....................................... 277

CHAPTER XXIII.

Path Résumed.—The Medal.—Musquito Pond.—Rawlins Pond.—Floodwood Pond.—The Sable.—A Network of Ponds.—Long Pond.—The Cranes.—Slang Pond.—Turtle Pond.—Hoel's Pond.—Boat Left.—Through the Woods.—Beaver Meadows.—Beaver Signs.—Beaver Pond.—Beaver Houses.—A Beaver.—The Bivouac................ 285

CHAPTER XXIV.

Return Path.—Clamshell Pond.—Song-birds.—Beaver-dam.—Beaver-talk.—Absence of Serpents.—Hoel's Pond.—Carry:—Green Pond.—UPPER SARANAC.—Eagle.—Water-thatch.—Tommy's Rock.—Goose Island.—Harvey's Opinion of Neighbors.—Phin's Idea of Subordination.—The Loons.—Loon Talk, ... 299

CHAPTER XXV.

Up Fish-Creek Waters.—Old Dam at Floodwood Pond.—Big Square Pond.—Maine Shanty.—Beaver-dam.—Wind on Upper Saranac.—Bear Point.—The Narrows.—Deer in Lake.—Camping on Point.—Moonlight Scene.—Dawn.—Trail in the Woods.—Down Lake to Bartlett's.—Moonlight Sail through Lower Saranac.—Baker's,...... 313

CHAPTER XXVI.

Whiteface.—Approach to Mountain.—Upward.—White Falls.—Chasm.—Little Slide.—Great Slide.—Summit.—Prospect.—Descent.—Baker's.—Backwoods' Dance.—Whiteface Notch.—Homeward 324

INTRODUCTION.

THE wilderness of Northern New York is a plateau ranging from fifteen to eighteen hundred feet above tide. It is one hundred miles in diameter. On the north and east it approaches within thirty or forty miles of the Canada line and Lake Champlain; on the south, within fifteen or twenty miles of the Mohawk River, and on the west, within the same distance of Black River. It embraces nearly the whole of Essex, Warren, and Hamilton Counties, the southwest portion of Clinton, the south half of Franklin, the southeastern third of St. Lawrence, the eastern third of Lewis, and the northern half of Herkimer.

Different portions of it are known under different names. The northern portion is called The Chateaugay Woods; The St. Regis Woods lie next below; then comes the Saranac Region; then that of Racket Lake; to the east extend the Adirondacks; and below, south and southwesterly, are The Lake Pleasant Region, and John Brown's Tract.

The eastern portion of the plateau is exceedingly mountainous. Here lies the Adirondack range, or group, the most northerly in the State, extending in a general northeast direction from Little Falls, on the Mohawk River, to Cape Trembleau at Lake Champlain. This range presents the conical summits cloven into sharp grey peaks peculiar to its hypersthene formation, and attains in some of its peaks nearly the height of one mile—almost the limit of eternal snow.

These peaks are Tahawus or Mount Marcy (which is the central and tallest, 5,400 feet high), Mount McIntyre, Mount St. Anthony (corrupted to Sanantoni), and Mount Colden.

These mountains are generally isolated, sloping somewhat moderately toward the north, but precipitous at the south.

Other summits rise north, south, and west, some equal in height to those named (except Tahawus) and others but little inferior—Dix's Peak, Nipple Top, Blue Mountain, Mount Seward (a cluster of peaks), Cove Hill, Moose Mountain, Mackenzie's Pond Mountain, and Whiteface. The last is the most northern of all the high crests of the wilderness, and hardly inferior in elevation to Tahawus. The region lying around the south base of Mount Seward was called by the Indians Cough-sa-ra-geh or "The Dismal Wilderness."

In the middle portion of the plateau, the mountains are generally rounded, and, like most of those mentioned above, waving from base to top with forest. The western portion is pleasantly varied by hill and plain.

One great valley shaped like a Y crosses the whole plateau in a northeast direction.

It begins at the junction of Moose River with the Black, continues seventy miles to a point six miles south of Upper Saranac Lake, here branching northerly to Potsdam in St. Lawrence County, and northeasterly to Plattsburg on Lake Champlain.

A remarkable chain of lakes and streams extends along this valley and its northeastern branch, linking (with a few carries, and with the exception of twenty miles of rapids on the lower end of Moose River) Lake Champlain, through the Saranac River and Lakes, the Racket River, Long, Forked, Racket Lakes, the Eight Lakes, and Moose and Black Rivers, with Lake Ontario. The River St. Lawrence is linked with this chain, by the Racket River traversing the northern branch of this valley.

The waters of this plateau fall naturally into four groups or systems, the Saranac, the Racket, the John Brown Tract, and Hudson River.

The first system lies mainly in the southern part of Franklin County, and comprises the Saranac River and Lakes, with the network of ponds and streams lying west and north of the Upper Saranac. All these are discharged into Lake Champlain.

The second lies just south, belonging to the south part of Franklin and the north of Hamilton Counties. It includes Racket River through those Counties; Long Lake; the two Forked Lakes; Racket Lake; Blue Mountain Lake (with its two lesser sheets, Eagle and Utowana Lakes, and Marion River), and Big and Little Tupper's Lakes; Blue Mountain Lake being the real source of the Racket River, although Racket Lake is generally so designated. These waters flow into the River St. Lawrence.

The third group includes the Eight Lakes: the Reservoir Lakes and other head waters of Black River, and the Moose and Beaver Rivers its branches. This group lies in the west part of Hamilton, the northern part of Herkimer, and eastern part of Lewis Counties, and its waters flow into Lake Ontario.

The fourth system produces the Hudson River, and occupies a portion of Essex County near the western line, and the east and south portions of Hamilton. It embraces the Upper Hudson, the Sacondaga, and Schroon branches of that river (the latter branch, however, is on the edge of the wilderness), Piseco, Round and Pleasant Lakes, and others. Thus, these sources pouring themselves forth to every point of compass form all the larger rivers of the State—besides those mentioned, the Ausable, the Salmon, the Grass, the St. Regis, the Oswegatchie, and the East and West Canada Creeks emptying into the Mohawk. And thus, upon this great watershed, and within a circuit of ten miles, rise springs whose waters seek the seas of Labrador and the Bay of New York.

The extraordinary arrangement of these sources is illustrated by the fact that the Upper Hudson ripples from the southwest portals of the Indian Pass, and the west branch of the Ausable River which empties into Lake Champlain from the northeast. Preston Ponds, through Cold River, feed the Racket River at the west; Fountain and Catlin Lakes, west of these, supply the Hudson at the east; and the Moose River, flowing southwest, almost twines with the Racket waters running north.

Other waters are scattered over the plateau, but not falling within the above systems: the east and west branches of the Ausable, Lake Placid, at the foot of Whiteface, Cranberry Lake, an enlargement of the Oswegatchie River, and Chateaugay, Ragged, and Chazy Lakes, near the northern edge of the forest.

Rich marbles are found in the plateau; valuable timber and beds of iron ore abound. The last-mentioned, although distributed generally throughout the forest, are found most abundantly in the eastern portion of the plateau, and are as extensive as any in the world. One bed on the Upper Hudson (between Lakes Henderson and Sanford) is worked easily, yields seventy-five per cent. of pure metal, and will produce a steel equal to that of the best Swedish or Russian ores.

The valleys of the eastern portion of the plateau, and the middle and western portions generally, are capable of supplying nearly all the agricultural products native to the State, such as rye, buckwheat, oats, pease, beans, turnips, and potatoes. The soil, however, is especially adapted to grazing. There is but a small quantity of arable land in the mountainous or eastern section; and even this, although strong (shown by its heavy growth of timber) is made less valuable by its low temperature, owing to its elevation and the surrounding mountains.

The soil is a gravelly loam, and is "deep, warm and rich" in many parts of the western division.

The trees are the pine, hemlock, spruce, white cedar, and fir, among the soft or evergreen kinds, and prevail on the lowest grounds and higher slopes and summits of the hills; and among the hard-wood species, the maple, beech, white and black ash, birch and elm on the intermediate surface. On the gentle swells between the lakes maple and beech abound.

The climate is the same as the mountainous portions of New England.

It is needless to enlarge upon the grandeur and picturesque beauty of the whole plateau.

Settlements throughout the plateau, of any extent, there are none. Here and there, on the edges of the wilderness, are clusters of rough habitations, and along the lakes and streams is an occasional log cabin, or hunter's shanty. The summer tent of the sportsman alone, in addition, dots the boundless sweep of forest verdure.

All the wild animals of our northern latitude, the panther, bear, wolf, and wild-cat, are here, with the moose, deer, fisher, sable, otter, mink, and muskrat.

The moose is the rarest of all. Still, not a year passes but one is slain in the deep, dark fastnesses which have now become the animal's haunt.

The eagle, the partridge, the loon, the duck are likewise found; lake trout swarm in the broad waters, and speckled trout in the cold, clear spring-brooks and rapid streams.

Eight or ten years ago, this wilderness hardly contained a hut or shanty, and was rarely invaded by visitors. But of late the number of sportsmen and explorers has gradually but greatly increased. The noble trout, however, are as abundant as ever, as are also the deer. But the latter have grown more timid, and are less certainly found along their once familiar waters. The shout of the loon, too — that symbol of the wildness and loneliness of the scenes haunted by this wildest and loneliest of birds—now rarely meets the ear.*

As suggested, the edges of this enormous wilderness are thinly inhabited by hunters and trappers, who pierce its deepest recesses in their light boats, and act as guides to visitors in summer.

The centre of the plateau comprises the region of the Saranac Lakes, the Racket River from Racket Lake to Perciefield Falls, and a tract around Tupper's Lake. In it are found all the distinctive features of the plateau—broad and beautiful expanses of water; the loveliest river of the forest; the prettiest cascades; one of the highest mountains, commanding the very grandest prospect of all; and, save one, the sublimest gorge. The chief and almost the only home of the moose lies within it; trout swarm in the myriad brooks; and the deer are as plentiful as in any other spot.

Into this centre, then—this wild heart of the wild northern forest—the reader is invited through the following pages.

* For some of the principal routes into the wilderness, see Appendix.

WOODS AND WATERS;

OR,

SUMMER IN THE SARANACS.

CHAPTER I.

Camp of the Indian Carrying-Place.—The Saranac Club and Guides.—A Bear.—Seeking Deer and finding Musquitoes.

SUNSET at the foot of the Upper Saranac! A golden light kindles a little clearing upon the southern border of the glittering lake: one sweep of dark green wilderness covers the remainder of the scene.

A log hut stands in the foreground of the clearing. Behind, on a gentle slope, lies a patch of rye and buckwheat, the rye scarce hiding the charred stumps within it, and the silver blossom of the buckwheat lending bright contrast to the coal-black soil.

Beyond, gleams a broad white space of calcined earth, with dark logs strewing it everywhere. Dead and living trees stand here and there moodily apart. A rough zigzag track leads up the slope, and is lost in the close woods of the background.

Down by the waterside, are two tents. The larger is open in front, displaying a layer of hemlock boughs upon the ground, and over them, blankets of grey, crimson and purple. On the front tent-pole, hang powder-flasks and shot-pouches: against a tall withered pine, lean fishing rods and rifles, while one of its skeleton limbs sustains the red forequarters of a deer. From a stick in a stump, dangles a cluster of dead partridges, their chequered hues warm in the sun-glow. One has fallen, and points with arched neck and hanging wings, as if for attack, at a black and white wood-duck, whose red bill is open to grasp, in appearance, the orange leg of a blue-winged teal, the leg drawn up seemingly from dread. A slanting beam glitters on a pile of trout between a brace of fish baskets, and a score of the same glossy prey, strung upon a birchen twig, lie carelessly on the neighboring moss.

Three hounds, white, with tawny spots, are nosing about, occasionally bending on their haunches to scratch their ears and lick their paws, crouching to stare open-mouthed, through their fore-legs, at the fire and snap the flies, or curling themselves for a nap, to start up again and resume their roamings.

Around a crackling fire of piled logs, four men are busy cooking. One, short but muscular, in a red hunting shirt, watches the roasting of a noble haunch of venison; another, tall and lank, in a shirt of blue, is frying trout in a bob-handled sauce-pan, while a third, with a hare-lip, and in a coarse blue check, is "toasting," on forked sticks, a brace of partridges spread out like fans.

The fourth is a man about fifty, of brawny shape, bronzed skin, an air ever on the alert, and eyes that, gazing at any object, protrude in keen glances. All the fingers of his right hand, except the first, are twisted into the palm, and there is no sign of a thumb, yet the limb is almost as ready as its neighbor.

He wears a purple check shirt, with pantaloons and felt hat, both of an earthen tint, and a woodknife sheathed in a belt of deerskin.

His actions correspond with the quickness of his looks. Now he tries a pair of ducks, roasting on sticks like the partridges; then stirs a layer of frying trout,; then hurries to a large Indian cake, arching and darkening into a rich brown; next turns a tawny wheat pancake, then stands a moment with arms a-kimbo, glancing round the forest and over the lake.

On the stump, a boy of sixteen is dressing a string of trout.

A little removed from the fire, is another group; two sitting on camp-stools, calmly smoking, one standing and loading his rifle, one reeling a fish-line, and one reclining on his elbow, with his shoulder against the pine-tree, gazing upon the scene.

Boats are resting their bows on the brown sandy margin, with their sterns buried in white water-lilies; a heap of dead prone hemlocks is on the left, half-drowned in the rushy water; and a couple of white cedars point horizontally, at the right of the scene, their jagged limbs resting on the bottom of the shallow, so as to lift their stiff, bristling foliage a little from the surface.

The whole picture is soft and rich, as well as wild, steeped as it is in the mellow charm of the deepening sunset.

"Here we are at the Indian Carrying-Place, and only two deer," said the one with the rifle. "That's miserable luck enough. I hope next year we'll find out a wilder hunting-ground; in Maine, for instance, where we can get not only as many deer as we want, but moose, gentlemen, moose!"

"What a restless mortal you are, Bingham," said one of the two on camp-stools, of erect, slender shape and gentlemanly air, and whose sporting garb of coarse grey even had a neat, trim look. "We shall find deer enough, before we're through with our trip; more than you'll shoot, I'll be bound! Harvey," turning to the guide with the maimed hand, "isn't it time for Mart and Will to be back?"

"Scurce yet, Mr. Gaylor," replied the old woodman, "they wont be likely to come afore they've got a deer. Sometimes though, it's mighty quick work gittin' one. Onst me and Phin," glancing at the young man with the hare-lip, "was at Floodwood Pond ketchin' fur. We——"

"Hark!" exclaimed the other of the two on camp-stools,

as a faint sound stole out of the far distance. He was in form and garb much like his companion, and wore an air of decision and careless self-reliance. "Wasn't that the hound, Harvey?"

"Jess so, Mr. Runnin'!" answered the latter. "Watch has sung out twyst afore. This last time, 'twas jess this side o' the Gut. I shouldn't wonder ef the deer takes to the water there. There's a runway at the p'int, isn't there, Corey?"

"There is so," answered the one at the haunch. "One day, the fust week I come to this place, as I was gittin' out the logs for my cabin there," nodding toward the hut, "I heerd my dog Drive—hullo!" as a dull report echoed at the right, where a large island seemingly blocked the lake, with a smaller one in advance. "That gun come from 'twixt Birch and Johnson Islands, and, I think, jest at the runway."

"That's Will's rifle, and we'll see the boat soon," said Harvey, shading his eyes, and gazing in the direction of the islands. "By goll, I thought I see 't then, but I didn't. 'Twas unly a loon making a flash. Besides, 'tisn't time yit."

"And why the deuce isn't it time!" broke in Bingham. "Are we to wait here all night, after hearing the gun, before Mart and Will come, and then it may be without the deer? When the hound speaks, the occasion demands, as old Webster says, prompt action; in other words, that I should be there; eh, gentlemen?"

"There it is again!" said the one on the camp-stool, who had called attention to the cry of the hound. "Bing, you do keep up such a horrible noise about your shooting qualities that——"

"And who has a better right, I should like to know, Ralph Renning?" returned the other loudly, bringing down his rifle with a thump. "I only wish I had gone with Mart and Will, I would have shown you what shooting qualities are, that is, if Watch drives a deer, eh, Cort?"

'Jess so, Mr. Bingham," answered the one at the fire,

with the blue hunting shirt; "and talkin' o' deer, I kin take ye to a place after supper, not fur from here nuther, where you'll hev a shot at a deer in no time 't all, and mebby two or three on 'm."

"Hurrah! let us be going immediately," said the other, shouldering his rifle and moving off almost on a run. "Good-bye, gentlemen, I'll show you what shooting is! Come, Cort, what are you waiting for? Which is the way?" pausing over a prostrate log, with his legs astride, and throwing back an impatient look.

"Hadn't you better get your supper first, Bing?" said Gaylor.

"Not when a deer is in question," answered Bingham, "or two or three, as Cort says. For my part, I think we shall find half a dozen. Cort, why don't you come?"

"Because Cort is engaged," said Renning. "I, as one member of the Club, object to his coming or going anywhere till supper is ready."

"Umph!" returned Bingham. "Well, if Cort can't come, Cort can tell me where to go, I suppose!"

"It's over to the last o' them three p'ints back o' Green Island and right agin' Fanny Island," said Cort, launching his arm, without looking, towards the large left-hand island which, with Birch Island, closed the water prospect.

"Hurrah! Smith, if you can leave your tree there, and Coburn can stop fiddling at his fish-line, we three 'll take the boat over to the point," exclaimed Bingham. "I'll show you how to shoot a deer—eh, what's that in the water there?"

"A bear, by golly!" exclaimed Harvey, seizing a rifle and hurrying towards one of the boats. "He's makin' torts Green Island!"

"A bear!" echoed Corey, leaving his venison and snatching also a rifle.

"A bear!" shouted Gaylor, Renning and Coburn, the two first overturning their camp-stools, and the last throwing down his rod, and all springing to their weapons.

"A bear!" yelled Bingham, plying his long legs in marvellous strides towards the water. "Hurrah, you Cort, don't be all day in getting the boat ready! Bears don't wait for people, a bit more than bucks. Only get me near enough, and if I don't plump that bear right through the head, or some other place, I'm a 'souced gurnet,' as old Falstaff says," and he tumbled into the boat, almost upsetting the light, buoyant thing.

In a few minutes, we all came up with the dark monster, who glanced round upon us his little, wicked, black eyes snapping with fury. Cort, in the excitement of the moment, urged on by Bingham, struck his boat against a sunken log, in line with the beast, who was by this time but a few feet from Green Island. Bingham was standing at the bow, looking as wild as a muskrat in a trap. His rifle was at his cheek as the boat struck, but fate was against the enthusiastic sportsman. Unprepared for the shock, over he toppled, upon a plat of marshy grass, just as he was about to fire. He fell upon his knees and one hand; fortunately, the rifle did not go off in the fall.

The bear, meanwhile, with his glittering tusks clicking like gunlocks, and jaws dripping with foam, had made his way to the bank of the island. As he leaped upwards, a mingled sound from several rifles echoed, and his black carcass seemed to wither down among the bushes.

"Good evenin', sir!" shouted Harvey, as he landed. "'hope you like bullet feed! As for myself, I al'ys take whiskey. Here, Phin! (who had come along in his boat), you kin carry the bear back to camp. This, Mr. Smith, is what I call rael old hunderd."

In a few minutes, we had all returned.

The sun had now sunk, and in the golden transparency of the first twilight, every object, from the leafy outline of the parallel shores to the minute tracery of the watergrasses, was pencilled more clear and sharp than even at noontide. The white lily blossoms looked like tiny cones of silver resting among their broad, heart-shaped leaves; for, like the birds, they fold themselves to slumber at the setting of the sun.

The clouds burn in vivid hues, the woods are golden brown, and the water seems as if a mine of varied jewels had there turned liquid.

Wrapt in the beauty of the scene, the Saranac Club hear an important call twice given before they heed it. It is "Supper! gentlemen!" in the voice of Corey, cook and camp-master to the club.

Just without the large tent, a table of forked poles has been thrown up, laid with bright, sweet flakes of spruce bark, and on it, smoke our wildwood viands.

Banquets in palaces! what are they, to the feast before us rovers of the greenwood, with the peerless scene in front and the radiant roof above!

The minutes do not vanish more rapidly than the fragrant spoils of stream and forest, prepared by the simple skill of our guides, who, with vigilant eye to our every want, wait upon us.

At length we fall back and the guides advance in turn. What heaps of crackling trout, what flakes of crusted venison, disappear! If there is an object in nature more voracious than a Saranac guide, I have yet to know it.

Suddenly Harvey rises with "There comes the boat! jest this side o' Johnson Island!"

A dark spot is relieved on the water in front of the smaller island in advance, at our right.

"They row so smart, I shouldn't wonder ef they'd got a deer," continued the old guide.

"Deer are not so plenty in this region, that you can imagine all that row fast have them," said Bingham, a little querulously.

Several minutes of silence followed.

"I bleeve I see the horns of a buck over the sides of the boat!" exclaimed Harvey, screwing down his right eye.

"Pho, pho! a couple of dry sticks!" said Bingham.

"Mart and Will feel well!" said Corey. "They're

tunin' their pipes like a couple of bullfrogs," as a hoarse strain swept across the water.

"Hev you got a deer?" cried Harvey, at length.

"Yes, and one more on top on't," answered a tall, powerful man, paddling at the stern, in a red hunting shirt, and leather belt with the usual wood-knife.

"Two deer did you say, Mart?" exclaimed Bingham, rushing to the water's edge.

"Shouldn't wonder!" said the one at the oars, in a pink-striped shirt and with the frame of a Hercules.

"Why, Will, where on earth did you come across such luck?" asked Bingham, excited as if some extraordinary event had happened.

"Oh, on the p'int, jest agin Birch Island, that is, one on 'em. The other we got—that is, the fust one, 'long in the Gut, nigh the carry to Bartlett's," answered Will, drawling his words in a slight nasal accent.

"Come, Cort, hurrah! now's the time for our deer! Come, Smith, 'can't wait a moment!" said Bingham, striding into his boat so as almost again to upset it, followed, as it righted, by myself.

"Take the stern, Smith! give us a shove off, Harvey! If I don't have one deer before it's dark," grasping the oars, "I'm a donkey!" giving them an enormous sweep.

"Don't go without me, Mr. Bingham!" exclaimed Cort, hurrying to the margin; "you can't find the spot without me!"

"Sure enough! I forgot all about you, Cort!" said Bingham, backing up. "But when we're in such a country for deer as this is, a man must be wide awake. Now, Cort, make her spin!"

Cort entered the boat and took the oars, while Bingham seated himself at the bow, fronting it.

"You show me a deer," continued the latter, examining the cap of his rifle, "or even a piece of one not bigger than the eye, and if I don't put a ball straight to the mark, call me a spooney, that's all!"

We were soon gliding round the first point. "We mus'n't make no noise now," whispered Cort, "we may come on a deer, the very fust thing."

Bingham raised his rifle from his lap, in readiness.

We turned the point. No living thing disturbed the solitude of the cove, except a black duck, which burst from the water and darted over Green Island to our right.

Bingham aimed.

"You'll skeer all the deer, ef you shoot!" said Cort eagerly.

"True!" returned Bingham, lowering his piece. "I didn't mean to shoot; at least I don't think I did, only the duck rose so sudden. But, hurrah, Cort! let's see what's behind the second point."

We rounded this with no better fortune. The broad surface of lily-pads lay unbroken; not a living shape was seen among the foliage of the banks.

"Where have all the deer gone to, Cort!" said Bingham, in a snappish whisper.

"I dunno!" answered honest Cort. "They ought to be here, by good rights. But less see what's round t'other p'int."

We did see: sleepy trees and lazy lily-pads and—nothing else.

Bingham began to fidget.

"We'll land here, ef you say so," continued Cort, "and I'll go back in the woods a leetle. We'll hev a deer yit!" cheerfully.

"I'll have one if I stay all night," said Bingham resolutely, as Cort brought the boat up to a dead tree jutting into the water and buried in moosehead-plants and rushes.

A few steps over this rounded bridge landed us on a strip of black mould, stamped into hieroglyphics with the sharp delicate prints of deer, many quite fresh; and crossing, we entered a little glade, shadowed by tall alders.

"I shan't be gone long, it's gittin' so late," said Cort, following a line of tracks leading from the glade up into the woods.

"I'm in no hurry," returned Bingham, seating himself on a log, "I'd as lief stay here till pitch dark, that is, as long as I could see to shoot at all. Now, Smith, isn't it pleasant here?"

The first grey which succeeds the gold after sun-setting, now trembled in the air. The colors of the water had lost their brilliancy; a soft sheen like the tints of the wood-pigeon's neck, had followed.

As I gazed, I felt some sensations more decided than pleasant. Still I said nothing.

"How our friends will open their eyes when we bring a buck home, this evening!" said Bingham, after (for him) an extraordinary pause of silence. "We'll have a good time around the camp-fire, eh (with a slap on his cheek), Smith!"

"Yes, when we bring the buck!"

"When we bring! why, of course (another slap), confound the musquitoes! we shall bring—(threshing his arms wildly about) let me get a sight of one, that's all! it 'll be good bite—night I mean to Mar—whew! why the air is full of the devils! I say, Smith, do the musquitoes trouble you so? I do wish the deer would come along! aha, wouldn't—I killed two this time! (scraping his cheek, with an emphasis.) What confounded little rascals they are! They come (jumping up, breaking off a branch hastily and whipping the air fiercely) not in companies, but in battalions, regiments, divisions, whole armies, tribes, nations; whizz, fizz, sizz, heavens! I shall go crazy! I hear them, I see them, the Lord knows I feel them—yes I fairly taste them! There's two in my mouth, three in each ear, and hang me! if there isn't one up my nose! I'm off!" and he moved towards the boat.

"But the deer, Bing, the deer!"

"Hang the deer! I couldn't shoot one, if he came. One might as well try to shoot with St. Vitus's Dance! You may stay if you choose, but I'm off! or stop though! Have you matches? we'll make a smudge!"

"Not a stick!" feeling in my pockets.

"Oh, of course not! nobody has anything when it's wanted! Cort, where are you? (yelling at the top of his voice). Come back here and make a smudge! I never saw the flies so thick, since the Lord made me!"

"But the deer!"

"Hang the deer, I say! let's get rid of the flies! I wouldn't stay in this place five minutes longer, without a smudge, for all the deer at the Saranacs!"

Just then, Cort made his appearance.

"I followed the tracks to a stream jest back o' here," said he, "and there I lost 'm and was lookin' round fur more, when I heerd you sing out, Mr. Bingham! Did you say you wanted a smudge?"

"There's nothing on earth I do want but that. I'd go back to camp quicker than lightning, if Renning and Gaylor wouldn't crack their jokes on me for a week. But hurry up the smudge, for conscience' sake!"

Cort left and returned in a moment, with a piece of damp wood.

"The flies is a leetle thick," said he, in his usual drawling way. "I dont keer for the skeeters so much," tearing off strips of mouldy bark from the old log where we were seated, making a pile, with the wood and several green hemlock boughs, and lighting it with matches and a few dry splinters. "It's these leetle midgets that bite so bad. I remember one night, on the Racket—there!" as the smoke streamed up. "You wont be troubled long with the critters now; they hate smoke as an owl does daylight."

"Ah, this is comfortable!" said Bingham, bending over the smudge till his visage looked as blear as one of the witches in Macbeth. "Yes, the flies are all gone, Corty, and now bring on your deer!"

But the deer would not be brought. So, after waiting an hour, we returned to the camp.

The gray of the twilight was now yielding to the darkness of the night. The shores and islands grew gloomy and mysterious, and the water soon was one expanse of starry purple. Comrades and guides had retired to the tents. Nothing disturbed the quiet of the summer night. The solitude was intense. The silence filled my heart. God seemed near in the solemn heavens. Far away was the world, with all its darkening sorrows and corroding cares. Here, I thought, would I abide and forget that world, that torturing, maddening world—here, close to the heart of Nature. The solitude would teach me peace, the quiet would yield me rest. Here would I abide, where the wilderness sweeps as sweeps the boundless sea. Sin blights not; pride, hatred, envy and ambition never enter. Here, the soul, mingling with Nature, would soar towards God. May Man, then, never pollute this realm with his breath, may he never plant his foul heel on its bosom of beauty! Free may its forests wave, teaching their stern, pure lessons of self-denial, self-reliance, endurance and courage; of the religion which dwells with Nature, where the bared soul

"Like Moses, shall espy,
Even in a bush, the radiant Deity!"

CHAPTER II.

The start from home.—The Yankee's story of the taking of Ticonderoga.—The Ausable Valley.—The driver's opinion of Deacon Brown.—Scenery on the road.—A quotation under difficulties.—Harvey Moody.—Scenery at Baker's.

How came we at the Indian Carrying-Place, in the wild forests of the Upper Saranac?

One day toward the last of July, I was debating whither I should go, to escape the heat. Now, the forest sang in the breezy tone of the pine, "Come!" Then the delicious rumble of the sea beach murmured, "Come!" and then the blended voices of some rural valley, the tinkle of sheep-bells, the rustle of wheatfields and the clinking of scythes uttered, "Come!" in most persuasive music.

"Where shall I go?"

"What do you mean?"

The voice was most familiar; I looked up and there was Ralph Renning, a fellow-townsman and a lawyer of eminence, who had just entered.

"I mean, where shall I go, to escape this dreadful weather?"

"Go? Why to the Saranac Lakes and Racket. Join our Saranac Club; Gaylor, Coburn, Bingham and myself. We start, to-morrow afternoon."

"Enough!" as a vision of that noble region of lake, stream and forest, of which I had heard so much from my friend, glowed before me. "But stay, what must I take for the trip?"

"Well, rifle, rod, powder, shot, hooks and lines, of course. Then a warm, wide blanket, to sleep in; a felt hat; your winter clothing and overcoat. Better take a flannel hunting-shirt, too. Then for the rain, take an india-rubber coat. Get a pair of large thick boots, reaching to the knee. As for stores, you will find them at Baker's, where we put up, before going into the woods. But I only dropped in to see how you were; so good bye, and be at the Northern Depot at five."

Accordingly, the next day, Renning, Coburn (Renning's partner) and myself left Albany in the cars, for Whitehall. At a neighboring station, we were joined by Gaylor and Bingham, the former a wealthy banker, and the latter a prominent lawyer; and the Saranac Club was fully mustered.

The beautiful evening saw us sailing down Lake Champlain in one of the fine steamers of its waters. All was sweet and peaceful; the boat skimmed rapidly over the star-dotted lake, and the night deepened in lovely quiet.

At midnight, we reached the ruined fortress of Ticonderoga. Darkly in view rose Mount Defiance, and my thoughts recurred to that July night, eighty years ago, when the columns of Burgoyne tore upward to the summit.

A slight movement attracted my attention to a form near me, looking earnestly at the hill.

"Ah," thought I, "here is one with whom I can interchange sentiments."

Apparently the figure thought so too, for it turned to me with

"Ahem!—I say—Mister!"

"Good evening, sir!" I replied, in my blandest manner, but not exactly liking his mode of salutation.

"Good evenin' ter yeu. But I say, there must be a tarnal heap o' snakes up on that aire hill!"

"Ah!" responded I, quite crestfallen, and observing the speaker more closely by the deck-lamps.

He was a tall, lank genius, with a hat like a saucepan and a mouth like a cat-fish. His vest was of immense black and white stripes, across which ran a steel watch-chain like a ship's cable.

"Yaas," continued he, with a nasal drawl, "I kinder consate so, from the looks on't and what I've heern tell. But I say!"

"Well!"

"Them black things up there's old Ty."

"Ah?"

"Yaas. I've heern my old grand'ther tell all abaout the time that tarnal critter Allen tuk the fort. Grandpop got it from grandmom, who got it from old Aunty Strides, as we used to call her, who got it from Miss Fellows, who al'ays said she heerd it straight from Miss Bunker, the wife o' one o' Allen's men. All these ere old wimming-folks lived in the place where I was raised, up on Connecticut River. Waal, as I was a sayin', grand'ther used to tell that when old Allen, with his Green Mounting b'ys, got up to the fort, there wasn't nobody nowhere's araound, no haow it could be fixed. 'Twas very airly in the mornin'. Allen, whilse the b'ys was a goin' one way inter the fort, went t'other, right smack up to the door where the Cap'n who was boss o' the whull consarn; Cap'n—let's me see—what war his name! he war a married man, teu. Waal, I dunno as I kin call his name naow; but 'twas where he done his sleepin'. Old Allen gin teu or mebby three smart bangs at the door, with the handle of his seword. Now, yer must kneow that though Allen war a tough old critter, yit when he war a mind teu, he could be as per-lite as a dancin' master.

"'Up with yer here!' says he, 'yeu tarnation lazy critter, and s'render, or I'll give the whull consarn to Old Sanko!'

"The door whips open quicker nor lightnin', and there stands the Cap'n, and who should be there but his woman teu, in her night-cap!

"Old Allen tuk his cap off with one hand and riz his seword with t'other.

"S'ze to the Cap'n, s'ze—but stop though—fust s'ze 'Haow air yer?' s'ze, 'haow d'yer come on?'

"'I'm all right!' says the Cap'n, for yer knows them

French fellers is jeest as per-lite and gin-teel as kin be. 'Haow de yeu come on?' s'ze.

"'Oh, stiddy by jerks,' says old Allen, 'but' s'ze—stop though, fust, s'ze, smilin' kinder to the woman, s'ze, 'I ax yer pairdon, mom,' in the per-litest way'" (here the fellow swung his leg up in a boorish bow) "'but,' s'ze, puttin' on a farse look at the Cap'n, s'ze, 'ye must s'render,' s'ze, 'but ye musn't be afeard, mom,' s'ze, fust-rate gin-teel agin, 'we don't make no war on the wimming-folks,' s'ze; 'but,' s'ze, to the Cap'n, farse agin, s'ze, 'ye must s'render!'

"'In whose name?' says the Cap'n, who but he? as peart as a crow on a tree-top.

"'In the name,' s'ze, 'of the Great Jehovy,' s'ze, 'and the Cont'nental Con-gress,' s'ze, by hokey! an' he got the fort, an' I'll be dod durned (slapping his thigh) ef he lost a single man!"

On the strength of this very reliable account of Ethan Allen's noble capture of Ticonderoga, I retired, with my comrades, to rest.

At daybreak, we were at Port Kent, where, with the morning star blazing on the water, we landed.

Up the long winding hill we creaked in the post-coach, toward Keeseville, four miles distant, passing trees all wrenched in one direction—signs of a past tornado. Suddenly, close by the road, a chasm opened, of sheer precipices and jutting crags, with leaning trees, and foam flashing through the downward gloom, while a low thunder rumbled upon the ear. It was one of the famous chasms of the Ausable Falls—a wild picture, shaded, as it was, by the morning mist that deepened the spectral lights and frowning shadows.

We breakfasted at the pretty and thriving village of Keeseville, on trout and venison (earnest of the region before us), and then started, in a public conveyance, for Baker's Lake House, two miles this side of the Lower Saranac Lake and forty-six from Keeseville.

The glow of a bright summer's morning was kindling the

landscape as we launched upon our planked road, which struck off southeasterly.

At our left, lay the beautiful Ausable valley, sloping up to wooded hills, showing points of wood in grassy bays; meadows with the hay-wagon loading; fields with cattle by the stream or under shades; large barns nearly drowned in lakes of yellow grain; and orchards of apple-trees contorted as by some vegetable spasm, with the small, red farm-house blinking through the branches.

In the centre of the scene was the Ausable river, flowing to Lake Champlain, in bends and reaches, rifts and stilly nooks, with tree and rock photographed upon it.

In front, was a streak of mountain pinnacles on the summer haze, giants of the enchanted realm we were to visit. Chief among them, pointed out by one of my comrades, was Whiteface.

We passed the little village of Clintonville and were now bowling toward the larger village of Ausable Forks, along a level, fringed on the left by trees, where the wild grape twined in lower bowers of foliage, through which glanced the scenery of the river.

"Hullo, Bill!" said our driver, to the Jehu of an advancing wagon, which a sudden turn in the road disclosed, "is that you? What's the news at the Forks?"

"Bad news enough!" answered Jehu, "the Morgan hoss is dead!"

"Dead!" exclaimed the other, pulling up suddenly and catching his breath, while his jaw fell, "the Morgan hoss dead? you don't say so! Gaul hang! that's bad news, sure enough! He was a feelin' tip-top, t'other day! When did he die, and what of?"

"He died, this mornin'. Nobody knows what of! He hadn't been ailin' more'n a few hours. Yes, he's gone!"

"Well, I swan! I should think the whull village 'ud be in mournin'. The Morgan hoss dead! Well, what kin be next! But it can't be helped, ef we mourned here all day! So good-bye, Bill! I s'pose there's nothin' else stirrin'!"

"No! good bye! git up there! but stop though, there is a leetle suthin' else! Deacon Brown's dead!"

"Whew, is he? But unly think, the Morgan hoss dead! Who'd a thought it! sich a stepper too! Well (sighing), good-bye, Bill!" and the worthies parted.

As we proceeded, bends of brooks and roads, breadths of rippling rye, white houses in green courtyards, and an occasional tavern, thrusting its gallows-shaped sign and large horse-trough into the traveller's eyes, met our glances.

From the Ausable Forks (where the east and west branches of the Ausable river unite), the country grew wilder. The wilderness stood close to the road, or left stony lots and black stumps transparent in thin grain. Forest summits with gray cliffs looked down, and barren slopes stretched away, with pines stripped nearly to the top, seeming, on the horizon, as if they might scud off.

We passed Black Brook, funereal with its furnace smoke: lines of dark charcoal arks drawn by mules and driven by glaring goblins; board-roofed mud hovels for charcoal burning, puffing black smoke from their loop-holed sides, with the huts of the charcoal burners crouching by in stumpy patches.

At Franklin Falls (where the plank road ends), we first encountered the Saranac river. This beautiful stream, flowing successively from the Upper, Round and Lower Saranac Lakes, unites after a score and a half of leagues, with Lake Champlain at Plattsburgh.

We dined at the tavern, which, with the red store opposite, had found miraculously one spot free from rocks, on which to rear itself; and again we started. Still wilder grew the scenery. The close forest thrust out the sharp ends of logs cut asunder for the track, and shaped a groined roof above. Corduroy bridges spanning the frequent marshes; fireslashes, one chaos of charred logs and stumps; wild pastures of fern and bramble, burying prostrate trunks; tumble-down log huts and new cabins in fresh-cleared lots, with patches of potatoes, rye and buckwheat, showed themselves at every turn.

The summits, sketched upon the morning mist, now stood boldly forth, mountains of purple.

Old King Whiteface towered loftier than ever, and I registered a vow to dare his summit, at some future period of my trip.

Suddenly, a pool near by was wrinkled as with a myriad waterflies; a humming in the woods began and soon a sunshower sparkled in the air. It melted in a few minutes, and then, almost without warning, a rain dashed upon us. We donned our india-rubbers, but supposing it a passing shower, agreed that it varied pleasantly the long ride, while Renning remarked it was a good breaking-in for the woods.

A half hour dragged along, and the fierce rain still streamed.

"I wish this breaking-in of yours, Renning, would break up," said Coburn, at length, querulously.

Renning said nothing.

At last the rain ceased, and soon the only reminder of it was a mist which Whiteface sent up; the old Sachem, smoking his calumet, on the return of peace.

Beyond the hamlet of Bloomingdale, we again encountered the Saranac river, lost as soon as seen, at Franklin Falls. Here it was gliding eastward, full of sylvan beauty.

A few miles farther and we encountered a corduroy road; logs laid across the track, at a swampy portion.

Bingham's tongue, ever since the rain, had been on a gallop. He was fond of quoting from his favorite authors and, as we struck the road, had fallen on Daniel Webster.

"I tell you what, gentlemen, this is great! 'Europe,' says the grand old fellow, 'within the same period, has been agitated by a mighty'—bump, bump, bump, all the time these logs are awful—'revolution, which, while it has been felt,' ugh! what a cadunk!—'in the individual'—it's out of the question, gentlemen, I can't talk—'condition'"—

(here we came to the most horrible piece of corduroy I ever saw, its huge logs lying or rather weltering, in a soil that shook like a jelly), "'and hap-pap-pap-iness of almum-mum-most every man has sha-sha-shaken to the cen-centre the po-po-po-litical fabric'—look out for that log! driver, can't you? it'll roll over as sure as a gun—'and d-d-d'—deuce take it—'dashed against one another thrones whoo-whoo-which had s-s-s-stood tr-tranquil for ages!'—thank heaven! boys, we're over that corduroy!"

The gold tangle of sunset glittered in the forests, the damp air was full of fragrance, and the Saranac river gave flash after flash, inviting us on, as we came in sight of the Lake House. A sharp turn to the left, the trample of our horses' hoofs over a little bridge, a slight ascent, and we were at Baker's.

"Now we've come," said Renning, after we had made ourselves comfortable in the little parlor of the inn, "the first question is, Where shall we go?"

"What think you of the Upper Saranac, or the St. Regis region?" suggested Gaylor.

"I should think Rawlins' and Floodwood Ponds and all that chain of waters west of the Upper Saranac would give us good hunting, if not fishing," said Bingham.

"I've a notion that a trip up the Racket to the falls, then down to our old camping spot on Tupper's Lake, would be pleasant, beside the fishing we should have," remarked Renning. "But suppose we send for Harvey Moody. I hear his voice pretty loud, in the bar-room; he will give us some good advice."

In a few moments, Harvey made his appearance. He was the oldest of several brothers, all living in that vicinity and nearly all guides; was the father of four or five sons, each a guide, and was an experienced one himself. He had been brought by his father to the region when a child, had always lived in it since, and, of course, was perfectly familiar with its localities.

He was dressed in the sober colors I found it his custom

to wear; thus blending himself with the natural hues of his haunts, so as not to startle his game—the hues of the oozy shore, where he set his mink-trap; of the bark of the runway trees, where he lurked for the deer; the log at the pool, where he stole to lure the trout; the sand-banks and gravel-beds of the stream, where he prowled for the otter; and the dawn and evening greys of the shallows, where he pried to waylay the fisher and the muskrat.

"Harvey!" said Ralph, after that worthy had paid his respects and expressed his joy at again seeing the four with whom he was acquainted, "we are considering where we shall go; whether to the Upper Saranac, to Rawlins' Pond, or to Racket Falls and then down to Tupper's Lake. What do you think?"

"Well, Mr. Runnin'!" answered Harvey, in his somewhat cracked voice, "as for Upper S'nac, I don't say there ain't as likely places in the world, but I do say there ain't no likelier. I——"

"But how about the fishing there, Harvey?" interrupted Ralph, who would not have cared if the waters of Paradise shone over the next ridge, were no trout to be found there.

"Well!" said Harvey, "I al'ays tell jest as 'tis. As fur the fishin,' 'tain't nothin' wuth speakin' on; but the huntin' is rael old hunderd. One day, 'twas jest about sundown, I and my son Will shot three bucks at Black Pond outlet, above Markham P'int, in less 'n no time. In the evenin', and 'twas a parfect inkstand of an evenin', too, as black as my dog Watch's mouth, we went floatin' for deer, and jest where a cat-tail p'int jets out from a cedar swamp above the Narrers, we come upon the goll darndest big buck——"

"That's the place!" said Bingham, with his eyes bulging out like a hooked trout's (he was a keen hunter, but cared little for fishing) and starting to his feet.

"Hold on!" said Renning, "don't go there to-night, Bing! We have time enough before us. You forget Rawlins' Pond and the waters along there! What do you think of that region, Harvey?"

"Well," answered Harvey, "Rawlins' is a rael tip-top place for huntin', too. You kin a'most al'ays kill a ven'son there. But the fishin' there ain't of no 'count, that is, when we talk about the Racket and Tupper's Lake; that is, there's good sport ketchin' whitefish at the old dam in the outlet o' Floodwood, which is next door to Rawlins, but you can't ketch 'em this time o' year, nohow. It's only in October. Still, ef you want to go to Rawl——"

"What do you think as to Racket Falls, before we go to the old spot, Tupper's Lake?" said Renning.

"Fust best!" returned Harvey, slapping his knee; "you can't git no better place than Racket Falls and all above there and then all the way down to Tupper's Lake. You know, Mr. Runnin' and Mr. Gaylor and Mr. Bingham and you, too, Mr. Coburn, all about the Racket, down from Stony Brook to Tupper's; but Racket Falls and them places up there, I bleeve you've never been to. Well, now, as fur fishin', you won't hev much till you git to Palmer's Brook—then there's the Falls—then Cold Brook —then Cold River. As for that Cold River, you may bleeve there's trout there, and some on 'em full grown, too. And as for huntin', Mr. Bingham, the deer's around, up about them slews. It's rael inkstand there with 'em. There's Stony Slew and Loon Slew and Moose Slew," counting on his fingers, "below the Falls, and Moose Creek, above. Ef there ain't the places fur night huntin', then there ain't none; and ef you, Mr. Bingham, could git only two or three of them big bucks I've seen at Moose Slew alone, you might hold up your head like a school-mam. It's all sorts of a nice place, I——"

"Suppose we say Racket Falls, and then down the Racket to Tupper's Lake!" said Bingham, transported by Harvey's suggestions of night-hunting.

"Agreed!" said we all, and the thing was settled.

Obeying now a summons from our host, whose portly form appeared at the parlor door, we ranged ourselves at the supper-table, which was abundantly supplied with the two staple luxuries of the woods, trout and venison. Piles of the delicious fish, browned and diffusing a most appetising fragrance, filled the space between a venison steak and an immense boiled lake-trout, lapped in golden cream. The tea and coffee also mantled in cream, whose rich clots looked like bits of golden ingots, while the white, crumbling biscuits almost melted on the tongue.

In answer to our queries, our host informed us that the trout (except the large one caught in the Lower Saranac) came from Rogers' Brook, and the venison from Colby Pond, both in the vicinity.

After supper, we strolled out in the twilight, to enjoy our surroundings. The Lake House was a low building, of two stories, partly white and partly in the wood's natural weather-stained hues, with a projecting gable. A white fence inclosed a little grassy courtyard. The borders of this space had once been devoted to flowers, but all traces were now being fast hidden by the grass. The Saranac river wound from the forests at the west (although its general course was from the south), and, broken into a small rapid, flowed northeasterly a short distance from the inn. A little wooden bridge spanned the rapid.

Rough upland fields, but lately wrested from the forest, lay around. The narrow river-flat northeast, however, was smooth in grass. Several buildings were scattered along the Keeseville road, with one or two not yet finished.

The Lake House was at the intersection of two roads; the Keeseville, which swept round at the foot of the building and wound to the Lower Saranac Lake; and the Elizabethtown, which ran hence to a village of that name and to Westport on Lake Champlain.

In the rear, or east of the tavern, a wild summit, known as Baker's Peak, heaved its dark, leafy cone against the sky. Mackenzie's Pond Mountain, cloven into two points like the antlers of a deer, printed the horizon next in that quarter, with other crests surging away to the south and east.

An irregular line of the wild forest was traced around the whole horizon.

The scene was enchanting with the soft semi-light, the rose-leaf clouds, the crimson west, the darkening fields, the blackening woods and the purpling mountains. Blended with the dreamy twitter from the shadowy trees, were the rush of the rapids and the distant cry of a huge bird—the black eagle of the woods—winging his stately way high overhead, toward the Lower Saranac.

We ascended the acclivity of the Elizabethtown road and made our way to the right, up a green hill, where was a flag-staff. The timid stars were stealing into the heavens. Deepest quiet prevailed, broken only by an occasional bay from a hound, at the cabin of Moody below.

My comrades descended the hill, but I lingered behind. I lingered and gazed and dreamed. The scene was so soothing, the tranquillity so holy! Nature seemed with folded hands to pray.

CHAPTER III.

The Saranac Boats.—The Buckboard.—Harvey Kills a Deer.—The Song of Glencoe.

WHEN I descended from my room, the next morning, day had just planted his golden sandals on the summit of Baker's Peak. The sky was a lapis lazuli; the atmosphere bland and cool. Early as was the hour, the tent intended for our trip was already pitched between the tavern and the barn, and round it our guides had gathered. These were Harvey Moody, with Cortez and Martin his brothers, and Phineas and William his sons.

Beside the barn door, on which sprawled a dried wolf-skin, two bear cubs were confined in a long, wooden cage. One was pacing to and fro, with quick startling motions, now and then thrusting his nose and paw through the bars in front; the other, lazily winking, was crouched on a cross-bar midway the height. While I was feeding them with blueberries from an adjoining field, Harvey sauntered up.

"Good mornin', good mornin'!" said he, in a hearty tone, "lookin' at the cubs and feedin' on 'm I see, Mr. Smith. They were got jest out here on Keene Mountain, and the skin of the old bear's in the loft there," pointing to a gable building, newly erected for a corner store. "I didn't git these ere, but I took two from a stump, last winter, at the lower Lake. The old 'un I shot, jest as he poked his head up. One o' the cubs died, but the other I've got chained up by my shop."

"You've killed bears enough in your lifetime, I suppose, Harvey?"

"Yes, and painters too. I was follerin' up a saple line onst, from Hoel's Pond a leetle north o' the Upper S'nac to the St. Regis waters, and jest by Catamount Mountain, I come crost the all-firedest big painter" —

"Good morning, Smith," said Renning, thrusting his head from his chamber window. "Good morning, Harvey! are the guides all ready for Rogers' Brook?"

"All ready, Mr. Runnin'," answered Harvey, "I've hed the b'ys here sin' afore sunrise, and the boats is in the pond by Cort's."

We had selected our guides, the evening before; Renning, Gaylor, Bingham and Coburn, choosing respectively Will, Mart, Cort and Phin, and I taking Harvey.

Renning and Gaylor were to try the trout at Rogers' Brook, and Bingham and Coburn to drive for deer at Colby's Pond. My choice was to wander around Baker's.

I was impressed, the more I saw of Harvey, with his skill as hunter and guide, and at a later day, as trapper. He not only thoroughly understood the region and the habits of its every bird, fish and animal, but was full of resources in his vocations. As guide, he was entirely reliable and always ready. He handled rifle, rod and oar with equal skill, and taught his woodcraft with a cheerful patience. His senses were wonderfully acute and continually alive. Not a sight or sound of the woods or waters escaped him.

As hunter, trapper and fisherman, he laid the whole forest under tribute. In the swamp, he opened the jaws of his wolf-trap; through leagues on leagues of woods, he blazed his sable line; on the borders of the waters, he built his deadfall for the mink; over the entire wilderness, he let slip his hound for the deer, while his fatal hook knew the buoy spots of every lake, and the mouths, eddies and rapids of every stream.

Renning and Gaylor started with their two guides, all fully equipped; and the morning was so beautiful, I determined to accompany them with Harvey, to their point of embarkation for the Brook.

We travelled up the Elizabethtown road, passing Harvey's cabin (half log, half clapboard) and his little log smithy in the corner of a small 'green space at the side of the hut.

We passed also the red farm house of Harvey's father and turned at the right into a grassy road, which soon brought us to the Saranac River. A dam at Harrietstown (a cluster of rough dwellings on the road between Baker's and the Lower Saranac) sets the waters broadly back for miles, and the overflow had killed the trees and thickets that crowded the former borders. A labyrinth of dead trees, prostrate trunks and withered branches, obstructed the waters, leaving but a narrow channel, midway. The live forest framed in the whole.

Drawn half way up the green bank, near a log hut, were four Saranac boats. These boats are dark-colored, slender as a pike, buoyant as a cork, made gracefully of thin pine, with knees of fir, their weight from ninety to one hundred and twenty pounds. Each has two oars on iron pins, a paddle, a neck-yoke for the "carries;" is made for three (it can hold five), and though so small and lightly built, will live in the roughest swells.

Renning and Gaylor embarked and glided rapidly and smoothly through the channel, Will and Mart handling their oars like playthings.

Harvey and I returned to Baker's. We reached it just as the buckboard (a board on four wheels with one seat) drove up for Bingham and Coburn, who were on their way to Colby Pond.

It was brought by a scarecrow of a boy, all broken out into tatters. The nag was a tottering mass of ribs and knuckle-bones with a skin drawn tightly over, and it seemed to have a constant inclination to fall on its nose.

Bingham borrowed a hickory goad and jumped on the buckboard with Coburn, and at last, between the two and amid the grins of the tavern loungers, old Mortality was punched and jerked into a funereal jog. Down the hill he shambled, his legs tangling and untangling in the most mysterious manner. But the moment he struck the level (I followed to see the sport), he subsided into his constitutional crawl. The woods echoed to Bingham's goad, but Bones only crinkled his hide, without budging a step the faster. I left them as they began the hill, with Bingham hallooing at the top of his voice, and boring the goad as if it were a gimlet, into the old nag's crupper.

After the buckboard had disappeared, Harvey and I strolled along the lane behind the barn, and he was in the middle of a "jack-hunt on Racket Pond onst, nigh the mouth of Wolf Brook," when he interrupted himself with "Hark! there's a hound runnin' a deer. It sounds like Watch; hark!"

Although I listened intently, I heard nothing but the rush of the rapids under the bridge above.

"It's Watch, by goll!" resumed Harvey. "He's bin missin' ever sin' yesterday. I was huntin' out on the Plains by Ray Brook, when he started a deer that run torts the Lower S'nac. He must a started another. There he goes agin! Goll, don't he sing!" and a yelp or two, followed by a burst of cries, came to my ear.

The sounds then retreated, floating fitfully here and there, lower, then louder, then lower again, and dwindling to a dreamy echo, then swelling once more until the tone illustrated the "wandering voice" of Wordsworth. At length, a peal sounded, like a clarion's.

"Here comes the deer, and a buck in the bargain; here, Mr. Smith, here! he's comin' this way!" exclaimed Harvey, slinging his rifle over his shoulder and running before me. "I'll hev a shot afore he reaches the river."

The deer had broke from the forest at the base of the Peak, and was now darting towards the stream. He cleared the stumpy field next the Peak and was crossing the river-flat, when Harvey fired. The buck gave one bound and fell headlong.

Harvey rushed to the spot and cut the animal's throat with his woodknife.

' Here's Watch!" said he, as a brindled hound came leaping over the field toward him.

"Good feller, good pup!" patting the head of the hound; "What did ye do with the deer yisterday, eh!" while the dog rubbed against him, whimpering, and twisting his lithe body with delight.

"Well," said Bingham, stretching his long legs on the chintz sofa of the inner parlor, just after tea, while we all sat round, "I'm about sick of this business, already. Here Coburn and I have been all day watching at Colby Pond and going over the worst road to get there that ever afflicted mortal man, all rocks and corduroy, and such a beast too, to take us!—why I've drilled so many holes with the gad into his leather carcass, that it looks like a sieve;—but as I was saying; here we've been watching all day for a shot, and not a shot do we get; not even a yelp to tell that one was wanted. And here Harvey Moody kills a deer right under Smith's nose, without stirring from Baker's. And here Renning and Gaylor come back from Rogers' Brook, and they too have a deer, without mentioning trout enough to break down that confounded tetering buckboard of ours, and without even leaving their boats. Well, so goes the world, Coburn, and suppose we take a drink. Ah, this liquor is good, at all events! and I say, boys, if I had got a shot, wouldn't I have given the deer fits?"

"That's so much a matter of course, Bing," said Gaylor, "there's no use of talking any longer about it. But here's Will Moody coming from the bar-room. Come in, Will, and sing us Glencoe."

Will entered, and after a few bashful excuses, struck up in a powerful but rather nasal tone, the following ballad, which I have translated into English from the Saranac vernacular.

> ' The young leaves of May had just feathered the trees,
> And the heatherbell's fragrance was filling the breeze;
> I went, as of old, to see day dipping low,
> On the wild, gloomy grandeur of rocky Glencoe.

'The bank of a burnie beside me that run,
　Displayed a bright lassie, as bright as the sun;
　All flowing in tartans, a lass long ago
　That loved young Macdonald, the Pride of Glencoe.

'With heart beating wildly, I slowly drew nigh,
　The lily and rose in her cheek seemed to vie;
　I asked in soft tones where her thought was to go,
　And she answered, I'm straying to gaze at Glencoe!

'Said I, lovely lassie, thy look and thy smile,
　My pathway for ever with joy can beguile!
　If thou thy affections on me wilt bestow,
　I'll bless the glad hour we met at Glencoe.

'Said she, My affections no more can I claim;
　I once had a true love, Macdonald his name;
　He went to the wars, alas! long years ago,
　And I live but to see him once more at Glencoe.

'It may be Macdonald thou'lt never more see,
　That he loves some far lassie more fondly than thee,
　That he thinks not of tartans so simple in flow,
　But of jewels that shine in disdain of Glencoe.

'False man! my Macdonald true-hearted will prove:
　The valiant in battle are faithful in love!
　And soon will the Spaniards in dust be laid low,
　And in joy will my true love return to Glencoe.

'So loyal I found her, I pulled out a glove
　She gave me at parting, her token of love;
　She hung on my bosom her tears all aflow,
　Oh, art thou Macdonald returned to Glencoe!

'Yes, Nannie, dear Nannie, thy sorrows are o'er!
　I come from the battles to wander no more!
　The rude winds of war at a distance may blow,
　And fond and contented, we'll dwell at Glencoe.'

CHAPTER IV.

The Lower Saranac Lake.—The Eagle.—Mount Tahawus.—The Loon.—The Gull.—Moose Mountain.—Cove Hill.—Mount Seward.—Whiteface.

THE next morning arose warm and threatening rain. Breakfast over, my four comrades and myself, with rifles, rods, blankets, overcoats and carpet-bags (holding as few articles as possible), left in Baker's wagon for the Lower Saranac Lake, to start thence upon our trip.

Up and down the winding road we merrily went, with the picturesque bends of the Saranac river at our right. One view particularly pleased us, soon after our departure from the Lake House: a graceful curve of the stream, lost at either end in woods, with one dry jagged tree slanting athwart, the only sign of decay amid the overflowing life.

We crossed the dam bridling the river at Harrietstown, by a bridge, and leaving the hamlet on our left, ascended a hill, and, with log-cabins and rough-clearings breaking the wilderness at either hand, soon saw the glancing blue of the lake in the background of the road.

We found our five boats in waiting, with as many guides; Corey, our cook and campman, meeting us here from the Indian Carrying-Place, with his son (little Jess, a boy of sixteen) as assistant, and two boats for the camp equipage and stores.

There was a party of sportsmen at Martin's (a tavern at our point of embarkation much frequented by visitors of the region), bound for Blue Mountain Lake. They were lolling on the green slope before the house and seated on the logs scattered around. The forest makes friends of all, and soon we were chatting and joking together like old acquaintances, exchanging little gifts, discussing plans and relating our adventures.

"You seem to want to know about the region, Mr. Smith," said Harvey to me, after he had placed his boat (the little Bluebird) in complete readiness; "So I'll tell ye that the Lower S'nac p'ints southwest and is six miles long by two wide. Then comes the S'nac River, three miles inter Round Lake, which is two miles long by that broad, and lays about west. Then a mile o' the river agin to Bartlett's, where there's rapids and a carry inter the Upper S'nac, which p'ints north agin. So you see the three lakes makes a horseshoe, with the two eends p'intin' one north and t' other tol'able nigh so."

"What are those islands south there named, Harvey?"

"Them two little ones over this spread o' water is the Two Sisters. On the left is Eagle Island, the largest island in the lake, three-quarters of a mile long. Burnt Island is on the right, and then comes the main shore. That fur mountain over Eagle Island, is Mount Morris, or Tupper's Lake Mountain, that we'll see clusser afore the trip's over. That peak north, is Baker's Peak. This is a great country fur mountains, and waters too. The lakes and ponds is like spots on a fa'n, and the streams is as thick as streaks on the moose-missee wood. As fur the woods, all in the State is packed away in this 'ere region, with now and then a clearin', like a bug on a chip floatin' in the S'nac here."

In a few minutes we were underway; each at the stern of his boat, leaning against the backboard, and the guide near the middle, plying smoothly and rapidly his oars.

Harvey had brought Watch with him, and he lay coiled at the Bluebird's bow. Sport, the other hound, had been consigned to the care of Will. Drive and the Pup completed the pack.

Onward the five boats swept toward the Two Sisters, with the store boats at the left crank and tottering under their loads.

On either side, was one grand sweep of mountain woods, swelling from the very verge of the water, which was scattered with manifold islands. Here and there trees, withered and scorched, strewed their gray and dull red tints, but they were hardly discoverable amid the universal green.

Heavy clouds with bright edges, filled the sky. The whole scene was fitful with brights and darks. Sometimes a beam lighted sudden and startling, on the top of a shadowed mountain, overflowing it with splendor. A new shadow then darted from the base, peeling off the light until the whole mass frowned again in gloom.

So with the lake. Now it showed one sullen hue; a gleam would then break forth, widening till dazzling diamonds danced upon the view, followed by a leaden tint, which closed like an enormous lid over its broad, sparkling eye.

Growls of thunder were echoing all around the scene, as if the mountains gave vent to fitful anger.

"Mackenzie's Pond Mountain, over there," said Harvey, "has his umb'rell up to-day," nodding to the east, where a dense mist touched the cloven crest. "It'll be a kind of on-the-fence day, nuther much rain nor shine, but a muxed up consarn, and mebby some wind. Well, in any blow that is reasonable, and some that might be unreasonable, this little Bluebird o' mine 'll live about as well (jerking his old hat in the most knowing manner, then spitting on his hand and sweeping wide his oars) as a loon, whether it's on Upper S'nac or Round Lake, and them two's about the wust in this region."

A breeze now crisped the lake, freshening till we danced onward over whitening swells I bared my head to the wind; I plunged my arm in the waves. Onward, good Harvey! swifter! let your oars play more merrily! How they dash, how they flash! onward, old fellow! on, old guide of the Saranacs!

3

On, on o'er the waters! song dwells in their sound,
Brave life in their tumult, and bliss in their bound!
Roam thou where the light wind makes love to the tree,
But a way o'er the wild rolling waters for me!

Oh the eagle, he darts through his mighty domain!
Oh the steed, with what triumph he tramples the plain!
But the bark, the bold bark, speeds as fleet and as free!
Then a way o'er the wild rolling waters for me!

Men say there is sorrow and darkness in life,
That the heart, it grows weary and worn in the strife;
But the bark has no heart-break; all cares from it flee;
Then a way o'er the wild rolling waters for me!

Bound onward, bold bark! leave the tame earth behind
Thy path is the white wave, thy breath is the wind!
Dash whiter thou white wave! wind heighten thy glee!
Ho! a way o'er the wild rolling waters for me!

At this glowing moment, when Pegasus had completely run off with me from the present scene and I was careering over the magnificent ocean, a stealthy dash of rain from Eagle Island extinguished my enthusiasm and wet me pretty thoroughly before I could don my India-rubber.

I could see Harvey grin as I clutched my coat; but I wrapped myself in my philosophy as well as my garment, and

" Did what they do in Spain—
Let it rain."

The pelted lake leaped into convulsions of foam, and through the mist the Two Sisters looked spectral.

The rain at length ceased, so suddenly, it seemed as if a wet curtain had in a twinkling been lifted; but mist still hung upon us.

"I had a rainy time on't, one time, in Lonesome Pond Bay, over there to the east," said Harvey, "watching for deer. Old Spot—he's dead now—was out, and as I hadn't heerd him for some time, I consated I'd fish. I ketched four big lake trout and bimeby I heerd Spot. How he did yelp! Jest as I drawed sight, for I knowed suthin' was a-comin', what should bust out of a lorrel swamp but an onmassifull big painter! I fired, but only wounded 'im. He sprung into a watermaple and sot openin' his green eyes on me as farse as a milishy cap'n on trainin' day. He was jest drawin' up for a jump, when I fired t'other barr'l right at his eye, and he tumbled as dead as—well, I won't say divil, 'case that's swearin'—but as dead as—well, I dunno—but he was as dead as—w-a-a-l, dead as kin be. I've got his skin now in my shanty to hum. But look at that eagle! He jest rose from Otter Island! How cluss he flies!"

As he spoke, a mass shot by so near, I caught the flash of a wild eye-ball. On the mass darted, into a range of stronger light. I saw his silver crest, his stately motion; he, the dark chieftain of the crag, swift of wing as the blast and keen of sight as the sunbeam!

"There he lights on Saple Island!" continued Harvey. "I kinder consate I'll hev a chance at 'im."

Swaying the head of a fir-tree downward, the eagle rose again and throned himself on the top of a tall hemlock, standing high and proud on his yellow-pillared feet. He cast his fierce eye down as we drew near, seeming to regard us with profound disdain and looking "every inch a king."

Harvey raised the rifle; but as he did so, the eagle launched forth again his black shape; but the rifle cracked, and the majestic bird swooped and fell, with a broken wing, into the lake. Watch leaped from the boat and in an instant was upon him. The wild orbs of the eagle flashed gleam upon gleam, as he darted his terrible beak at the eyes of the hound and struck with his sinewy claws and one massive wing, while Watch, eluding his enemy with quick motions, made at him rapid dashes of attack. The water foamed with the strife, almost concealing at times the combatants in a showery veil. Gallantly did the superb creature battle for his life; but his bristling neck was at last grasped by the hound, who shook him, as it were in triumph. In a few moments, the streaming blood and relaxed frame of the victim showed that the strife was ended.

Harvey pulled the hound and his prey into the boat, patting the back of the former proudly and lovingly, while I looked with pity on the latter. There he lay, the conqueror of the clouds, so lately careering in the glory of his strength, mangled, at my feet, and weltering like a warrior in his blood. Haughty and dauntless to the end, he fastened his grand, tawny eye upon me, flashing even through the mists of death, until he shook in his last tremor.

Harvey, however, was not troubled with any sentimentalities about the bird.

"They're a wild, cruel sort o' critter," said he, "them eagles, and boss it over the whull wing kind in the woods. They've bin known to ketch fa'ns when they was sleepin', and pick their eyes out as quick as a wink. They're great robbers, too. When a fish hawk has took a fish, an eagle 'll bust, as 'twere, right out o' the air, pounce on the hawk, kill him and steal the fish. Now that hawk had as good a right to that fish as I hev to any trout I ketch, and I should like to see a man take away my trout. He'd stand a mighty good chance to feel what's in my rifle, that's all. I don't hev no kind of pity for the greedy rascals, when they are killed. I'll skin 'im fur ye, when we git to the Injin Carry, and you kin git him stuffed and show folks what kind o' critters comes from the S'nac country. But you was askin' me t'other day about Mount Tawwus, or Mount Maircy as some people calls it, and why they should I dunno; it's only the name of a big man, it don't mean nothin'; but Mount Tawwus means a good deal, it means—lets me see—it's suthin' about split, but whether it's case it goes full split up into the clouds, or it splits folks most in two straddlin' up 't, I can't say now—rowin' kinder muxes up things in my head. You kin jest git a squint," resting on his oars and pointing eastward; then dipping an old battered, tin coffee-pot into the lake and drinking from the half-flattened spout.

A gauzy summit on a blue background of cloud and kindled by a stray glance of the sun, met my gaze, seeming, every moment, as if it would melt away. Was that dreamy shape, tender as memory and bright as hope, the grim god that piles one on another his defiant crags, and tosses with scorn the thunderbolt from his breast? There it shone in almost transparent beauty, more like a fairy painting than a terrific mountain whose crest pierced the clouds and froze in the cold of the sunshine.

A point in front now concealed the other boats, and we entered a channel between two islands.

The water is smooth; the trees are quiet in the lull of the wind; the solitude is complete. "The gentleness of heaven is on the "—hey! what the deuce is that?

A sound burst upon me, making me jump in my seat. It was like the laugh of a maniac; more—the jeering laugh of a demon over a fallen victim—a bitter, taunting laugh and yell mingled. It came from the opposite side of the island, to the left.

I looked at Harvey with wonder.

Harvey grinned.

"Wait a little, Mr. Smith, till we pass Buck Island here! There! d'ye see that black speck?"

"Why, yes; but you don't mean to say the infernal sound I heard, came from that speck?"

"Wait!"

Again the demoniac laugh. It sounded evidently from the speck. It echoed and re-echoed over the lake, now from the neighboring point and now from the little island in our rear, until the air seemed filled with a diabolical gabble.

"Hoo, hoo! yes, you may hoo, hoo, there; but look out! don't be sassen us too much!" said Harvey.

"But what the plague is this hoo-hoo thing of yours, Harvey? I never before heard such a sound, out of Bedlam!"

"That's a loon, Mr. Smith!"

"A loon!"

"Yes, and he's the sassiest thing——"

"Well, Harvey!" said I, "I've often heard the saying, 'crazy as a loon,' but I never realized the truth of it before. His cry is horrible!"

"Yes, siree! fightin' tom cats and owls stirred up by jacklights aint nothin' to a loon when he's a mind to holler, sayin' nothin' of a couple on 'em. There he goes agin' ho-ooooooo-ah-ho-ooooooo-ah-hoooooo-eee-e-e. Don't you be a sassen us all the time! I've killed loons afore I ever see you, you sassy tyke! He's comin' up quite cluss!" as a swell (we were now out upon the lake again) lifted him so that I could see, against a background of island, his glancing shape of black and white.

Harvey lifted his rifle.

"I bleeve I'll—there I consated he'd pop under, the sassy villyan!"

And pop under he did. Lightning could hardly have been quicker. Minutes elapsed.

"Why, where has he gone, Harvey?"

"He'll be up in a minute. There he comes!"

Sure enough, and reappearing as suddenly as he vanished; so near too that I could see his sharp beak and even the white strips round his dark, graceful neck. But he had hardly risen, before he gave a quick, frightened cry, and once more shot downward. Minutes again passed and I saw the black speck of his head a quarter of a mile away, floating near an island.

"There was a feller, ho! ho! ho!" said Harvey, "from York; he was out with me, one time, on Tupper's Lake, and a loon hollered out and then ducked under and staid—w-e-l-l, I should say ten minutes; and he wanted to know, ho! ho! ho! ef 't'adn't got so feared at us 't'ad drownded itself. I thought I should split; but see that gull! there, on that little bare rock jest afore Schooner Island, where them two trees stands up."

There it stood, relieved against the leaden hue of a ledge

upon the island, as if formed from white water lilies, and filling entirely its little pedestal.

"I bleeve I must make short work of that critter, at any rate. I'm gettin' rayther hungry for a shot!" said the old hunter, aiming his rifle.

"Don't shoot that bright thing, Harvey!"

"Too late, Mr. Smith!" crack went the rifle, and the gull—flew away.

Yes, positively. I looked at Harvey, and Harvey, he— why he tried to whistle. But it was of no use—he couldn't. He had shot and—the bird wasn't there. He—the deadly rifle of the Saranacs! To be sure, an hour afterward, he broke a silence of fifteen minutes by telling me that it was "all Watch's doin's! that he stuck his consarned nose right agin my elbow jest as I was pullin';" but I noticed a slinking air in the old woodman, the rest of the day.

But just now, he tried to change the topic.

"Don't you think that island looks suthin' like a schooner, Mr. Smith?" in a subdued voice, and giving a sweep with his oars.

It certainly did. It was about a quarter of an acre in extent, rocky, with groups of thickets and two tall trees resembling masts.

"There's old Moose!" exclaimed Harvey, shortly after, pointing to a vast mountain, smooth with its woods and blocking the horizon to the south-east.

"Next is Cove Hill. You'll see this and Mount Morris, all the way crost Round Lake, till you come nigh abouts to Bartlett's. Cove Hill agin comes out plain at the fust of the Stony Creek Ponds, crost the Injin Carry. On t'other side o' Moose Mountain, twixt it and Mount Seward, is Ampersand Pond; that sends out agin Ampersand Brook, which j'ines the last of the Stony Creek Ponds jest where Stony Creek goes out."

Harvey now rowed for a considerable distance in silence.

The sun had marched into a broad space of blue sky, the breeze had fallen and the lake was glassy. We passed island after island, heaped with their forest foliage, some like green domes, others broken with ledges. Counterparts were painted on the crystal of the lake—the rocks to the most delicate lichen stain and tiniest moss cup, the trees to the most spider-webbed fibre, and even the waterplants to their most fairy blossom. We glided over these green pictures, as if skimming the air in some magic bark above the real rock and forest. The furrows from the oars ruffled them for a moment, but they reunited, fragment to rock, branch to tree, blossom to plant, as the gentle water pulses ceased; and all was once more perfect.

"There's Outlet Island, where the S'nac river leaves the lake for Plattsburgh on Old Champlain," said Harvey, jerking his head to the east. "A queer thing happened there onst; I set my trap fur a bear on the island, nigh a deadfall fur mink. Well, I didn't go nigh it agin fur a fortnight. Finally, at last, I consated I'd go and see what luck I'd had. Afore I got to the trap, I found the trees all gnawed and stripped round, and the bushes stamped flat, and some old logs all bruk up; and, by goll! ef there wasn't bear tracks round, enough to set a dozen school mams a-puzzlin'! Finally at last, I come to a little holler, and there was the biggest bear I'd seen that season, dead; with the trap all bent and battered up, hanging to his hind leg. The deadfall was bruk up too, with a mossle o' mink's hair nigh it. My idee was, that the bear 'ad got into the trap shortly after I'd set it, and finally at last starved to death, after he'd eat a mink that 'ad got into the deadfall; but see that wood-duck steerin' by Loon Island!" pointing to a small rock in the middle of the lake.

"Why, how many islands are there, Harvey? It seems to me they form a perfect network."

"There's fifty-two! The lake looks like speck-maple from Boot Bay Mountain with 'm. But there's Mount Tawwus agin, and Mount McIntyre by it. That's where the great Ingin Pass is, and a mighty grand place 'tis too."

"You've been there, Harvey?" said I, pricking up my ears.

"Onst," resting on his oars, to dip his old coffee-pot again and drink. "How the rock on one side o' the Pass could get up so high into the clouds, isn't inkstand with me. Why, it scoots up right afore ye, as if 'twasn't never goin' to stop till it bunks its head agin' the moon or some other place up there. That air pine," pointing to a vegetable Anak on shore, "wouldn't look bigger on top there, than a deer-weed. And there's holes in the rocks you hev to scramble over, to git through the passage, big enough to hide all Gen'ral Jackson's army at Orleens. But speakin' o' the mountains, there's Mount Seward next to Mount McIntyre and risin' over old Moose."

I looked and saw the blue summit, with a spot like a star sparkling high upon its breast.

Since then, I have grown familiar with that star.

Once, in the fearful wilderness that stretches from the base of the mountain, I became accidentally separated from my comrades. I knew not where to turn. A tempest was near and I looked forward with dread to a night passed alone in that forest, exposed to the storm's fury and to the chance prowlings of the savage animals roaming the gloomy depths which were unknown even to the oldest hunters. The shanty of an Indian trapper was within an hour's distance, but where? Above me, soared the vast mountain, and it frowned more darkly than ever, in the shadow of the coming storm.

Just as I had surrendered all hope of extricating myself, a spot flashed out on the breast of the mountain, to a sudden gleam of sunshine. It was the star; and guided by it, I found, before the night fell, the kindly cabin, and heard against the protecting walls, the wild tempest thundering through the pauses of my slumber.

"That flashy place there on Seward is a ledge with a waterfall over it, and it al'ays shines jess like a tin platter in the sun," continued Harvey, "but fur a shiny thing, the slide on Old Whiteface, standin' up out there, is the most flashiest! It looks as much like a white riband, as any that a pooty schoolmam puts in her hair, when she's riggin' out fur a dancin' bee."

"Aha! Whiteface! have you been up it, Harvey?"

"I hev so! Gittin' up gives yer a high old time. Hadn't I better put a stop to that crane's flyin' any furder?" pointing his rifle, as the slim bird, stretching her snaky neck, and towing her spindle legs, moved heavily athwart the green mainshore; "but let her go" (remembering probably the gull). "As I was sayin', gittin' up that mountain is mighty bad sleddin'! It's a rael old Dutch ruff of a consarn, and afore ye strike the slide, you tug right up straight a'most with your hands and feet, about the same as a bear 'ud go up a tree. Risin' the slide is a good deal like mountin' a ladder from the top of a meetin'-'ouse up to the steeple. It makes ye fairly dizzy. But it's old hunderd when yer git there, Mr. Smith. You kin see miles on miles, all round yer. It makes yer feel as ef, as a body may say, you was one o' them eagles high up in the air a-lookin' down'ards, and ef a feller could make himself into a ball like a bear and roll down agin, you'd feel all the better. But you can't stay up long, unless you camp all night, for there's no housen within miles on ye, even from the foot of the mountain, lettin' alone the mountain itself."

"Oncle Joe Estis," continued the old guide, a moment after, "see that slide made. He was roofin' a barn, nigh Lake Placid—'twas about thirty years ago—and all of a sudden, he heerd a sound like thunder from the mountain, and see smoke, with rocks and trees tumblin' kinder dim like through 't, down, down the side, a crashin' and a roarin'; and when the cloud of smoke cleared away, there was the grey slide o' rock half way down to the foot, the same as 'tis now."

CHAPTER V.

Lower Saranac Lake.—A Talk on Trapping.—A Moose Story.—Saranac River.—Moose Mountain.—Middle Falls.—Round Lake.—Umbrella Point.—Bartlett's.—Upper Saranac Lake.

WE had been skimming, for some little time, in sight of a long mountain at the right, or west side of the lake, and now came abreast of a beautiful bay, opening in the same direction.

"I've camped often at the lower eend o' Boot Bay here," continued the old woodman. "It winds and twists south along 'twixt Boot Bay Mountain that you see there, and Loomis' P'int. Pope's Bay winds on t'other side, with Mack's P'int twixt the bay and lake. Both's old hunderd for ketchin' fur. There's as much as a dozen of old deadfalls o' mine tucked away 'long the shores of each on 'm, at this very time."

"What do you trap for, Harvey?"

"Muskrat and otter and mink and saple and fisher. The two last is gittin' scurce about here. But I'll tell ye suthin', Mr. Smith, ef you'll keep it cluss. I know where there's beaver!"

"Beaver! Harvey, beaver! Can ye take me to them?"

"I kin take ye to the waters where they hev their housen and where I've trapped 'm fur years, every fall a'most."

"Where?"

"Up in the St. Regis' woods, off north-east o' the head of the Upper S'nac."

"Good! we'll make that expedition, before I leave this region, Harvey!"

"I'm with ye!" answered the old trapper, "and we'll consider the consarn settled on!"

"How do you take the animals you have mentioned, Harvey?"

"Muskrats and beaver and otter, gin'rally in common steel traps. But we make deadfalls fur saple and mink. They're made this way: You cut large chips or blocks of wood and fix 'em in the ground in a tight half round, and cover the top over with hemlock or spruce or other thick boughs. That's called the boxin'. Then yer lay down a piece o' wood along the openin', called the bed-wood. Then yer lay a round stick, called the spindle, crost the bed-wood, with a piece of ven'son or trout on the eend, that's in the boxin'. On the forred part o' the spindle, yer stand up another round stick, called the standard, and on top o' that yer lay a heavy piece o' timber, a tree or big bough, that's called the top pole. So when the mink or saple crawls in and nibbles the bait, down comes the top pole squash, and there's an eend o' the critter. Them kind o' traps is scattered all along these waters; and as fur the saple traps, we make a line on 'm forty, fifty miles through the woods, and hack the trees along, which we call blazin', and scatter the traps, a dozen or mebby twenty to the mile; and some take fresh deer entrails, when they kin, and scent up the traps, fur the mink and saple to smell and foller 'm. As fur the fisher, he's al'ys breakin' inter the back o' the boxin' and stealin' the bait in these traps, so we hev a trap or contrivance fur him, in these saple lines. We bend down a saplin' so as to hev the eend in a notch we make in a root or log cluss to the ground; then we fasten a common trap to this eend, baited; so when the fisher pulls on the bait, the saplin' flies up out o' the notch with Mr. fisher danglin' with his foot in the trap, and there he hangs till he dies or the trappers comes 'long and bags the tarnal sputterin' thief. Sometimes he gnaws his foot off to git away, but gin'rally we find him danglin' there like a piece o' smoked ven'son; but shell I git ye a taste of the spring up there?"

Receiving my assent, he rowed to the shore, through a broad aisle of lily-pads, disappeared up the steep bank, and returning with his coffee-pot brimmed with the liquid, offered me a draught.

Of all beverages, commend me the spring water of this region. The crystal of the lakes and streams is sweet and refreshing, but the cold nectar that bubbles up from the grainy silver, at some old mossy root or lichened ledge, is worthy the lips of

> "Heroes in history, and gods in song."

"Look at that rock up there!" said Harvey, after we had resumed our way; pointing to a ledge rearing its mural front upon a bank three-hundred feet high, near the inlet or entrance of the Saranac River.

The cliff looked like some grey rampart of the dark ages, frowning from its steep upon its vassal waters.

"There was an old hunter by the name o' Ramrod, that had an adventur up there," continued he. "Well, fust of all, there used to be in a corner of the rock, an old dead pine with prongs all down its sides. It come up to a level with the head of the rock. One day, he telled me, he rousted up a bull moose and unly wownded him. Did ye ever hev a mad bull make at ye? I tell ye that's some, but 'twant nothin' to the way that moose made at Old Ramrod, 'cordin' to his tell, full trot. 'Twant but a leetle way from the head o' the ledge, and I tell ye, he put it. A half a minute fetched him to the top o' that air pine, and he throwed himself on the prongs, and down he went. But he hadn't tuk more'n four steps, afore the moose come to the edge o' the rock, and over he went, licketty split. Ho! ho! ho! wa'n't there a dead moose ketched in some spruces, a'most down to the edge o' the water, after he'd bin knocked from rock to rock down the precipyce, 'cordin' to Ramrod! and wa'n't he glad! I tell ye it sot him up, as he said, for the rest o' the day, fur it wouldn't ha' bin no b'y's play, ef that dod-blamed wownded, cross-grained old moose had a ketched him afore he'd got to that air pine, now I tell ye. I know suthin' about that, myself. They're a terr'ble farse critter, when they're riz up, and I'd ruther eat dumplins any day than fight one on 'm. There's an otter slide!" pointing to a smooth path down a bank of the main shore. "But here we are, at the S'nac River! The rest of the boats is out o' sight, but we'll overhaul 'm at Middle Falls, where they'll stop, I've a notion, to fish. It's a good place for trout there! or mebby they'll stop this side; there's a good brook there, too!"

As the old guide was speaking, we entered the river. Directly at the entrance, on our right, lay an expanse of wild grass, and thickets, with a deep fringing of water-plants.

The views now changed suddenly as the scenes of a theatre. The banks became low, the woods frequently yielding to broad spaces of natural grass, called indifferently by the guides, parks and wild-meadows. They were skirted, next the water, either with thickets or trees, the green levels beyond being seen through the loops and vistas of the foliage.

Sometimes, these meadows wound like bays into the recesses of the background forest, beckoning the fancy to distant nooks of beauty.

Here and there, in the forked head of a dry tree, was the nest of the fish-hawk, a rounded mass of grey withered sticks. From the abundance of the water in these woods, this bird haunts almost every scene, and its huge nest, frequently met, gives a wild picturesqueness to the monotony of the verdure.

Spread over the shallows, was a broad floor of lily-pads, glistening in green varnish and brilliant with white and yellow blossoms, the pearly scallops of the former resting on the surface, and the globes of the latter erect upon their short, thick stems.

The dark red Mohawk-tassel and the scarlet-berried

Solomon's-seal gleamed upon the banks, and on their tall stems, tufted in the water, shone the purple blossoms of the moosehead.

Between these meadows, the forest thronged to the river's edge so densely as to slant many of the skirting trees nearly athwart the stream. We skimmed over the shadows in the water, where some jagged branch was so accurately depicted, it seemed that the little Bluebird would be torn while gliding over.

Black, soaking logs, almost buried in the waterweeds, lay along or pointed from the banks, whence the twittering stream-birds vanished at our approach, while from among the plants, the duck whizzed and the frog and occasional muskrat plunged.

"Look out fur the fifth bend o' the river, Mr. Smith, fur a nice sight, as you seem to hev a notion of seein' mountains," said Harvey; "but here's all the party, and they've bin fishin' like sixty."

Sure enough, comrades and guides were just leaving the mouth of a little brook which joins the river at the east.

"Here comes the loiterer!" shouted Bingham. "What have you been about, Smith? Here we've been pulling up trout as fast as Joe Bunker, the pettifogger, can lie. But whew! The musquitoes! We've been like the Jews in building the walls of Jerusalem, fighting with one hand and working with the other. Ralph and Gaylor don't seem to have minded them, though! I lay it to the thickness of their skins! But poor Coburn! he——"

"Do, for Heaven's sake, stop that tongue of yours, Bing!" exclaimed Gaylor. "It's like a runaway horse!"

"It runs to some purpose, then, or you wouldn't try to stop it!" retorted Bingham. "I'll gird ye, as Falstaff says, if the musquitoes can't."

"These musquitoes are terrible, there's no mistake about it!" said Coburn, his usually bluff, hearty tone, now low and slightly fretful. "I-I hardly—bel ve—I can stand it all the way, if the whole trip is to be so. I don't know but I begin a little to repent coming."

"Nonsense, Coburn," exclaimed Bingham, "pluck up what spirit you have and put it through!"

"Exactly!" returned poor Coburn, plaintively, "put it through—that's what I complain of. There's been nothing but putting it through, ever since we've been at this plaguey spot."

"Didn't I hear you singing, 'The woodpecker tapping the hollow beech tree,' pretty loud, on the lake, Coburn?" said Gaylor, smiling.

"Yes! but I didn't bargain for the tapping I've had here," returned Coburn, fidgetting in his seat.

"Well, come, let us tap on our way. We've caught our fish, don't let us waste any time in talking," said Ralph, who was smoking like a locomotive.

"On, Stanley, on!" roared Bingham, and we all again started.

"Now look out for the view, Mr. Smith!" said Harvey, shortly after.

We opened upon a bend, and, filling the horizon, a mountain broke out with an expanse of its broad breast, so sudden as to be startling.

"Old Moose agin!" said Harvey, "but look, Mr. Smith, look!" dropping the oars and grasping his rifle which lay within reach, fitted into the side of the boat.

On a little glade of smooth grass, at my right, were two deer, one with head erect looking at the boat, and the other crouched at its feet.

Mine was a mere glance, for before Harvey could point his weapon, the two had vanished, more like shapes of smoke dissolving into air, than living things shooting into the foliage.

A dashing, crashing sound now filled the air, and we saw the gleam of foam in the channel of the stream. It was the "Middle Falls," where the water was broken by scattered rocks, into a rapid.

Here was our first carrying-place. Landing, I made my way through the narrow footpath, up and along the bank clustered with aspens, spruces and maples, to the broad ledges at the side of the falls, where Ralph and Gaylor fell as greedily to the task of deluding the trout on their hooks, as if they had never before thrown a line. Bingham commenced spouting "The Falls of Lodore;" Coburn, taking a seat, began rubbing his musquito bites; I looked about the spot and watched the two anglers.

Gaylor. A jerk; a "squttering" (as Harvey says) in the water; curl of trout on surface; frantic slap on nose at musquito; mosquito nowhere; trout ditto.

Renning. Twitch; twitch and jerk up; hook in air; nothing on it; growls; hook swings into rapid; three grabs at gnats; gnats nowhere; trout ditto. Scene ended.

For the boats have by this time been dragged through the rapids by the guides, and all is ready once more for a start.

During this process, my eye had been fastened on Harvey. Each boat was towed by a rope at the bow, with a guiding oar in the middle. The old guide was most industrious. Planted to his waist in the white waters, now he dragged at the bow, now kept the boat from the rocks by the oar. But the greatest trial of skill was in running the two storeboats. With his keen eyes widening, his whole form alive with excitement, yelling, pulling, pushing off with the oar from the rocks; shouting quick commands, as the stern of Corey's boat once nearly buried itself in the foam and then keeled as if to spill her load in the rapids, the old boatman showed himself, as his after bearing proved him, the master spirit of the guides.

"We'll hev a dancin' time on't, over Round Lake," said he, resuming his rowing and jerking his head at the swaying of the trees, even on this sheltered stream. "But the swells 'll be with us instid of agin us, and that's jest all the diff'rence. One's a boost in the back and t'other's a punch in the belly."

A curve of the river was passed, and Round Lake, rolling and dark, now opened. Here we stopped for lunch. An enormous, prone hemlock on the left bank of the stream, was our table, with myriads of wild roses, which spangled the thickets as if a pink snow storm had fallen there, perfuming the air, and with the low roar of the lake for our accompanying music.

We were soon on its angry waters. Gallantly did old Harvey swing his oars, and boldly did the little Bluebird dance along, after rustling through the long, dense rushes of the shallows at the entrance, the swells threatening, every moment, to bury our little bark. Onward, however, she went safely, although with shifting walls of water on either hand, and ridges swelling in front, while the other boats were rising and sinking in deep see-saws. The white-edged rollers were climbing wrathfully the sides of the islands, and the air was filled with the hoarse voice of the lake.

Eastward, Moose Mountain, the whole grand breast of Cove Hill and the summit of Mount Morris, bounded the horizon, without an opening or scorched tint in the fresh smooth foliage, with tall pines and hemlocks, "the haughty senators of mighty woods," rising here and there above the general surface.

Over these mountains, sailed swift lights and shades, like the play of color upon velvet. Occasionally, the breast of a ridge glowed in golden sheen; an immense shadow then rose from the lake like the Afrite from his crystal vase, and clambered the acclivity, the startled sunshine shrinking before it, until it vanished over the summit.

"There's somebody taking a snack on Bark Canoe Island to the right there!" said Harvey, looking over his shoulder towards a blue streak of smoke undulating through the trees. In a few minutes, we were abreast a noon camp. In the foreground of a little green dingle, the carcass of a deer hung from a limb; a camp fire crimsoned a ledge in the back ground; and a spotted hound crouched by a bush.

In the middle picture, were two men in red hunting-shirts; one toasting, on a stick, a flake of venison, and one seated on a stump, examining his rifle.

"Halloo, Harve!" shouted the former, as we danced past, "you're hevin' a Scotch jig on the lake there, aint ye?"

"Yes, it's lively times here!" answered Harvey, "but where did you kill your deer?"

"Nigh Duck Island, out there! He took to the water from Bartlett's clearin' and run down Umb'rell P'int. He swum lively, but 'twas no go. Loot settled him afore he got to the island!"

"Stearns Williams and Loot Evans!" said Harvey, "they live with Bartlett. But there's Umb'rell P'int!" glancing toward a tongue of wood thrust into the lake at the west, near an upland which had been burned over, displaying darkened rocks, charred logs, and standing trees of a dull red, scattered over a partially blackened soil.

"That pine, lookin' so like an umb'rell, gives the name to the p'int," pointing to a tree standing far above the other foliage of the spot, with a trunk bare nearly to the top, where a few large branches curved out, the whole very like the object mentioned.

"I remember the time well," added Harvey, "when that tree had all its branches like any other pine. But there's a story round the woods about it: how one time, Old Nick wanted to go a-fishin' in the lake when 'twas rainin'; so he tore up the tree and whipped off the branches with his big jack-knife, carried it with him into the lake and stood under it whilst he grabbed the all-firedest big trout that ever was seen in these waters; then as soon as it come to the top and see his eyes, it turned all cooked to his hands, and when he got through fishin', he put the pine back agin, and went ridin' over on a streak o' blue sulphur to Tupper's Lake Mountain or Mount Morris, that you see over there to the south-west. There's no eend of sich stories in the woods, Mr. Smith, but it takes a fool to believe half on 'm."

"Ought not this lake, Harvey, to be called the Middle Saranac?"

"That's jest as folks has a mind to. It's gin'rally called Round Lake 'cause 'tis round; but then it's about in the middle 'twixt Upper and Lower S'nac."

"How many islands has it?"

"There's Duck Island and Buck Island and Feather Bed Island, Bark Canoe Island, Bear and Amelia Islands, west; and Watch, Hatchet and Fawn Islands, east; nine in all."

"You see that burnt ridge over there by the p'int," continued he; "'twas burnt over three years ago, and a rousin' time 'twas, I tell ye. Ef all the furnaces in Black Brook could be brought to blaze away t'gether, 'twouldn't be nothing to what that fire was. Why, the pines and hemlocks quirled up like caterpillars, and as fur the bushes, they went off like blottin'-paper, and the leaves fell jest like bugs inter a camp-fire. 'Twas night, and I was on the lake at the time. Sich a roarin' and sich a red it throwed on the sky and on the lake! Why, my two b'ys, Sim and Phin, that was with me, looked like a couple o' red divils. And, sanko! how the sparks flew! All of a sudden, I heerd sich a screech. 'Twas so shrill-like and pitiful, it cut right through me. Onst, twyst, three times it come, then there was four or five doleful whines, and 'twas all still. 'Twas a painter, I've a notion, ketched in some holler in the rocks where it couldn't git out, and was burnt to death."

We had now crossed the lake. We entered once more the Saranac river, losing, as we did so, the influence of the wind.

The ripples from the oars washed over the broad, thick lily-pads, the water quickly peeling from the oily varnish or shrinking upon it into large drops. The white lily leaves, where they had been stirred up by the oar or feeding deer, showed in their inner lining a dull crimson, and those of the yellow, only a lighter green.

A mile farther brought us in sight of Bartlett's. We threw our lines at the mouth of a brook on our left, and a brief half hour rewarded us with a dozen trout, of a pound each. We then crossed and landed among the rest of our boats, close to a large slab boat-house.

At this point, began a quarter-mile carry westward, along the rapids of the river, to the Upper Saranac Lake.

The clearing contained but an acre or so, on the north bank of the river. Here stood Bartlett's two-story, unpainted, frame tavern, and its shadow lay cool and black upon the gentle, grassy slope, as I passed toward the entrance. Our guides were clustered at the open door of a log hut at one side, with several gaunt hounds that, I found, belonged to Bartlett.

A huge, savage-looking bull-dog, with porcupine quills clinging to his coat, and his black lips curled over his white fangs, stalked near the hut, looking powerful enough to bring down even a moose, while Bartlett himself, a short but strong, square-built man, with a hat that seemed made of dingy jackstraws, talked to one, laughed with another and kicked the hounds generally out of his way, with expletives more emphatic than pious.

In the sitting room, I found my comrades louder than usual in conversation, for which the empty glasses, telling clearly of punch, probably accounted.

The boats and luggage having been carried on wheels over the portage to the Upper Lake, we followed, leaving Bartlett in the act of applying his right foot to the ribs of an unlucky hound, and the bull-dog gazing after us with a face grim enough to darken daylight.

The afternoon sun sprinkled the bushes and trees of the ridge like golden rain, and soon the bright waters of the Upper Saranac gleamed before us. We watched the guides as they reloaded the boats; steadying them by the bows, while we entered to our places at the stern. The wind had lulled; the lake lay in smooth sleep; no more symptoms of rain were visible. Gaily we launched upon the water, here narrowed into a bay, and merrily rose our songs.

Sometimes a playful breeze stooped to the surface brushing it into darkening ripples, then fanned our brows with its delicate wings and melted away.

We soon turned the point at the east, whence we could see the lake stretching upward to the north, narrowed by islands into winding channels. As I glanced through these liquid paths, I longed to thread them toward the upper waters, which, the guides united in saying, were so exquisite in their beauty.

Pointing southwest, we passed Birch and Johnson Islands, crossed the intervening basin and landed, an hour before sunset, at the Indian Carrying-Place.

CHAPTER VI.

Sunrise.—Indian Legend.—The Saranac Wizards.—Mode of Carrying the Boats.—The Beaver-Pond Hunt.—The Stony Ponds.

I RETIRED to rest in the tent about midnight and awoke at day-break. There was a cool, grey light over the lake, which lay like glass. The fronts of the islands rose indistinctly as if reared in air, with dark pictures below them. The atmosphere was fresh almost to chilliness, and sweet with the odors of the woods. The tent looked ghostly, the forest gloomy. A brace of loons near the margin were sending out their wild halloos like Indian warwhoops, awakening a hundred quavering echoes. An eagle was sailing over the lake; a drowsy twitter was creeping through the woods. The smokeless cabin looked dead. The camp fire was smouldering in brown ashes, with embers melting along the charred back-log.

The largest of the stars were still shining, although dimly, through the sombre tints of the sky.

Soon, however, the ash color of the east commenced to clear into semi-transparent grey, then to kindle into pale yellow. Trees began to creep out from the massed forest, and a streak of distant mist to crawl along the lake. The islands stood out more boldly. The twitter from the woods increased to chirps, swelling occasionally into song. The lake showed differing though still sober tints; here a space of marble grey, there of polished black.

At length, the cheeks of the clouds at the zenith blushed into rose: one long cloud in the east began to glow into ruby, then burn into gold. Gemmed colors—sapphire, emerald, topaz and amethyst—glanced upon the lake.

Gold ran along the tops of the tallest trees. The east gleamed with royal crimsons and imperial purples. At last, through a vista of the background ridge, striking the landscape into gladdening light, poured the lustre of the risen sun.

The scene was now astir. The guides left the smaller tent (where they had slept with the exception of Harvey, who had preferred, wrapped in his blanket, to make his bed in a neighboring thicket) and began preparing the morning meal. My comrades appeared from the larger tent, Bingham's face opened with a yawn like a cavern, while Ralph's seemed swollen as if all his diabolical snores of the past night (he is a most horrible and provoking snorer, that Ralph) had settled there for the day. He also wore a hang-dog look, as though he felt guilty for his disturbance (may the Lord forgive him!) of at least one suffering individual.

The smoke of the camp-fire commenced curling, and, as if it were a signal, the rough chimney of the log-cabin began to breathe. The guides, bending over the crackling blaze, toasted slices of ruddy venison and spread the trout on the winking coals for broiling, while the sauce-pans began to carol and the head of the tin teapot to strike up a clattering jig.

Our sylvan meal ended, we lighted our pipes for a social smoke on the grass.

"Ralph!" said Bingham, "you must feel quite exhausted by your last night's performance!"

"How is that?" returned Ralph, with a twinge of his shoulder, as if conscious of what was coming.

"Why, those sounds that, more than human, echoed through the tent! those unearthly snores, fit to wake the dead, let alone live people!"

"Pish!" said Renning, pettishly, "do let my snores alone!"

"But your snores won't let other people alone. Poor Smith there, looks as if he were becoming insane from want of sleep. It is really villanous! I—really—I—

with my delicate nerves too (with a languishing look), I—I—won't be able to stand it. I shall break down; at the beginning of the trip too! What *will* you do, when the air, out here, and the exercise have made you even stronger and heartier? I really dread to think of it!" and the inveterate tease affected to shudder.

"I move we let each other's little peculiarities alone, and confine ourselves to general subjects," said Renning, twisting uncomfortably in his position.

"Little!" returned Bingham, putting on a stare. "Little! Here's impudence! And peculiarities! Well, I never heard full, deep-chested, air-shaking, sleep-murdering roars, called little peculiarities before. Why, gentlemen," rising as if for a harangue, "he ascends the scale regularly, from the double bass of the biggest bullfrog to a height where he is in imminent danger of choking. There is no use in shaking him; it only breaks the sound into numerous particles and distributes them over a wider surface, splintering, as it were, one monotonous note into counter, tenor and treble; the scale then proceeding with more rascally vehemence than before. I'll match him against a dozen, I was going to say a regiment, of loons, any day or rather night; for like the whippoorwill, this interesting friend of ours only sings at that season. I move we proceed against him as an outlaw, on the spot!"

"How about the musquitoes, Bing?" said Renning, recovering his good-humor, and charging in his turn upon the enemy—the common enemy, I might say. "You were going to outlaw them, last night."

"Bing is better in denouncing snores and musquitoes than in killing deer," said Gaylor quietly.

"Deer!" exclaimed Bingham, "where's the deer I've missed, I should like to know?"

"Where's the deer you've shot?" enquired Coburn.

"Shot!" returned Bingham crossly. "How the deuce can you shoot a deer, when you don't see any? I've shot all the deer I've seen!"

"And that's *nil!*" said Gaylor.

"Nil, sure enough! I would have shot one of the deer, if not both, that Mart and Will brought in, last evening, had I seen them first. It *is* nil, sure enough! All the hunting stories that sportsmen and writers tell, of finding deer on every point and island and drinking at every creek in this wilderness, should be scouted, denounced, gentlemen! by all decent men. They talk as if deer are to be found in every alder-bush, and trout in every little ripple, no bigger than Coburn's conscience here; and if, gentlemen! (waving his hand), you can find anything smaller than that, you must turn your eyes into microscopes, that's all!"

"Smith says you found the musquitoes rather troublesome at the point, last evening," said Coburn, with a grim smile.

"Oh, Smith!" said Bingham, turning to me. "Smith's tongue is the only thing about him that is even reasonably alive. I've wondered ever since we started, why we've admitted him among us. Killing deer and catching trout are as much beyond him as Ralph's nasal accomplishments here are beyond a whole orchestra of hoot-owls, or even a moderate knowledge of men and things is beyond my friend Coburn here. But what on earth is that?"

A long, open box of wood, mounted on round wooden blocks, about a foot from the ground, drawn by shadowy oxen and driven by a tatterdemalion that looked like a scarecrow from Corey's cornfield, met our sight. This picturesque conveyance, moving with most diabolical screeches as if laboring under a wooden rheumatism, we found was to transport our luggage over the carry (a mile of travel), while our guides would bear our boats, and we betake ourselves to our independent feet.

Shouldering our rifles and rods, up the ascent we started. I subsequently learned the legend connected with the clearing.

About a hundred years ago, a large tribe of the Saranac Indians inhabited the forests through which runs the

Indian Carrying-Place; an old path, named by them, the Eaglenest Trail of the Saranacs. The site of the clearing held their village and Council-Place. They claimed as their exclusive hunting-grounds, not only the Eaglenest Forests, but those of the Wampum Waters,* the Stream of the Snake,† and the Sounding River,‡ from the Lake of the Blue Mountain to Wild Mountain at the Leap of the Foaming Panther.§

Two young warriors, stately and brave, divided the admiration of the Tribe; Ta-yo-neh, the Wolf, and Do-ne-on-dah, the Eagle.

Whenever the war-path led to the lodges of the fierce Tahawi, on the slopes of grand Tahawus,—The Splitter of the Sky—the young warriors vied with each other as to which should win the most scalps to his belt. Ta-yo-neh was brief in talk and his chants at the war-dance were few, but his eye burned with the fire of his heart. Do-ne-on-dah was frank in speech, and his song in the dance was loud. Although rivals on the war-path, the young braves smoked together the calumet of friendship. Love had made soft the heart of Ta-yo-neh and he had gathered to his lodge O-we-yo, the Blossom of the Tribe, but no maiden's eye as yet had kindled the breast of Do-ne-on-dah. The old men looked at both with pride, and the young with admiration. Each could skim the Lake of the Silver Sky at the head of the Eaglenest Trail, in his yellow canoe, as the eagle skims the air. The Lake of the Great Star‖ saw the prints of each on his margin, after the deer, at noon; the Stream of the Snake beheld on his winding banks at eve, the trail of the same feet unwearied. The Tribe, at length, became divided as to the merits of the two, but the strife was friendly.

So rolled on the suns, and now the two young warriors were to visit the torrent of the Wild Mountain in search

---

* The Stony Ponds.   † Stony Creek.   ‡ Racket River.
§ Perciefield Falls.   ‖ Racket Lake.

of the stately moose. Both departed in their birch canoes, over the Wampum Waters at the foot of the Trail of the Eaglenest.

The moon of the month of young leaves hung its bow to the glittering orb of the early evening, then grew round as the red ring in the eye of the loon, and nought was heard of the warriors.

At last, as that same moon was quenched in its rising by the sun, Ta-yo-neh appeared but no Do-ne-on-dah.

"Where is the Eagle of the Tribe?" asked old O-qua-rah, the Bear of the Saranacs, the Sachem of his Tribe.

"He went with his brother to the Falls of the Wild Mountain, after the trotting moose," answered Ta-yo-neh— "but the Black Terror of the woods was not to be seen even by the keen-sighted Eagle. Ta-yo-neh and his brother then paddled through the Eye of Hah-wen-ne-yo* up the Lonely River† to the Dark Lake,‡ where the Black Terror fell before the arrows of Do-ne-on-dah and Ta-yo-neh. As the bright Sachem of the sky touched his feet upon the Hill of the Raven, Ta-yo-neh and his brother went out upon the trail of a deer. They climbed a tongue of the wood by the Dark Lake and Ta-yo-neh left his brother to follow a panther's trail leading from the trail they were treading. Since then, Ta-yo-neh has mourned for the sight of his brother."

"Wolf!" shouted O-qua-rah, while his eye gleamed like the fire in the wood, "the Sachem of the Saranacs hears a forked tongue—Ta-yo-neh has torn with his claws the heart from Do-ne-on-dah!"

"Ta-yo-neh cannot lie," answered the other firmly. "He knows not what has happened to his brother the Eagle. He searched the tongue and the dark waters beneath it. He was a whippoorwill, all night calling 'Do-ne-on-dah! Do-ne-on-dah!' but nought answered, save the mocking spirit that only speaks what the voice utters."

---

* Tupper's Lake.   † Bog River.   ‡ Mud Lake.

"Wolf!" again shouted O-qua-rah; and this time, he clutched his tomahawk. "Where is Do-ne-on-dah?"

"Ta-yo-neh has said," answered the other.

"Die!" yelled the Sachem, and swung on high his tomahawk, but a light form shrieking flew between it and Ta-yo-neh and the glittering axe sank into the brain of O-we-yo.

Ta-yo-neh started as his bride fell dead at his feet, clutched his tomahawk in his turn and swung it toward the head of the Sachem. But the blow was arrested by one of the old men of the Tribe.

"Go!" said he, "the old Bear of the Saranacs—the Sachem of the Tribe—must not be torn by the young Wolf. O-kah also asks, where is Do-ne-on-dah?"

"Do-ne-on-dah! Do-ne-on-dah!" rose in notes of wailing and anger from a portion of the Tribe; "Ta-yo-neh! Ta-yo-neh!" mingled with "O-we-yo," in accents of grief, broke out from the others. Knives and hatchets flashed and a terrible conflict had commenced, when old O-qua-rah, with Ta-yo-neh's knife plunged in his heart, fell headlong among the combatants. The strife was arrested; the arm of Hah-wen-ne-yo had interposed; the sacrifice to justice had been made. The heart of Ta-yo-neh had been cloven by the death of O-we-yo; O-qua-rah had been stricken down by the bereaved Ta-yo-neh.

But though the combat ceased, the feelings springing from these events soon caused a separation of the Tribe. One portion, under Ta-yo-neh, went down the Sounding River to the Green Council-Place, close to the beautiful lake, the Eye of Hah-wen-ne-yo; the other, under O-kah, remained at the Eaglenest Trail of the Saranacs. Moons upon moons passed away, while the two portions of the Tribe became more and more angry with each other. Ta-yo-neh claimed the hunting-grounds down the Sounding River to the Council-Place, O-kah those of the Eaglenest, the Wampum Waters and upward to the Lake of the Blue Mountain; but the Stream of the Snake that winds from the Wampum Waters saw often the gleam of the hatchet between the two and his own bright brow stained with Saranac blood drawn by kindred, but now alien, Saranacs. Hundreds of moons passed. Ta-yo-neh grew into a withered pine, with grey moss fluttering thinly from his top, and then a fallen trunk, which the Tribe reverently hid within the earth.

One day, the Tribe of the Eaglenest saw a canoe coming upon the Lake of the Silver Sky. It touched the shore and an old man tottered out and with feeble steps approached them.

"Has the tribe of the Saranacs forgotten Do-ne-on-dah?" he asked, in faltering accents.

"The dead still lives in the Tribe," answered O-nech-tah, the son of O-kah, who had in turn become the Sachem, "but it is as the song of a bird heard when the heart was young, lingering faintly in the thoughts of the aged."

"Do-ne-on-dah is here!" answered the stranger, laying his hand feebly on his breast.

Doubt flitted across the face of O-nech-tah. The stranger opened the beaver skin from his bosom, and lo! there, stamped upon his heart, shone the totem of the Eagle. Then knew the Tribe it was indeed Do-ne-on-dah tottering before them. A shrill cry of joy and welcome went up, and "Do-ne-on-dah! Do-ne-on-dah!" echoed in the woods of the Eaglenest and over the waters of the Silver Sky.

"How did Do-ne-on-dah return from the bright Land of the Happy?" asked O-nech-tah. "Has Hah-wen-ne-yo spared him for a while from the Feast of the Strawberry, to gladden the hearts of his people the Saranacs?"

"Do-ne-on-dah's feet have not yet trod the trail that leads to the land of Hah-wen-ne-yo," answered the other. "He lingers like the hemlock that the moss covers, but must soon fall and mingle with the dead leaves of the forest."

He then told them how, after Ta-yo-neh left him, he had fallen through a cleft into a cave, where he had lain helpless, until discovered by hunters on their way to Canada; how he had joined the British against the French in the war between the two countries; was rescued from death in battle by an Indian Chief, who gave him his daughter, and whose Tribe made him Chief after the death of his preserver; how he had lived since happily, surrounded by his children and children's children in the distant spot where the Tribe had dwelt, and how, lately, the whole Tribe had been swept away by the Hurons and he had now come to die among the people of his youthful love.

Joy took possession of the Tribe of the Eaglenest, as they listened. A runner was despatched with the tidings, to the Tribe at the Eye of Hah-wen-ne-yo, and the next day, at sunset, both tribes were assembled in the Council-Place of the Eaglenest. Do-ne-on-dah took his seat upon a mound with O-nech-tah and Ko-nu-teh, Chief of the lower Tribe, at either hand supporting him, for he drooped like the elm when the water is washing under its roots. The old man then repeated his story and ended by solemnly enjoining both Tribes to live together hereafter in amity. They as solemnly promised, raising in unison the shrill whoop of friendship. As the last quavering note died away, Do-ne-on-dah, with a quick motion, bent his ear, reared himself suddenly on high, flung his arm aloft and saying loudly, "The Eagle hears the voice of Hah-wen-ne-yo! He comes!" stepped forward a few paces and fell dead in the sight of all the people.

The two Tribes buried him, just as he had sat upon the mound, by the side of Ta-yo-neh, on the margin of the Eye of Hah-wen-ne-yo, and ever after lived in harmony and peace. When the sad time came to leave the Green Council-Place and the woods of the Eaglenest, together their canoes rippled the Lake of the Silver Sky and together they sought the waters of the Ottawa in the hunting-grounds of Canada. There, remnants of the Tribe still live in contentment and prosperity.

We had a delightful walk over the carry. The track

was broad and passably smooth, with here and there huge roots running across and bordered with luxuriant wood plants. It dipped into hollows and wound pleasantly along, with the fresh morning sunshine lighting up the whole.

Upon one side, was the curiosity of the carry. Withered, jagged limbs projected from the bark of living trees like struggling skeletons. The sight was truly death in life.

The legend runs thus. While the Saranacs inhabited the carry, certain wizards from the lonely waters of Ampersand Pond in the wild region between Moose Mountain, Cove Hill and Mount Seward, so troubled the Tribe that a feast was holden on Turtle Island; and the old Patriarch Priest of the Tribes, forsaking his cave in a gorge of Cove Hill, prayed for help to Hah-wen-ne-yo. The Great Spirit listened to the prayer. One night of lightning and rain, the wizards who were slumbering in hollow trees, were awakened (so said one who had been least guilty and who escaped to tell the tale) by finding themselves walled in with growing bark. In their despairing struggles, they thrust forth their arms, which were caught by the bark and there they withered. To this day, when the fall wind wails in the forest, sounds of sorrow float upon it from these magic trees, the coffins of the wizards of the Saranacs.

At the end of the carry, on the shore of the first of the three Stony or Spectacle Ponds, we found one of our American ruins, a dilapidated log hut, with a dead clearing around it, dotted with dark stumps and strewed with half-burned logs.

Here we basked in the sunshine, after drinking from a spring that bubbled through the overgrown border, awaiting the transportation of our boats over the carry.

The conical breast of Cove Hill, dark with wood, heaved grandly up eastward. Ampersand Pond is cradled at its foot and sends out a brook, which, after a rocky and tortuous course, links itself with the last of the three

Stony-Ponds, its mouth being a famous resort for large trout.

The scene was quiet and delightful. Faint cries from hawks dotted around a distant fir, touched the ear; a kingfisher, with his purple back gleaming in the light, watched the water, from a dry limb; and a little family of black ducks steered out from a hollow in the bank and pushing through a broad field of lily-pads, made their way diagonally down the pond.

Bingham had just seized his rifle for a shot, when a couple of legs appeared, working nimbly under the long curve of a boat. The bow being rested on a stump, let from under it a man, no other personage than Cort, somewhat red in the face from his exertions. And here let me notice farther the mode of transporting boats practised throughout the forest.

The guide balances his upward-turned craft by a wooden yoke clasping the base of his neck, the ends fitting in iron rings at the sides of the boat, and the weight also resting on his upturned arms. He thus bears his burden over the portages of the innumerable waters that make one vast Venice of the wilderness.

When the portage is long, the guide rests himself for a moment, by leaning the boat's bow against some tall stump, broken sapling or small rock and withdrawing from beneath it.

Our comrades started to fish the mouth of Ampersand Brook, but the restless Bingham resolved to visit a beaver pond a mile or two off (the knowledge of which had been infused into him by Cort) for his favorite sport, deer-hunting. He (unlucky Bingham) invited me to accompany him and, propelled by Cort's oars, we were soon furrowing the mirror of the pond. We crossed; entered the second pond; skirted on the left a bank of open trees, and passing an island fronting a bay, pushed into a creek which twisted through a wild meadow.

"Turkle Island there is a great place for the black

snappin' turkles," said Cort. "There's a turkle's nest on't where the critters lay their eggs. D'ye see that streak o' brown sand? That's where they crawl up from the water."

We left the boat a short way up the meadow, and wading through the long, coarse grass, reached at last a wooded point. Here Cort whispered to be "keerful and not make the least bit o' noise, for round it, he'd no doubt but there was mebby two or three deer feedin'."

Treading softly, in Indian file, Cort foremost, we rounded the point. As usual, in taking the utmost care, my unlucky feet would keep cracking all the dry twigs in the path; and it was ludicrous to see Bingham's impatient face turned towards me as some crisp snap broke the stillness. I knew I should pay at the camp-fire for every crackle, in his stinging jests and provoking raillery; but the more gingerly I tried to tread, the more I kept up the snapping.

No deer was in sight; but another point was ahead, and, Indian fashion again, we neared it.

Crack, crack, snap, snap, crackle, snap. At last, Bingham lost all patience.

"Confound you, Smith!" jerking his head alternately as he whispered, "has the devil, if I must say so, got into —what do you see, Cort? Heavens! are those big feet of yours shambling around without any control or—do you see anything, Cort? Have all the bones in your body got loose—eh, what is it, Cort? Where on earth Smith do you manage to find so many twigs to step on!"

"Hush–sh!" said Cort, who was now peering round another headland. The next moment, he beckoned to Bingham, who quickly, though quietly, advanced. I followed. In a lily-pad pond, with head and earflaps erect and one forefoot lifted, stood a large buck. Bingham aimed, but at the critical juncture, my unlucky pedals struck another twig—snap—whew! Didn't that deer run? Bingham fired; but the buck still bounded through the scattering lilies. Another shot—this time from Cort—and the deer fell. Cort rushed forward with his wood-knife, which he carried, like the other guides, sheathed in his leathern belt; and by the time Bingham and I had reached him, he had cut the throat of the victim. The ball had, however, pierced its heart.

Bingham looked narrowly at the wound.

"I say, Cort! couldn't it have been possible that I hit the buck before you did?"

"There isn't but one hole there!" answered Cort.

"Ah, Smith!" said Bingham, shaking his head, "you're an unlucky creature, or rather I'm the unluckiest of mortals in bringing you. I was as sure of that buck as I am that you're my evil genius. What on earth got into those hoofs of yours! But no matter now; let's join the boys at Ampersand Brook, or the next thing, I shan't be able to get even a trout!"

Cort swung the deer over his stalwart shoulders and we returned to the boat, left the second pond behind and, pushing through the long grass and lily-pads of the connecting channel, opened into the third.

This and the first of these linked sheets of water are a mile in diameter and of exquisite beauty; round, as if traced by a compass; rimmed with a belt of snowy sand, and ringed with the dark green woods. Not a shape or color of decay can be seen on any side.

The second is much larger and quite irregular.

The forests were tranced in the morning calm, and the pond, as we crossed it, was a reflected picture of blue and white. Now we cut through a wreath of pearl and now ruffled a belt of sapphire.

"There they are, at the mouth of the Ampersand!" said Cort, glancing round.

"And whipping up the trout like Old Sanko!" added Bingham. "Pull away, Cort, and let's have a chance among them. Jupiter! if Renning isn't bringing up a two-pounder in that landing-net of his! Pull, pull, Cort! Good morning, gentlemen. Have you left any trout for a luckless lawyer and one Smith, gentlemen, whose name has been adjudged by the Supreme Court to be no name, and who would be the life of our party if he could only crack jokes as he can twigs! Why,"——

"For heaven's sake, stop that bawling of yours, Bingham!" exclaimed Renning, who had just dropped his prize with a broken neck, into his boat, "you'd frighten all the trout in the universe."

"And if I did, I'd but follow Smith's example here in the way of bucks. What do you think, gentlemen! Instead of

'Stepping like Fear in a wide wilderness,'

which, by the way, is a very appropriate line in these old woods, he stepped like a cart-horse on paving-stones, and the consequence was—I—hem!—have the honor to announce that a deer is in the bottom of the boat. What do you think of opening the day with a fat buck, gentlemen? What do you think?"

"I think I shall pull out of this place," said Coburn. "Bingham's tongue has got loose again, and the Lord knows now when it will stop."

"Are ye afraid, gentlemen, I shall rival you all in my trout exploits also, that you go as soon as I appear?" retorted Bingham. "However, I'll follow. Smith, please get into your own boat. I'll say this of ye, before we part, that your feet in size and shape, are more like snowshoes than any natural extremities I am acquainted with, and make a noise to match."

Again I found myself in the little Bluebird with my friend Harvey, and we all filed into Stony Creek, whose source lies but a rod or two from the mouth of the Ampersand.

CHAPTER VII.

Stony Creek.—Origin of the Indian Plume.—The Racket River.—Moose Talk
—Panther Story.—Palmer Brook.—Racket-Falls Camp.

STONY CREEK, or Wahpolichan-igan—its Indian (St. Regis) name—flows in a succession of sharp oxbows, three miles, into the Racket River, principally through wild meadows skirted, at the stream, as is usual, with trees. Among these, the most conspicuous are the elm and white or water maple; some of the latter, grouped into a score of stems from one root. This tree is the Banyan of these woods, and its "pillared shade" is one of the most noticeable objects along their streams. Particularly along the Racket, is it seen clustering its trunks on the grassy banks, coverts for the deer and "leafy house" for the birds.

The Creek was quiet and beautiful, stealing beneath the gothic roof of branches in gold-speckled green and sometimes laughing in open light from the meadows or parks. Pointed logs frequently narrowed the channel to a few feet in width and sunken trunks now and then stretched entirely across, obliging my guide to sink them deeper with his paddle for he had abandoned the oars from the continual windings. As I sat at the bow, with my eyes half shut, steeped in the wild beauty of the scene and shaping some chance moulding of leaves and sunshine into an ambushed hunter or crouching panther, my attention was at length caught by glowing flakes among the dense herbage of the low borders.

"What is that beautiful flower, Harvey?"

"That's the Injin Plume!"

"The Indian Plume! A pretty name and most lovely flower!"

It rose in a slender spire of superb scarlet, about a foot high, its delicate petals like the geranium's. The plant seemed nearly to blaze in the sunshine and to kindle into ruby light the green nooks where it nestled.

As I looked at the flower, glowing almost like live coals against the grasses of the banks, I shrined it in my memory and heard afterward from a St. Regis Indian, this legend of its birth.

A very long time ago, long before the incidents related of the Indian Carrying-Place, Onwee was the Sachem of the Saranacs, dwelling by the Stream of the Snake. One daughter shone in his lodge, beautiful as a star, and pure as a snowflake on the wintry summit of Whiteface. She was betrothed to Ka-no-ah, named "The Arrow," from his swiftness on the trail, whether of the deer or the foe. All went happily, and the life of Len-a-wee or "The Indian Plume" was like the mellow days that the Indian Summer smiling in the stern face of Winter, breathes in purple mist through the wood. But at last, the Demon of the Quick Death darkened over her people. Right and left he swung his startling tomahawk, and the white hair—the frolic boy—the strong warrior and the blossoming maiden fell alike beneath it. All trembled before the viewless foe. Onwee bowed his old head and died, and the Swift Arrow was launched upon the shadowy trail. The Tribe veiled their faces in dread; Hah-wen-ne-yo was angry with his children. In vain the Great Calumet sent its smoke from the lips of the Prophet toward His Dwelling-Place. In vain was the White Dog slaughtered, to bear upward the sins of the people. At last, the old Prophet proclaimed that Hah-wen-ne-yo had appeared to him. He came in dazzling splendor, one night of lightning, on the top of the Tempest-Darer that looks upon the first of the Wampum Waters. And thus he said, "Not the breath of the Great Calumet and not the blood of the dog of snow will soften my wrath.

The warm blood from a human heart will alone appease it. That spilled, my smile will again beam upon my children!"

The old Prophet spoke and deep silence hushed the tribe. But a moment after, Len-a-wee glided into the ring of warriors ranged around the Prophet on the banks of the winding stream.

"Len-a-wee is a blighted flower;" said she, in her tones of music, but now sad as the wail of the wind in the time of the falling leaves; "let the blood of her heart atone for the sins of her people!"

She said, and grasping the knife from the belt of the Prophet, darted close to the stream which she and her Ka-no-ah had so often skimmed together in their birch canoe, and plunged it into her bosom. The red blood flowed upon the earth; the keen weapon had cleft her heart. Reverently and sorrowfully did the warriors of the Tribe raise her in their arms, and solemnly did they lay her form by that of Onwee and Ka-no-ah. As the next Morning trod through the forest, his golden fingers touched the spot which had been stained by the blood of the maiden. No blood was there, but instead, a slender flower, red as the flush that kindles the cheek of the Sunset as it sinks in the gloom of night. The Demon of the Quick Death plied his tomahawk slower and slower from the birth of the flower, and soon his presence darkened no more the hearts of the people. And ever after, was the flower loved by the Saranacs. The warriors twined its blossoms in their scalp-locks, the maidens spangled its glowing sparks over their tresses of darkness. When the Autumn blighted it, they mourned; when the late Summer told it to bloom, they were glad. A feast was instituted in its honor, for it glowed in their minds as the emblem of unselfish devotion to the common good.

Another curve of Stony Creek, and, darkening for an instant under a log bridge, we came to the junction of the stream with the Racket, where two leaning water-maples watched like Dryads the wedding of the lovely Naiad. We turned to the left, or eastward, up the river, as the last of the other boats, containing Bingham's tall form, vanished beyond a bend.

Broad in comparison with the channel we had just quitted (which is about a rod in width), this truly beautiful river, like the Saranac Lakes, impresses its character upon the region it traverses. Its source is Racket Lake; thence it expands into the Forked and Long Lakes, and after flowing one hundred and fifty miles, in two bold sweeps, to the north-east and north-west, falls into the St. Lawrence, north of its source. From crystal cradle to grass-green grave, its shadowy footsteps glide through an unbroken wilderness. I say unbroken, for the dots of clearings only heighten by contrast the general wildness of the scene.

Its name, as some suppose, is derived from the French Canadian hunters, in old times, hunting the moose in winter by means of the raquette (the French for snow-shoe), around the waters now known as Raquette or Racket Lake.

Others affirm the name to be taken from a small marsh which a Frenchman, accompanying Indians who were exploring upward from the river's mouth, thought to be shaped like a snow-shoe.

"But I've al'ys heerd," said Harvey, "the name come from the tarnal racket the river keeps up with the falls and rifts and what not, on't."

Its three Indian names are Mas-le-gui (St. Francis), Ta-na-wa-deh and Ni-ha-na-wa-te (both Iroquois), the last signifying "full of rapids."

"We are now 'mongst another set o' waters from what we was at the S'nac Lakes," continued Harvey, after he had given his idea of the name of the river. "The ridge that the Injin Carry runs over, is the dividin' place. The Stunny Ponds runs, as you know, by way of the Creek, inter the Racket. This ridge, about thirty miles west or mebby northwest o' here, turns the Big and Little Wolf Pond waters inter the Racket too. On the other side o' the ridge the waters of the Musquiter and Rawlins and Floodwood and other ponds round there, go inter the Upper S'nac."

A short distance east, we found the river bending short to the south. Two or three miles from the bend, glimpses of an opening broke upon us through the foliage of the border on our right.

"Big Meadow," said Harvey. "I'll see if there's a deer there."

He landed, taking his rifle, and ascended the bank, followed by myself. The wild meadow contained about a hundred acres, moulded into bays by points of wood and grouped with groves like islets. Irregular streaks of stemless cedars, like green tents planted on the ground, and tamaracks, with their graceful limbs, skirted here and there the grassy surface.

We cast our glances around; no living shape disturbed the loneliness. We entered deeper; and Harvey, stopping suddenly at the muddy margin of a thread of water, exclaimed—

"By golly, I raally hed a notion at fust glance this track b'longed to a moose," pointing to a large, rounded hoof-print stamped in the ooze. "How on airth could oxen 'ave strayed out here! We're miles away from any clearin' or where any human critter lives. Let me see! Oh, I hev it! The lumber people, workin' on Cold River, 'bove Racket Falls, must ha' drove their oxen 'cross here."

"Is a moose-track like that of an ox?" I inquired, as we were gliding again upward.

"It's longer and more peaked. The time has bin when I've seen a good many moose-tracks, but not of late years. Of'en and of'en, when I was a young man, I've hunted 'em on snow-shoes, on the sides of old Tawwus, but they've gone, most, from there now."

"They've gone almost entirely from this region, haven't they, Harvey?"

"Jest round here, they hev. But in them woods south

o' Mount Seward, they say they kin be found yit. Them woods, though, I don't know nothin' about, nur nobody else that I ever see, but the Injun guide, Mitchell Sabatis. I dunno but some o' the Keene Mountain trappers, too, may go 'long the edges in winter, layin' saple lines on snow-shoes. And they finds 'em round at Mud Lake"——

"I suppose you've shot numbers of them, Harvey, in your time?"

"You're right, I hev. But they're a terr'ble critter to kill."

"Why so?"

"Oh, they're so farse when they're wounded or brought to bay. There isn't no critter in the woods that I wouldn't fight, sunner than a moose. A bear or a painter ain't nothin' to 'em. I've fit a good many and killed a good many and I tell ye, when their blood is up, by goll! it's lively times. They jump at ye with their mane on eend, and glarin' as though they'd eat ye up; and them broad horns o' theirn, too, look mighty ugly. You've got to be consid'ble smart in dodgin' about the trees and watchin' your time to fire, or let 'em hev it with your knife whiles the hound tugs at their flanks, or it's kingdom come with ye. I've fit 'em when 'twas about an even chance whether I should be killed or them. And there's no give up to 'em, nuther. They'll fight as long as there's breath left. And you take a critter five or six foot high, and weighin' eight hunderd or a thousand pounds, with great horns, and feet that'll cut into ye like a knife, and you may hev a notion it's no child's play fightin' 'em. I've heerd a bull-moose roar afore now and was glad he was miles off!"

"What sort of sound does he make, Harvey?"

"Well, I can't scurce tell ye. It's a loud, shrill, ringin', twangin' sound, like—I'll tell ye—'tis more like the twangin' of a tin horn than anything I kin think on, and kin be heard through the woods a-ringin' and echoin' fur miles."

"What does the animal feed on?"

"Water-lilies jest like the deer; but they're more fond o' the tap-borers or moose-heads or pick'rel weeds, as some calls 'em; and they say in the woods that the pick'rel come from these weeds. They're old hunderd on 'em. The big upper lip o' the moose, when it's feedin', goes flop, flop, in twistin' in their fud, so that a body kin hear it, a mile or more. I remember, one time, at the head o' Cold River—'twas one still night in the airly part o' July. Them queer things, the tree-toads, was singin' away— quir-r-r-r-r, and as for the lightnin' bugs, by goll! I never see 'em so plenty. Well, I sot in my boat—'twas Little Mary, afore I'd built the Bluebird—and the fust I knowed, I heerd, kinder faint-like, that flop, flop, flop. The moose was either in a lily-pad pond, more'n a mile off, or in the second o' the Preston Ponds not so fur, but over a mile at enny rate. They're a big critter and don't do things like a mink by a derned sight."

"You say you would rather meet a panther than an angry moose, Harvey!"

"Pooh! painters ain't nothin'. I'd about as lieve meet a dog as one on 'm. They're a good deal more skeered at you than you at them, and 'll run, that is, when they ain't got no cubs to fight fur. I've hunted and trapped in these woods and fished in these waters about forty-two year and I've never seen a tarnal sight on 'em. I've camped, too, alone of'en, right under Catamount Peak, that lays off in the St. Regis' Woods, nigh the head waters of the Upper S'nac, and never even then heerd a great many. I remember one time, though. I'd bin trappin' beaver on a pond right under the Peak and 'ad killed a doe and dressed her jest outside my camp. I call it camp, but I hadn't no shanty nur tent, unly the ground to sleep on. I was alone, unly I hed Watch. Well, I made a rousin' big fire, fur 'twas a leetle cold and there'd bin a flurry o' snow at sundown. About midnight, I was woke up by the dolefullest sounds—well, they was more like a woman cryin' out fur help in the woods than anything else—a pitiful, kind o' whinin', wailin' cry. 'Twas comin' clusser and clusser, and at fust my head was so twistified by bein' woke up so sudden, I raally consated some one was lost in the woods; so I sung out and the doleful cries stopped right off and I knowed then 'twas a painter. Well, I was jest a goin' to turn over and go to sleep agin, when Watch begun to show his teeth and growl, and the hair on his neck riz up. I couldn't see nothin', and yit, as I stared round the camp, I consated I see a blazin' kind o' eyeballs nigh the fire. But Watch wouldn't stir, fur the catamount would a killed 'im with one blow of his paw. Finally at last, I heerd a creep, creep, creep, off through the woods, and that was the last on't; and sun I fell asleep agin. But talkin' o' moose: when he's riled or wounded or crowded up too cluss, look out fur 'im, that's all. You must git out o' his way, fur he won't git out o' yourn, take my word for't."

"I should like to see a moose, Harvey!"

"I'll take ye to Mud Lake, up Bog River, that comes in at the head o' Tupper's Lake, where you'll be tol'ble sure o' secin' one and p'raps git a shot."

I expressed myself delighted with this arrangement and he resumed.

"It's a dreary, skeery, dark hole of a place, that Mud Lake. There's a wild meader or slew, some ways from it, the biggest I ever see. You can't much more 'n look crost it, and there's the place where the moose find their feedin'. This meader isn't known much. I never knowed but one man beside myself that ever spoke on't. Well, I've saw the time when I've skeert up in that meader two, or even three moose, in a day, and shot one or two on 'em. But it can't be done now. Talkin' o' trappin' too. I've ketched fisher and mink and saple and black foxes on Tupper's Lake, 'twixt sunrise and sundown, enough to kiver the little Bluebird all over. But that can't be done now nuther;—see how the deer 've turned up old sanko there, and no later than last night, too!" pointing to a broad shallow, bristling with the cropped stems and heaped with the tumbled pads of the yellow lily, interspersed with the upturned dull red leaves of the white. "What say ye for a jack-hunt to-night? There's fust rate slews all along here, up to Racket Falls, where we camp for a day or so, as I onderstand!"

Gladly did I express my readiness, for I had long wished to witness this mode of hunting deer.

These slews (*i. e.* sloughs) are frequent in the forest and are either low, marshy spots with narrow streams and covered with wild grass which affords pasturage for the deer, or shallow basins of water, mantled in water-lilies, of which the yellow species is the animal's favorite luxury. The principal hours for feeding are from sunset to early morning. The day is generally passed by the deer in covert.

In about an hour, we reached Palmer Brook, a charming little stream meandering through the usual wild meadow, where trees single and clustered, and shrubbery-like thickets, all disposed as by the hand of taste, gave the scene not only a picturesque but habitable look, so that the eye involuntarily wandered to discover the country-seat.

There we found the whole party landed, with their boats drawn up the shore. They had decided to send their three hounds out for a drive and were waiting for Harvey to bring Watch.

It was now deep in the afternoon.

Mart, Will and Cort each led off a hound, to let him loose; my comrades started for their several stations, while Harvey and I set out, he leading Watch by his chain.

We entered the forest, and the old woodman undid the collar from the hound, who looked up with his bright, intelligent eye, waving his tail delightedly. Harvey bade the dog start. Watch bounded off with a yelp and then moved in a quick walk, with his nose to the ground. After completing a circle, he returned and gazed up at Harvey, as if to say, "No deer there." Harvey waved him off again, and vaulting logs, threading thickets, searching bushes and spruce caverns and nosing the underwood generally, in another and still wider circle, once more he returned with his mute message as before. A third time Harvey sent him away, but a half hour now elapsed without the return of the dog. The old guide then turned to me and said,

"The pup has got the trail at last, so we'd best make tracks torts the brook again. Bimeby we'll hear him tell his luck."

Returning, we found Coburn at the mouth of the brook; Corey and Little Jess had pushed on to Racket Falls with the baggage boats, to prepare the camp before night.

My station was also at the brook's mouth on my left. Beyond, was the runway.

The scene,—late alive with shapes of hurrying men and eager hounds, flitting colors of red and blue hunting-shirts and flashes of guns and wood-knives, boats gliding up and down the river to their stations, with loud talk and calls and short, joyful yelps,—was now quiet and solitary, with only the common sights and sounds of the wilderness. The falsetto of the jay; the bass note, softened by distance, of the raven; the harsh cry of the wheeling hawk, the tap of the woodpecker, and the pervading monotone of the river, soothed the ear and deepened the loneliness. Occasionally I hushed my breath for a cry from the hounds, but nothing was heard. My boat lay with quiet ripples sparkling around its stern, and bushes burying its bow. The sunlight glanced from the river, twinkled on the leaves and bathed the grass. Minute after minute crept by; no cry from the dogs, no human sound; my rifle lay idle at my knee. Seated near me, on a mound of moss, was Harvey, with his rifle also across his knee; and over a clump of tall ferns, close to the borders of the stream, I saw the motionless head and shoulders of Coburn.

At last, a burst of music from a hound made the woods echo. A rifle shot succeeded; then came a fainter yelping, followed by another report, dull and lengthened, down the river.

Soon Bingham and Cort appeared, skimming down the Racket, the face of Bingham radiant with pleasure, and Cort rowing with buoyant speed. As the boat came nearer, I saw a buck at the bottom and Watch curled at the bow.

"I fixed him this time!" shouted Bingham, "Right through the heart, or I'm a humbug! By goll!" landing, "as old Harvey here says, it was a splendid sight! How Watch yelled and how the deer flew! And how he stopped too—and fell—right flat in his tracks! But I suppose it will be all Cort, Cort, at the camp-fire. Renning will say, in that confounded cool way of his, 'Why, of course, Cort shot the deer; who doubts it!' And then Gaylor will say, 'There's one thing Bing can't do; he can't shoot!' And then you, Coburn and Smith here, will chime in. Well, I've heard such before. But it doesn't affect me! I tower above it all, 'like some tall cliff'—Ah, here comes Gaylor and Renning—and—hang me if there isn't—yes—there is—a deer, by Jupiter! in Gay's boat! Well now I call this last superfluous. It's really robbing the forest! Of course, Gaylor," as the last party landed, " you shot the deer, and not Will."

"Of course I shot him," responded Gaylor in a cheery tone. "There's one in your boat, I see. When did Cort shoot him?"

"There it is!" said Bingham. "But I shall enter into no controversy on the subject. I shall merely mention I shot him and say no more."

"Ha, ha, ha!" exploded from the whole company.

"Oh laugh away!" said Bingham, taking a seat. "There's the buck though, and here's the tool," slapping his rifle, "that did the business. Cort! hand me my flask!"

After enjoying the quiet and leafy beauty of Palmer Brook, a little while longer, we all moved gaily up toward Racket Falls, which we reached at sunset. We found the tents pitched and the camp-fire kindled upon an elevated point or headland, on the east bank, at the foot of the falls or rather rapids, the foam of which gleamed red among the scattered rocks.

The tents stood in a grassy space, with a background of firs and cedars intermingled with the birch, aspen and maple. One large white pine towered on either side, with one near the front of the headland looking upon the Racket, which glided swift and dark, with large blots of foam from the falls, whirling and loosening in their downward way. In one corner, a tamarack hung its beautiful foliage.

The opposite shore rose into an acclivity, with here and there a dry pine like a flag-staff, above the verdure, and fluttering with pennons of grey moss. Paths meandered from the headland (which was a well-known camping-spot) down to the river on either side and into the background of forest.

After our usual meal, we disposed ourselves for a genial smoke before the crackling camp-fire.

The lucent gold of the twilight tinged the scene and vanished; the dusk darkened into night.

A breeze crept through the high woods opposite; above me, the white pine, that tree of sorrow, heaved its long deep sigh, and the low crashings of the rapids filled the air. Ralph and Gaylor had left to lie down in the tent, the grassy floor of which had been spread deep by the guides with mattresses of hemlock. Coburn had taken his seat on the end of a log, close to the camp-fire, to smoke and cogitate perhaps his next speech in Congress (as he was a member and a powerful speaker), while I had gone aside to observe, if not also to meditate.

At first, my eye was caught by the camp-fire shedding its gloss in a wide circle over the grass blades, brakes and tiny wood-sprouts, cutting the nearest trees into gigantic yellow cameos on a sable background and touching with wild scarlet the black river below; the dark figures of the guides flitting athwart the flame like goblins, with Coburn shown in sharp relief, his countenance fixed and arm slightly raised as if thrusting an argument upon "Mr. Speaker," and the sparks whirling through the smoke like fiery insects.

I thought then of the vast expanse of this sea-like wilderness, almost unchanged since its creation, and of the wild freedom of that savage life known upon our continent before the "White Throats" came. I asked myself whether man has gained greater happiness with his boasted civilization. Do all the trophies won by that civilization, its treasures of science, its enchanted realms of painting, poetry, sculpture, music, eloquence, its elegancies and luxuries, outweigh its sufferings, cares and crimes, the daily anxieties and toils and battles for its miscalled prizes; its galling conventionalities, its scourging necessities, its malignant rivalries, its treacherous smiles—real ability failing where grinning trickery succeeds; mere poverty despised and mere gold adored; genius trampled beneath the hoofs of pompous dulness; frank honesty supplanted by wary villany; right throttled by the ruffian hand of power; all these, the rank weeds that choke the hotbed of our artificial existence? I, for one, am sick of the griefs and strifes and follies of the world. Oh men! when will ye cease to torture and crush your fellow-men? Thy wailing winds, oh earth! are but the echoes of our human sighs, thy very throes the emblems of our agonies!

Here, thought I once more, would I live; here, in this fresh, free wilderness, this tranquil realm of content, where honor is not measured by success, where pretension does not trample upon merit, where genius is not a jest, goodness not a seeming and devotion not a sham. Here, where the light of day is undarkened by wrong, where silence is the parent of pure meditation and the solitude is eloquent of God. Here would I live, listening the forest's calls to self-communing, and all those teachings that guide the insight, soften the heart, and purify, while they expand, the soul.

CHAPTER VIII.

Floating for Deer.—Night Scenery on the Racket.—Owls.—A Camp Scene.

I WAS awakened from my reverie by the voice of Harvey at my side.

"Come, Mr. Smith! it's about time now for our night-hunt, and a rael inkstand of a night 'tis, too, dark and not windy; and I think one deer, ef not two, 's jest about 's good 's dead. Ready?"

I slipped on my overcoat and grasped a blanket to defend my knees against the chill of the night air. At the boat I found Corey, who was to go with us as marksman (as I had had little experience with the rifle), while Harvey was to handle the paddle. The latter duty required consummate skill, which the old boatman proved himself to possess. He seated himself in the stern while Corey took the oars; I sat in the middle, and the Bluebird skimmed rapidly down the river, a bend of which soon hid the camp-fire.

Our jack was a semicircular piece of birch bark, painted dark; the top and bottom of wood, with two oil lamps behind a glass front, and planted on a wooden handle at the prow. It was not yet lighted.

The black woods looked threatening, but the water, although dark, seemed more companionable sprinkled with the stars, and even the wilderness did not appear entirely abandoned, with the same dots of light glittering among the breaks in the gloom.

Nor was the solitude completely silent. Now and then came the chirp of some bird startled by our oars, while the owl's prolonged hoo hoohoo, hoo hoohoo-o-o-o-o-o-o-o-o-o-ah, rounding into a deep-throated, peevish caw, frequently came on the ear.

Here and there a skeleton tree, leaning over, made a thick black streak in the air, or a protruding branch dropped an arch, while dark bulks told the margin logs.

"We're nigh Palmer Brook," at length said Harvey, in a guarded voice. "I forgot to put ile in the lamps or trim 'em to-day, so we'd best land to light up the jack, hadn't we?"

We landed on the steep bank, in a cavern of the foliage. We had not much more than entered it, however, before my face and hands broke out as it were into an intolerable tickling.

"Whew, the flies is comin'," said Corey. "How quick they smell a feller out! Plague take these mitchets; but we'll fix 'em, skeeters and all!"

The charges of these winged lancers were indeed terrible. They, the mixed legion of musquitoes and gnats or midges, are the serious annoyance of the summer woods. They seem to lie in wait, and the moment one ventures from the boat on shore, they swarm in myriads; like fire on invisible ink, your very coming strikes the atmosphere into gnats and musquitoes.

If you open your mouth, in they go; if you inhale through your nose, up they go; they play an unceasing fife to the drum of your ear, and dart in as if to assault your brain. Just as you motion to slap your forehead, there is a quick sting on your temple, and you don't know which to slap first. If you rub your cheek— w-h-i-z-p—there is a terrific bite on your eyelid. You crush the sight out of your optics with a finger that has three little fiends tacked to it; you try to rub both your prickling hands at once, while your elbows are suffering; you shrug your shoulders and begin to wriggle your back in your shirt, at the same time your legs are twitching as if in a galvanic battery; in short, you are defending the tip of your nose, while the aggregate flesh of your body is creeping off your bones.

"Yes, yes! we'll fix 'em!" repeated Corey, as he and Harvey gathered the materials of combustion at the foot of a pine tree. Soon a snapping blaze was licking the rough bark, bringing out the immense tree from its dark background and tinging the leaves and stems around into ruddy gold. With the light flickering over their persons, the two guides then prepared the jack, kindled it, and we re-embarked, leaving the fire to burn down, like a red eye-ball alternately winking and glaring in the darkness of the bank.

Corey examined his rifle, to see if all was right, then seated himself directly behind the jack, so as to front the water, with his weapon across his lap.

A red glare played upon the shore and the stream ahead, while the boat remained in deep shadow. The unnatural light dazzles and bewilders the deer, which frequent the banks and shallows and particularly the sloughs, at night, to feed upon the water-lilies, and it strikes them motionless, the boat and its occupants being concealed in gloom. They stand gazing out from the dark background, quite covered with the light, affording a near and generally fatal shot.

The boat seemed now to glide of its own volition, Harvey drawing his paddle so still, as not to wake even the whisper of a bursting bubble. Once dipped, the paddle is not withdrawn, but worked by the wrist and elbow noiseless as the fin of a fish.

As I hushed my breath while thus borne along, there was a weird effect from the glide, making me feel, with Hecate,

"Oh, what a dainty pleasure 'tis,
To sail i' the air!"

The water-flies entering the glare of the jack-light glittered like specks of gold. As the broad crimson gleam startled up the banks, a gigantic shadow seemed to chase the boat and swallow the trees, touching them first, then meandering over the branches down to their very tips.

The red beams flitted athwart the bushes and water-plants of the margin near us and turned the bushes into moving gold, upon which and the gleaming lily-pads, we would rustle suddenly, as suddenly leaving for the still water. A quick dropping shot of splashes in the shallows told the "plops" (one of Harvey's Saranac words) of the startled muskrats, as they tumbled into the water from the logs and borders. Their little black heads spotted the water all around in the jack's radiance, vanishing when out the stream of light, with the quickness of thought.

We were now gliding across the opening of Palmer Brook. Suddenly I heard a slight rustling close to the bank and then two or three light, paddling sounds in the water. Corey raised his rifle and motioned toward a black thicket. The boat glided up, as if sentient. The click of Corey's springing gunlocks followed; I saw two spots of pale fire in front of an immense black tree; Corey caught his weapon to an aim; the figure of a deer, motionless as a sculptured image, with head turned toward the jack, started out; a rifle-crack; the deer sank; the boat shot to the bank and Corey, drawing his wood-knife, leaped out. The deer scrambled up, fell and then lay motionless.

"It's down among the rushes O! with that ven'son!" said Harvey, laughing.

"'Tisn't nothin' else!" answered Corey, dragging the doe into the boat, with her throat cut. "I sent her my 'spects right 'twixt her eyes!"

"Old hunderd, and all the folks jine in!" cried Harvey. "Now for the slews below," singing,

"Oh, Susy was her name!
Sich a purty little dame—zip!"

Again we were skimming along the margin, Harvey

dipping without care, as no feeding-places were afforded by the bolder shores now presented.

The ripples clinked along the sides of the boat in the quiet, like little, muffled bells, and I heard the gulp or guttural yelp of a frog, sounding like a blow on a tree, awakening an echo.

At length the dash of the paddle and ripple-taps at the prow stopped and we were again gliding along, with the stillness of death. Corey would motion first with one hand and then the other and the boat would, as if human, obey. Now it turned and stole into a little cove, looking this way and that with its broad, red glance, like a Chinese candle-bug, and then it drew itself backward and resumed its course. Now it felt along an opening, glided beside a pavement of lily-pads, pushed its face into a space of rushes or crept athwart a cluster of alders. Often, some dark object seemed to me a deer, but the light turned it into a small rock or an immense log foreshortened or an upturned root. Occasionally there would be a splash or paddling near the margin, but Corey would whisper, "a bullfrog" or "a muskrat."

At length, we turned into a basin of lily-pads.

"Loon Slew," whispered Harvey.

On we rustled; the newness, the picturesqueness, the romance of the entire scene delighted me. Gliding as if by magic over these wild waters, hemmed in by the trackless forest; not a human creature (but our own party) probably within leagues of us; not one human habitation, the stars our only watchers; my two companions, inhabitants of the wilderness, caring for or knowing little else than its sports and laughing at its hardships; the whole, presenting such utter contrast to my usual experience of life, impressed me with the profoundest interest.

We had now approached a low point covered with tall, dense thickets. The jack-light played upon the edges but failed to penetrate the interior. Corey raised his hand as if warning us to perfect stillness. A light, quick smacking or chopping sound within the alders—an animal feeding! Corey raised himself cautiously; the sound ceased but was instantly resumed. He peered on this and then on that side the jack; swung it either way; then motioned now on one side, now on the other, the boat turning as if chained to his gestures. At last, another light, paddling sound came, then a trickle or two of drops. Corey aimed with lightning quickness, but with the motion a loud startling huh-h-u-u-u, huh-huh rose from the thickets, followed by a rapid crash through them. As if the first sounds were signals, three more like them burst from the shore, a rod or two from us. Light boundings were heard; a few moments elapsed and then for some distance within the forest, echoed the same thick, fierce sounds between a snort and a scream, only fainter.

"Confound 'em!" said Corey, in a tone of vexation. "Five whistles and every deer off!"

"And no leave axed," added Harvey. "But let's try the other places below! Them deer by this time is mindin' their own business. 'Ef it's all the same to you,' says they, ' we'll bid ye good evenin'; we don't like no sich company!' But didn't they whistle!"

Making our way out of the slough, to the usual terror of the frogs and muskrats, who were "floppin' and ploppin' and poppin' and squigglin'" (whatever that was), as Harvey said, all around, we once more glided down the river.

We passed several low openings, which the Bluebird swept with her searching eye, but fortune had deserted us; no more deer were seen; no sounds were heard that told even of their vicinity.

"The deer has all gone to night meetin'," said Harvey, at last. "I felt quite sarten of one, at Moose Slew, but 'taint no more go. 'Spos'n we turn back to camp, Corey! Shell we, Mr. Smith?"

The boat's direction was accordingly changed up stream. The same caution was still observed but it was fruitless. By the wheel of the magic paddle, the little Bluebird would turn her gaze full in front of the openings and sweep them with red scrutiny, but nothing was seen across the flat expanses. Wheeling her great eyeball half round again, onward the boat would steal, bringing the various dark objects of the shore into momentary crimson life. Up Loon Slough once more we moved, starting out over the rustling surface, as if by an enchanter's wand, the stemmed balls of the yellow lilies with their broad, glistening leaves, but we could hear or discern nothing that showed a deer had even visited the spot. We reached the point. The bushes moved gently in the faint night breeze; but there was no sound upon the bank, no ripple on the water.

Out of the slough again we glided.

"I guess the deer has all gone to bed!" said Harvey at length, giving a plunge with his paddle. "There's no use tryin' any longer, so we'll git on to camp as fast as we kin; hey, Corey! What say ye, Mr. Smith?"

"Yes!" answered Corey, "let's git out o' this, jest as soon as we kin go. For my part I'm tired o' lookin' without seein'. Hang the deer say I!"

I was also in favor of moving camp-ward, as the air was increasing in its damp chilliness, and every limb felt cramped in keeping my position with such entire quietude; so we turned and pulled rapidly up the river; Corey extinguishing the jack and betaking himself once more to the oars.

Again came the distant hoot of the owl floating over the dark silence.

"Shut up there!" exclaimed Corey. "What d'ye think we care for you!"

"Them owls is a sassy thing; them and loons," said Harvey, lighting his pipe with a match. "They seem to hev a notion nobody haint no business in the woods but them."

"I tell ye, shut up and mind yer business!" said Corey, as another hooting was heard, but this time appearing to come from a considerable distance. "If I hear another word, I'll give ye a bullet to feed on."

"How can you shoot him, Corey?" said I. "He must be, from the sound, certainly a quarter, if not half a mile away."

"He isn't twenty rods!" replied Corey; "that's a way the critters hev of hootin' in their throat so as to seem a long way off, when they're close by."

"That's a true bill," chimed in Harvey. "And they're just the revarse o' wolves. Let them howl and you'd think yourself nigh enough to look down their throats a'most, when they're mebby so fur off they couldn't smell ye, if their noses was as long as pine-trees. They'll go y-o-w-l, y-o-w-l, one beginnin' fust and the rest strikin' in, jest as they sing in meetin', when the parson lines the hymn."

"Hear that owl snap his jaws!" said Corey, as a clicking sound in front met my ear. "Look!" continued he, after the boat had moved a few rods, "there he stands!" pointing to a dry tree leaning over the water a short distance before us. Sure enough, there, dimly seen, was a large bird perched on the top of the tree and shaking his head sidewise and up and down, like a political orator in a paroxysm of patriotism.

"He don't appear to mind us much," said I.

"They're the sassiest——" Harvey was commencing, when another hoo hoo, broken short by the report of Corey's rifle, intervened. Whether it was the jar I gave the boat in my desire to see, or carelessness on Corey's part, from being too sure of his aim, the bird, instead of tumbling dead as I expected, glided away smooth and noiseless as thistle-down, showing for a moment athwart us, and then swallowed in the gloom.

"These stump speakers can't always be killed off, Corey!" I observed.

"Specially when the place you shoot from plays teter!" said Corey in a slightly vexed tone. "But no matter, misfortins will happen."

"In the best regilated fam'lies," added Harvey.

"Tootle too loo, too loo, too looty,
Tootle loo—whew, whew, whe—whew whew"—
a sudden crack sounded, and then a dull, reverberating report.

"A tree fallin'," said Corey, as I gave a slight start. "They'll fall sometimes in the woods without any warnin', jest as human bein's will in apoplex."

"That's so," said Harvey. "I've bin out afore now, and a tree that looked jest as sound as a trout 'ud give a quick skrick like, as a deer'll bleat when tackled by the hounds, and then fall with a most onmassyful noise. It takes a two-hoss pettyfogger to git out o' the way."

At this moment came the most singular sound I ever heard. It was a sharp whine, half smothered in a thick wheeze, or a loud hiss with a fine whistle cutting through it, like an exhausted blacksmith's bellows or a person breathing in an asthma.

"What on earth is that, Corey?" asked I.

"It's a young owl tryin' to whistle!" answered he, "and a rael doleful sound 'tis. It sounds as if his throat was dry, and he couldn't pucker his mouth."

"It sounds as if he had the phthisic," said Harvey, "and was tryin' to breathe through a holler knittin'-needle."

A hollow, choking ubble-bubble now sounded close at hand.

"There's somebody drowning there in the river, boys! do make haste—quick!"

But the "boys" only laughed.

"That's another of the owls agin; the big horned critters, or cat owls, as they're called," said Corey.

"An owl again!" exclaimed I; "why, how many noises do the creatures make?"

"As many a'most as ridin' skimington," answered Harvey. "Sometimes they'll screech like a catamount; then they'll whine like an old woman at camp-meetin'. Another sounds like a bell—a leetle owl, not much bigger'n a couple o' white lily-blows. Another sounds for all the world like the whet-whet of a saw—and that isn't a great sight bigger'n a pine-knot. I've heerd some bark like a dog, some mew like a cat, and spit 'pit 'pit they will and snarl and growl as ugly as Satan. Others agin 'll c-r-y out so doleful, you'd think they had the belly-ache. Others agin 'll whu-i-stle clear as a nigger. They're great hands to steal, too, 'specially the big horned ones. I've seen 'em spyin' round my traps for what they could git, time and agin. And I've ketched 'em tearin' rats they've found in traps all to pieces, and lookin' farse as wild-cats."

"What do they live on?"

"Well, ducks, and patridges, and dead fish; the last is old hunderd to 'em. I've seen 'em skim cluss to the ground, and then fall quick as a wink on a squirrel, or muskrat, or rabbit, mebby. I've shot, afore now, and wounded 'em, and they'd throw themselves on their back, and lift up their long, black claws, and snap their beaks, and wink their round eyes, they would, and sw-e-l-l like a big puff-ball. They're all sorts o' colors, too, grey and brown, and white and brindle; and one kind's red at fust, as ef 'twas singed by the camp fire, and then grows mottled like. This 'ere makes sounds like a body's teeth a-chatterin' and clickin' t'gether with the cold. The fust time I heerd one I couldn't think what on airth 'twas. I looked round and round, and finally at last I see the leetle red sarpent a p-e-e-kin' out of a holler low down in a maple, lookin' like a konkus on a pine-tree."

We now glided along in silence past the grim, ghostly trees. I almost fancied we were spectres flitting through a phantom scene, bound in a spell, and I feared to draw breath lest I should break it, and incur some dreadful punishment. Now and then I imagined the darkness gathering into a vast demon, and threatening to whelm us in the gloom of his frown; sometimes I thought the sombre walls on each side were closing to annihilate us.

Suddenly another hissing was heard, but this time accompanied with a sound between a snarl and a snore. It filled the woods in the stillness, until I thought it might be the demon napping on his lonely vigil.

Corey clattered one of the oars, and immediately, with a keen shriek, a large black object burst from the shore, and sailing over our heads, became lost in the darkness.

"An eagle," said Corey, unconcernedly. "He was sleepin'; and though he snores like a nor'wester, the least leetle sound 'll wake him, and off he goes."

A sudden light now gleamed from the gloom in front, and Harvey exclaimed—

"Here we are cluss to camp. I'm glad on't; my j'ints feel rayther creaky in the damp air so long!" Then croaking:

> "And it's are you-u-eu Macdon-ald, returned to Glenco-o-o
> Oh! it's hung on my—hay! hul-lo!"—

At this instant there came out of the camp the voices of Renning and Gaylor raised in a song. I could hardly believe my ears, as I knew they had no more idea of music than a brace of loons. And yet, there they were, tangling their voices together in an ear-splitting discord of—

> "Some love to roam
> O'er the wild sea foam,
> Where the shrill winds whistle free!
> But a mountain la—(No, Ralph, you're wrong.)
> But a chosen band,
> In a mountain land,
> And a life in the woods (a tremendous roar) for me!
> Oho ho oh! ho, ho, ho, ho!
> But a chosen ba—(No, no, not yet, Ralph.)
> Oho oh oh! ho, ho, ho, ho-o-o-o!
>   (Like the blast of a cracked trumpet.)
> But a chosen band,
> (With a clap, as if they had joined hands in eternal friendship.)
> In a mountain land,
> And a life in the woods for (clear up in the air) me."
>   (With a sudden drop into a long groan.)

"That last sound 's a good deal like the c-a-w-w-w of one of them owls we've bin speakin' about," said Harvey. "I've knowed my two tom-cats sing better 'n that."

"I've got two b'ys to hum," said Corey, "that kin beat that noise on a couple o' punkin vines."

The two singers recommenced—

"Some love to"——

I had now reached the camp, and the fire revealed me to them. They were seated on one end of a green log, the other end lying in the camp-fire, and smoking like a huge calumet.

The song broke off short.

"Why, Smith, is that you?" said Renning. "Come, take a punch. By the way, what luck have you had?"

"We've one deer!"

"Good. I may say very good. But I don't care much for deer-shooting. Give me trout (loudly, and clutching the air with a swing) eh, Gay?"

"Certainly," returned Gaylor.

"Trout! that's the word—trout! Come, Smith, take a punch: a moderate punch! But I say, Smith, put me in a boat, and Gay, here, in his, and you in a third: no, not you! you can't catch trout: but Bingham: no, nor Bing either: he's only down on deer. Well—we'll say Coburn, that is, if he wasn't so afraid of the flies! But the truth is, Smith, the flies are rather bad in the woods. They do bite, old boy! sometimes better than the trout—and as I was saying, put me and Gay in our boats, and—whoever you've a mind to, I don't care a fig—at Half Way Brook, down there on the Racket, or at Redside Brook, on Tupper's Lake; wouldn't we have lively times there with the trout? from one pound to two, eh, Gay?"

"Precisely!"

"The punch is in the pitcher, by the partridges there, Smith. Isn't that good punch? Stop! I'll take a little!

Gaylor and I have been so busy conversing, we quite forgot the punch—eh, Gay ?"

"Umph !" said Gaylor.

"Talking of punch," resumed Ralph, "Gay, here, makes the best"——

"Hold your jacklight a little more around, Cort !" a loud voice here broke in, which we recognised as Bingham's, sounding from the woods a little above. "It appears to be a sort of 'facilis descensus Averni' here, Cort !—in other words, a most diabolical mud-hole. Lord, one of my boots is gone ! Ah ! here it is, all right ! Hurrah, there, Cort, come back a moment ! your long legs don't recognise the difficulties of a pair not brought up in the woods. I've lost the path to the camp, and I'm down here by the river. These woods are 'a mighty maze,' and deucedly 'without a plan,' and in the night time they're a good deal 'like the light,' as Byron says, 'of a dark eye in woman'—that is, the dark with the light left out. Ah ! here we are ! Good evening, gentlemen. What ! are ye thieves of the night, cutpurses, that you sit up so late ?"

"What have you got ?" asked Ralph, laconically.

"Got ! a pair of barked shins and a cold, I'm afraid, on this confounded river !"

"Where's your deer, Bing ?" said Gaylor.

"Deer !" repeated Bingham; "I don't believe there's a deer on the Racket. Here we've been floating from the head of the falls, up as far as Moose Creek; into the Creek for a mile, and back again, and I pledge you my word there are no more signs of deer to be found than of common sense in our friend Smith, here. There were signs of musquitoes, though. In fact, I may say, my face is one great sign. Every pore is a bite. But there's an awful smell of punch here. It truly

"'Wastes its sweetness on the desert air.'"

"You'll find some in the pitcher there," said Ralph. "Help yourself. That's the way we did."

"So I should think," said Bingham, looking into the pitcher at the camp fire; "and 'we' have helped ourselves so thoroughly, the pitcher is as dry as a President's message. Why, you must have used a forcing-pump here! there isn't even a seed left. Cort, make me a glass of punch!" sitting down on a log.

"So you found no deer, Bing!" said Gaylor.

"Deer, poh, deer! Why not say elephants, hippopotami? One can find the last as well as the first in these woods. Take my word for it, gentlemen, there's no deer here. I shall certainly go to Maine next year, if I have to go alone. You can there—why, Cort, what on earth is in this punch? it's as black as old Harvey's tom-cat," holding the cup containing it at the camp-fire.

"I ax your pardon, Mr. Bingham," said Cort aghast, "but I do bleeve I've mixed it in the cup that had black pepper in't."

"Black pepper!" said poor Bing, clapping his hand to his stomach, "gunpowder, you mean; and from the heat in my throat and all the way down, I think it has exploded there. . Black pepper, Cort, is good in its place, but it's confounded bad in the place it has got to now!"

Gaylor and Renning soon after this went to their tent, whither Coburn had gone early; the guides sought lairs in the thickets, preferring them to the close air of the lesser tent. Bingham, after giving birth to a diabolical yawn, followed his comrades, and I was alone.

The black river below; the dark bank in front; the murky woods around; the hollow rush of the falls; the hoot of a neighboring owl and the distant cry of a wolf —a long drawn melancholy cry—all made a scene of the deepest solitude. Man! how far off he appeared and how near God!

The wilderness is one great tongue, speaking constantly to our hearts; inciting to knowledge of ourselves and to love of the Supreme Maker, Benefactor, Father. Not in the solitude of the desert, nor on the mighty ocean do we more deeply realize the Great Presence that pervades all loneliness. Here, with the grand forest for our worshipping temple, our hearts expanding, our thoughts rising unfettered, we behold Him, face to face.

I walked to the end of the point; I surrendered myself to the influence of the hour and the scene. From the starry heavens and the solemn landscape, breathed the Invisible Presence; and from the depths of my heart rose an aspiration of unbounded faith and love. And I knew I was immortal—I knew, despite the sin and weakness of my wrecked humanity, I was still in some poor measure one with Deity.

CHAPTER IX.

Carry at Racket Falls.—Up the Racket.—Cold River.—Bowen's Camp.—
Long Lake.—The River Driver.—Harvey's Woods-Almanac.

WE rose with the sun for an excursion up the river, to the foot of Long Lake (Wee-cho-bad-cho-nee-pus, lake abounding in bass-wood), belonging to the Racket System of waters.

As I awoke, a path of gold gleamed into the tent through an aperture in front left for air.

Upon the sun-streaked space before it, the camp-fire was merrily blazing, and around were the guides busy for the breakfast, the first symptom of which appeared as I left the tent, in a gridiron grinning at a gaping lake trout, as if anticipating the lively broil to which it would shortly put him.

The scene was fresh and cheerful. The tips of the white pines, and the upper rim of the bank opposite, were of a yellow burnish; a brown, decayed stump, against which stood a jack, a neck-yoke and a landing net, looked mellow and rich in the light, and the stem of a silver birch, touched by a finger of the sun, gleamed like a pillar of pearl.

A carry of a mile and a half led around the falls over a steep ridge.

Each guide, except Corey (who, with Jess, remained to keep the camp), shouldered his boat, and up through the fresh, odorous woods, we moved over an undulating track, a foot in width, with the accompanying music of the rapids and forest. The guides strode steadily on, with firm and even buoyant step; around huge roots, over prone trunks, and through tangling underbrush, although the burden upon them was over six score pounds.

We passed the Titanic pine, with its long tassels; the hemlock, with its stiff fringes; the pointed cedar poised on the ledge and clinging to the cleft; the dense cones of the spruce; the perfect pyramid and finger-like apex of the balsam fir; the maple, the beech, the birch, with their varieties and differing hues; the streaked moose-wood; the low-branched hopple; hundreds of seamed columns around, a firmament of foliage above; sprouts, herbs and plants, ferns and mosses, lichened rocks, tall thickets, low bushes and creeping vines forming the floor; the whole scene bewildering the eye and stimulating the fancy.

The landscape, too, was full of life. A wandering breeze put all the leaves in a flutter; the golden-winged woodpecker, with an upward slide, clutched the bark of some old tree and rattled with his black beak till echo laughed again; the raven winnowed his sable shape over the tallest trees; the ground squirrel made a brown streak across the green log; and the rabbit, jerking his long ears, bounded athwart our winding track.

At the summit of the ridge we found the remains of a camp but lately deserted; the black remains of the fire, and the beds of hemlock boughs showing the locality of the tent. A deer's head lay under a neighboring thicket, with its brush lodged in the leaves; and a large trout, freshly dressed, hung from a forked stick in the dead leaves, where it had probably been forgotten. We respected, however, the law of the woods, which says, "Thou shalt not touch thy neighbor's traps, nor his venison, nor his trout, nor anything which is his, not even a jack-knife." Everybody honors that law. In the loneliest shanty, the hunter may find a rifle, a fishing rod, a haunch of venison, a basket of fish, and, lawless as he may be otherwise, he thinks no more of disturbing it than if the owner were present.

There is another law. Every empty cabin is taken possession of for the time being as if the intruder were the lawful occupant.

We descended to the head of the falls, and launching our boats, moved up the river sparkling before us like a track of diamonds. The trout leaped into the light like a flying fish; the duck rose with a splash and shot before us; the brown heron spread his wide sails from the sandy islet. Sprinkles of hawks were pin-pointed around a dry pine in the background; a flock of blue jays scolded in a near clump of trees; and a black eagle swept lessening over the rolling surface of the woods, alighting at length on a hemlock, like a musquito on a finger.

We presently came to a beautiful headland of open trees and luxuriant grass scattered with firs and cedars. Near it, was a wild meadow, softened and smoothed over with such a rural home-look that I almost bent my ear to hear the sheep-bell, and glanced to see the boy ride the farm-horse in his rattling harness to water.

At Cold Brook we stopped to fish, as also at the mouth of Moose Creek, and soon after we reached Clear, or Cold River, presenting at its intersection a much broader surface than the Racket. Cold River rises in the Preston Ponds at the south foot of Mount Seward, and empties here after a flow of forty miles. It being noted for trout, we entered, and soon scores of the speckled fellows were flapping in our boats.

We then explored farther up the beautiful stream, and at length a distant sound of axes touched our ears. "The lumber people that I told you of at Big Meadow!" said Harvey.

Now the bank thrust some black tongue of a log into the stream to collect the floating twigs and water-weeds; now the elm leaned over so as to touch the sparkling water-break as if to drink, and now the lady birch gleamed out with her waxen skin and flowing tresses.

At our right, or to the north-east, Harvey pointed out Mount Seward, some six or eight miles distant and mellow with aerial tints.

A mile farther on we passed a little opening in the woods. A fire was sparkling there, and around it were several stalwart fellows in red flannel shirts engaged at their dinner. Among them the copper skin and long dark locks of an Indian were conspicuous. A yoke of oxen were near, one ox lying down and the other feeding.

Following the example of the lumbermen, we shot into a little cove and swallowed our lunch on the back of a prostrate cedar, with our knees buried in herbage.

We then returned, and taking the cross cut of a small channel to our left came again into the Racket. Up we pulled once more, and, after a few miles, landed on the right bank, whence a half-mile carry led to Long Lake.

A path that touched along through the woods soon brought us to a small stumpy clearing, where stood "Bowen's Camp," a little four by six shanty of spruce bark and sloping to the earth from a cross stick on forked poles. The recess contained a chest and a bed of boughs. A sapling fish-pole stood in a corner. Outside was the kitchen—an upturned, propped scow, with a gridiron, a saucepan, an iron pot, and a tin cup or two underneath. Blackened stones showed the fire-place, with a pole planted in a rocky cleft whereby to hang the pot; the whole disclosing a very primitive mode of life.

It was the home of Bowen, a solitary hunter and trapper, who cultivated also a small patch of potatoes, rye and buckwheat on the adjacent hillside.

We skirted the clearing, passing the grey eye of Bowen's spring sparkling between long fern leaves, ascended a height, and the lake burst upon us. Reflecting in its broad bosom the blue and white of the soft heaven, it stretched down toward the south, until an abrupt curve closed the view. In front was a charming bay, a leafy mountain beyond. A bare rock stood by a green island in the mid-distance, with another bay rounding to the right. Thence the vision was closed by the curve, although it still would fain have roved beyond where fancy imaged a hundred fairy coves and stately reaches and romantic shades.

I gazed at the lake in its enchanting beauty, with playful breezes darting over its gloss and the sunlight kissing it into radiant smiles, and thought how it pierced onward and downward into this splendid wilderness, so lonely in its surrounding details, so imposing in its sweep of grandeur. Far to the east, towered I knew the sublime Indian Pass and the cloud-cleaving Tahawus with the wild lakes gemming like dew drops his giant feet. Southward from its head, down through the great forest glittered a network of water to Lake George, that storied lake of mountains. To the west wound the savage Bog River, dim artery to the core of the whole region's heart, its gloomy fastnesses offering, with the Mount Seward wilderness and the lonely shades of Indian Lake, the only home now of the almost mythic moose.

We returned to our boats and were soon on our downward way toward the camp. The dash of the oars echoed pleasantly and the ripple of the wake made hollow gurgles and pulsated among the lilies and rushes of the margin.

As we passed the mouth of Cold River, a boatman, descending the stream, joined us. He was a river driver; and belonged to the lumber crew we had seen, but for a week had been hunting with success near Mount Seward; had heard the roaring of a moose in the distance, had caught a fine lot of trout, and was now on his way to his shanty near Tupper's Lake. He was a frank, talkative fellow, and we gave him an invitation to camp with us the coming night, which he accepted.

"We'll hev rain shortly," said Harvey, pointing to the sky. "When I'm off the lakes and can't hear the loons, I look out for other signs o' rain in Natur. Now the weather seems jest at this time fair enough, but do ye see up there how them white clouds take to one another jest like b'ys and gals. That's a sign I've scurce ever knowed to fail that rain's a comin'. Ef they hang off though, meltin' away in the sky, that's the sign of a dry spell. There's another sign I see too! Look at that popple flutt'rin!" directing my attention to a quivering aspen or wild poplar. "There aint no other leaves stirrin'. Them trees know jest as well as the loons when wet weather's ahead. Ef I hear the owls to-night I shell be more sarten than ever."

"A deer, a deer!" at this moment shouted Gaylor, who was leading the van. I caught a glimpse of a pair of antlers skimming the surface of the stream in front of Gaylor's boat, and then a sudden turn concealed them.

Both the boats dashed round the bend, but we were only in time to catch a glimpse of a white brush disappearing by a thicket in a small, wild meadow on our right.

After this little incident, nothing occurred to waken our attention until we heard the note of a kingfisher perched on an old rotting tree.

"Did ye ever see them little critturs, 'bout breedin' time?" asked Harvey. "They're cute, they be. I come nigh a nest, one day, in a hole in a bank, and one on 'em made a sudden flop onto the water and went flounderin' and spluttcrin' about as ef he was a-dyin', and t'other stood on the bank, all bristlin' up and his tail a-shakin', and makin' a squawkin'. They cut them didoes jest fur to git me off the nest. It beats me how much critters without sense knows. They know a great deal more'n some men!" and with this aphorism he comforted himself with a portion of "stick."

We shortly reached the head of the falls. It presented a sweet, peaceful water scene of scattered rock and leaning tree, with dark spots of cedars, and logs laving their jackets of golden green in the crystal; a marked contrast to the dash and foam of the stream immediately below. We traversed the carry, and found the camp-fire merrily blazing under Corey's superintendence, and the camp in perfect order.

Our sylvan meal was soon spread and cheerily we despatched it.

> Merry merry outlaws
>   Of the greenwood free,
> Far from toil and trouble,
>   Self-made monarchs we!
> Over us its banner
>   Waves the windy tree,
> Waters round us warble,
>   Oh how blithesome we!

Night draws around; the stars jewel the trees and we prepare for slumber.

Just as we had slouched our felt hats over our ears and were wrapping ourselves in our blankets, a most horrible uproar burst from the opposite bank. It sounded like imps in convulsions of laughter. The tones and the echoes were so blended it was impossible to tell the number of the voices.

"Harvey!" shouted Bingham to that worthy at the camp-fire. "Are the ghosts of the Saranac Tribe pealing out their warwhoops preparatory to an onslaught, or have all the panthers in the woods become suddenly mad, and are coming to attack the camp?"

"Them's owls!" said Harvey laconically.

"Owls once more!" cried I. "Are the woods made of owls, and every owl with a different voice?"

"The sort of owl that makes this noise," said Harvey, "is a part of my almynack of the weather. We shell hev a rainy day tomorrer depend on't!"

CHAPTER X.

Camp Sketches in a Rain Storm.—Lumbering and River Driving.

I HAD been dreaming of floating through a forest, with a jack-light for an eye and trying to halloo between a scream and a hiss, when a humming like an enormous beehive wakened me. Harvey had proved a true prophet; the rain had come. I rose, and opening a fold of the tent in front looked out. It was early dawn. Through a brown light, masses of the landscape were dimly breaking. Across the background of the opposite bank the fine rain was glimmering. A rainy mist mantled the sky and shut in the farther view.

As the grey dawn strengthened, near outlines came out, but the whole view looked sulky and promised only a day of unvarying wet. The guides were soon astir, and the camp-fire was at length spluttering and flaming, our only comfort in the dreariness.

Presently my comrades awoke. The front of the tent was open for the fire to shed its genial, cheerful light within.

"A nebulous prospect!" exclaimed Bingham rising, "everything looks like a wet sponge. How watery these forests are! Every appearance of a social day in camp, eh, fellows?"

"A very good time to kill that buck you're always talking about, but never doing, Bing!" said Gaylor.

"Who killed that buck at the Beaver Pond I should like to know?" said Bingham with some heat.

"Cort!" answered Coburn laconically.

"Ah! h—e—m! but who shot the other at Palmer Brook?" triumphantly.

"Heaven knows!" said Renning. "You said you did. But what shall we do to-day, boys!"

"A capital day, Ralph, for you to fish the river!" retorted Bingham. "A little water by absorption may possibly neutralize something else in your system!"

The odors of breakfast now filled the air; the frying-pan hissed, and the teapot bubbled.

Tea, in the woods, hot or cold, is most delicious, refreshing and invigorating. The air of the forest, sparkling with vitality, requires not the aid of spirits to make the blood glow and the heart bound. Tea adjusts and sustains the true equilibrium.

The meal finished, we quartered ourselves comfortably in the tent, pipe in mouth, to pass the day as pleasantly as we could.

Our canvas room presented quite a picturesque appearance. Guns and fishing-rods, in their woollen covers, were piled in a corner. Blankets were spread over layers of hemlock, the warm reds and purples of some contrasting with the cool greys of the others, as well as the greens of the foliage, to which red and blue hunting-shirts added their colors. Camp-stools stood legs up; pipes and meerschaums, boxes of cigars and papers of tobacco littered one nook; partridges chequered another; one overcoat hung loosely by the neck from the tent-pole and one was sprawling below; carpet-bags, pillows of the night before, were strewed about; the skin of our bear stood rolled up in a corner near a pair of moccasins and a neck-yoke accidentally left and on which my luckless cranium had slipped in my jack-light dream, adding to its sensations a feeling as if the owls were busy with my brain.

Outside, was another picture composed entirely of forest touches. In the hollow of a tree was a slain wood-chuck, its grey dimly relieved by the gloom of the cavity; a rifle, slanted low against a stump, was pointed at a dead deer propped against a tree; on another stump forked a pair of antlers; half screened by a twisted root stood a jack; on a flake of bark, covering a camp-kettle, glistened a glutinous pile of trout; and a dead mink showed its teeth at a mud-hen, which trailed her brown wing in seeming defiance.

Of the guides, two were at the entrance of the small tent smoking with the river driver, who had decided to spend the day with us; two within were playing a game of cards; and one next them was turning a sapling into a ramrod. Corey, his red shirt lighting up the covert, was under a stooping cedar, cutting venison steaks, and Little Jess was by him, dressing a wood-duck.

Add to these, the glimmering air; the dripping trees; the tamarack drooping its boughs as a lurcher its ears, and the aspens in hysterics from the ceaseless pelting; the river pricked into one continual twitching by the rainy needles; with the dense grey blanket of the mist spread over all, and the scene is complete.

"Well, boys, how we shall spend the day, out in these rainy woods, where the sun has hardly room to shine in the best of times, I can't imagine," yawned Bingham.

At this moment the river driver passed, and, hearing the last remark, stopped and, with the latitude of the region, spoke.

"Onst in a while," said he, "we hed jest sich times in the lumber woods when we didn't know what to do with ourselves, but 'twas in the wust kind o' snow-storms instid o' this mite o' rain."

"Come in and tell us about this lumber life!" said Renning.

"Well," said the boatman entering, and settling down against an overturned camp-stool; "in the fust place, there's big comp'nies in Maine that follers lumb'rin' for a business. In the fall they send out their timber hunters to find out where the thickest white pine clumps is, for this pine mebby you know lives t'gether like parents and children and grows not a great ways from the water.

"Then the buildin' hands come, and bush out a spot for a camp, and build up the shanties. The shanties are nice ones and they're scatterered all round in the woods, p'tic'ly round the Upper S'nac Lake. They're called Maine Shanties. Then other hands comes and lays out the roads; fust the main—that's the big road through the woods—and then the branch roads leadin' to the pine clumps. Then the crews is made up, and comes inter the woods fur the winter.

"All our fam'ly's bin in them crews and bin everything but Boss and Cook. The old man's bin swamper, I've bin chopper, Tim and Hank, my two brothers, lumb'rin' up Cold River with Joe Slack and Injin Jake, they've bin barker and teamster, and 'ave tuk keer o' the bateau with the tents, cookin' things and victuals."

"What do you mean by swamper and barker?" asked I.

"The swampers bush out the roads to the pines that's felled, and the barkers strip the bark off the eends of the logs that slides on the snow from the bob-sleds that carries 'em to the landin's.

"I've been chopper, as I said afore, and though I say't myself, it takes a smart man to be a good chopper. Fust, you must look out and not take pines that's got the rot, or the konkus as we call it. You've got to look out purty sharp fur that. The tree on the whull is jest as good lookin' as one that's sound, and it's unly by lookin' cluss that you see a brown blotch even with the bark, not fur from the butt, and from the size of a popple leaf to the biggest size hopple's and there you see the konkus. And then you must hev jedgement about fallin' a pine, or mebby you'll be knocked by 't inter kingdom come. I've knowed pines to fall contr'y a'most from the skid."

"Skid!"

"Yes! the bed-piece or little cord'roy road o' poles we lay on the snow fur the tree to fall on, and not bury itself in the banks; and there you hev 't handy to strip the limbs off, and cut it inter logs.

"Well, as sun as the snow sets in the crews go ter work in the woods, fur ye see the snow makes it rael handy in these thick woods to drag the timber. After the pines 's down we chop 'em inter good-sized logs, and mark every one so we kin pick 'em out agin at the booms along and p'tic'lar at the big boom at the eend. They're then hauled to the water by the teamsters with bob-sleds and oxen. But about the choppin'! I tell *you* when we're all to work we make the old woods ring agin fur miles round the shanty. Sich a whack, whack, and sich a crackin' and roarin' as the pines fall! And then the draggin'! It's gee up and gee ho! and whoo, and go 'lang, and the sleds they go a screechin' through the snow with the weight o' the logs on 'em; and the woods is in a parfect hallerbelloo with it all. So we gets 'em to places handy fur the high water, and the river drivers come, and drive 'em down to the big boom at Plattsburgh.

"What waters do they drive the logs through?" asked Gaylor.

"Gin'rally through the Upper S'nac, Round Lake, and Lower S'nac into S'nac River and then down. But there's waters all round the Upper S'nac that they drive through. There's Musketer, and Rawlins and Floodwood Ponds and the Fish-creek waters, and twenty more up and round there. Now about the drivin'. That's stirrin' work I tell ye. It's bad enough in runnin' the bateau to keep right sides up through the logs and rapids along, but this is, I was a goin' to say, the very old Harry. A stavin' off the logs from the rocks, and one another, and pushin' on 'em down with your pike-poles, and jumpin' on 'em and strikin' up a dance as they roll over to keep up straight, and straddle 'em when they come to a rift; I tell ye it's some!

"The river drivers 's a hard set. It's rum, rum, with 'em most all the time, and when they aint drinkin' they're fightin', that is when they aint workin'. But after all, ef rum must be drinked, I don't know any folks that ought to hev it more than them Maine river drivers. They're in the water a'most all the time, and you know as well as I doos what the water is in Mairch. There's a good deal o' fun, though, afore the rael drivin' begins. The fun is gittin' the logs into the water. All go to work with their pries and hand-spicks and cant-dogs, and it's tug, and it's roll, till swash go the logs into the stream that's all swelled up and comes a rushin' and a roarin', hur-r-r-r-r-a b'ys! down through the woods like a nor'-wester or a hail-storm. In the logs go; swirlin' round; turnin' eend over eend; a dartin' here and slap-dash agin a rock there; knockin' agin each other, cadunk, cadunk, makin' the splinters fly; divin' down and stickin' up their noses agin like North River sturgeons, or jumpin' half-way out o' water like a hungry trout, and all the while a rushin' down with the current. When there's a high bank for 'em to roll down, I tell ye, it's some to look at 'em. I've seen 'em often roll down them steep hills by Fish Creek waters up there on Upper S'nac. Down they go, topsy-turvy, eends up, head over heels, any way, a crushin' down the small trees, bringin' up agin the bigger ones, and jumpin' over the rocks and rollin' like thunder and lightnin' both down over the ledges till they come to the water, and, Jesse! what a splashin'. I've seen the stream as white as a cloth with 'em.

"Now comes the work. Sometimes they'll go fur a consid'able ways, jest like a flock o' sheep, till the stream looks as ef 'twas made o' logs a'most; and we walk over 'em as ef 'twas one big raft. Then there comes a little bay like or eddy, and fust one, then a dozen or twenty mebby gits a kant, and noses up torts shore, and then the others comes along and jams up the forred ones, and I tell ye there's fightin' fur a consid'able time and the foam flies, but the rael old jam mebby don't come yit.

"Bimeby that comes. We'll spose there's a little island or a rock in the narrer part o' the channel, or a sharp crook in the stream, and a log or two gits ketched; then a dozen or fifty so as to make a boom like; and then them that's behind comes dunk, dunk, bum, bum, and the big ones rides down the smaller ones, and the others comin' down shoots up on them and others come a crashin' on them and workin' under, and the jam gets bigger and bigger, and the stream roars down through and over, enny way it kin to git along; and the whull kit that's a comin' down comes a tumblin' and a dashin' and a rollin' and grindin' agin one another, and flyin' back and rarin' up and divin' down, and the waves wash up, and you'd think all cr'ation was a breakin' to pieces. All this ere unly makes the jam bigger and stronger. It lays all eends and p'ints, and it must be got rid on. So when the stream has high rocks over it, a man is let down by a rope round his waist, with his pickaroons on, to cut or pry away at the lower eend o' the jam where the trouble is. This is gin'rally in a small spot, a log or so, and ef the log, the key-log some calls it, has the bigger part o' the weight on't, a few cuts with the axe doos the business; the log breaks and hurra! the man's jerked up by the rope ag'in and the jam comes a tumblin' down like old Sanko. Ef the trouble can't be got rid on so, the man knots a rope round the log and the hands go down stream with the rope and tug and tug and he pries or cuts, or both, and the jam starts that way.

"Other times and when there aint no high banks, one, sometimes more, 'cordin' as the jam is, goes with his axe and hand-spick and pickaroons agin—you knows what them is! No? Well, they're lectle steel spikes druv into the heels and soles o' their boots so as to keep 'em from slippin'. Well, he goes a treadin' over the jam as well as he kin, for it's dusty trav'lin', I tell ye, to cut away and pry off the trouble, and he tugs and h-e-a-v-e-s and s-t-r-a-i-n-s and cuts, and sometimes one nip or blow doos it, and all gives way at onst, with a roar like the breakin' up o' the ice in Tupper's Lake, and down the logs come tumble-te-tumble. The thing is now fur the man to git away. There he is in the middle mebby of the logs, and it's mighty hard sleddin' there, all a rollin' and tumblin', and it's some to git ashore. He runs and he jumps (these river drivers are as spry as cats) and he goes cornerin' round ana twists, and sometimes what he steps on turns over, and afore he knows it, down he goes 'twixt two logs and he hes to dive down and come up where he kin ketch it, and sometimes don't come up at all. There was Will Timball, he was as nice a young feller fur a river driver as ever I see; a sober (fur all on 'em don't drink), good, honest feller, as merry as a cricket all day long, and couldn't he sing! I tell ye, there's no use o' talkin', but some of his songs they fairly witched your heart out. Well, he went in a heavy jam to pry off, and he went down and he never come up agin. I see him onst with his hands up above his head twixt some logs, but they shut up tight like the wink o' your eye, and that was the last of him. Poor Will, he must ha' got hurt as he fell, fur a spunkier feller never lived, and strong and nimble, and knowed how to drive as well as the best on 'em. There was Betsey Chase, his sweethcart, he was to be married to her as sun as he got to Plattsburgh, as nice a young gal as ever growed. Oh how she took on! Them that see her at Plattsburgh when she was told on't, said it e'en a'most bruk their hearts to see her take on so; she was kinder onsarten after that about the head, and finally at last died. Well, when the logs druv past, we found the body and took it to Plattsburgh, and we buried him alongside of his mother.

"I see another terr'ble sight onst in a jam. The jam was jest above a long stretch o' rapids, and rael bad rapids they was too, about fifteen mile above Plattsburgh, in the S'nac River. Well, there the jam was, and a feller they called Dare Devil Dick—his name was Dick Siples—and he was one on 'em, now I tell ye! one o' yer rael harum-scarum kind o' critters that didn't know what bein' skeert was. He'd al'ys go right head foremost into scrapes, and somehow or other he'd al'ys git out on 'em too. I see him fight two men one time and they was the bullies of Plattsburgh too. Well, he licked 'em both. I tell ye he fit spiteful. He was the sassiest feller to strike I ever see, and I've seen a good many fightin' charackters too in my day. Well, as I was sayin', Dick spoke out, says he, 'I know jest where the trouble is, and I bleeve I kin set it right,' and with that he jumped with his hand-spick right out on the logs, and ef he didn't spring and jump over 'em—I tell yer! Well, he come to a sarten spot and he tugged and pried and tugged agin, and finally at last, quick as that (slapping his hands) it 'peared to me, the whull give way. Dick sprang, but the log he was on went slap-dash right into the rapids, and what did he do but fall right a straddle, and down he shot, and all the logs a tumblin' after him. I tell ye we all quaked. There was Dick, a riding the log jest like a hoss, and a tossin' and a plungin' a leetle ahead o' the rest, but precious little though. Now he'd shoot twixt rocks where the foam flew six foot high, and now he'd seem to be a goin' right on a bed on 'em; but somehow or the other he'd fly as 'twere past; and now he'd dive down into a great white swell o' foam, like a loon, and up he'd come agin. All this while the logs behind was a strikin' agin' the rocks and keelin' up and rollin' over and over and s-w-a-s-hin' down agin. I tell ye 'twas an orful sight. And sich a roarin' and crackin' and splittin' as there was. Two or three times we all had an idee he was gone. Onst he grazed a log so cluss he had to throw his legs up, and hang on by his knees, and then on t'other side a log come p'intin' right agin him, and 'twould ha' tore him all to pieces ef it had a hit him; but he kinder twirled himself round and it unly struck the log. It keeled that over though, and down he went and made what you may call a summerset in the water. Up he comes agin a gripin' and holdin' on like death. He hadn't though got more'n sot up agin afore a tre-*men*-jious log come a strikin' on a bed o' rocks. It jumped up I should raally say six foot and then rolled over and over right upon him as we had an idee. It didn't though, but it struck the log he was on, jest on the eend, and it tipped it up like a rarin' colt. Down it come agin caswash, and the foam flew, and we could jest see Dick through it, but down stream he went and wasn't hurt a hair. But now come the wust thing of all. There was a passle o' logs struck a smooth ledge o' rock that Dick had shot aside of. They come a cornerin' like, and hung jest like a ruff right over Dick's head. We all thought nothin' now could save him from bein' crushed flat as a shingle. Down come the logs, whonk, and Dick's log flew up on eend and then fell back'ards on the other logs. But where was Dick all this time! Why I'm afeard you'll set me down as a liar ef I tell ye that he see the logs a comin' (for his eyes appeared to fly round his head like a hum-bird's in a tumbler) and he sprung and he hit on another log jest along side, and the next we see of 'im he was a shootin' right into a swift place where the stream was a runnin' like a mill-tail; and here was the very wust place, fur 'twas where it pitched a foamin' like a bear's mouth when he's riled, down about six foot into a hole where 'twas a bilin' jest like a pot. Ef he'd a gone down there, nothin' could ha' saved him, I bleeve, fur that aire hole was jest one bed o' sharp p'inted rocks and he knowed it. Well, I'll be swizzled ef that aire critter, jest as that aire log was a pitchin' down that aire cobumbus like o' water, didn't reach out and ketch hold on a branch o' hemlock a growin' from a pint o' the bank, and swing himself up jest like a squirrel. Didn't we hooray! I tell ye, we did, some; and Dick he hoorayed too, and he got a straddle of the branch, and 'Hail Columbee!' s'ze he, and he clapped his sides and gin a crow and s-s-pun it out so long, you could ha heerd him a mild. Then he slipped down from the tree and the fust thing he said, s'ze, 'Gimme a drink,' s'ze, 'fur I'm so tarnal dry,' s'ze, 'fur all I'm so wet,' s'ze, 'and so chilled through,' s'ze, 'that I don't know,' s'ze, 'but I'd go off,' s'ze, 'ef my teeth should happen to strike fire,' s'ze, and he gin a laugh and then a jump as ef he was a goin' to jump down his own throat.

"Poor Dick, poor Dick! he didn't fare so well the next scrape he got into; fur the very next year he got inter a jam, and a couple o' logs come t'gether and cut him right in two, they did. Poor Dick! I see the eends of the logs all red fur a minute afterwards, and down he went, and we buried him at Plattsburgh, jest as we did Will Timball.

"Yes, yes, it's a danng'rous life, and a hard life this drivin' the river. It's a good deal like drivin' a passle o' onrooly cattle in the woods. Some o' the hands go behind in boats and a wadin' where they kin, and ridin' on the logs to see that they don't stick by the way; and pole 'em and hand-spick 'em along, and drive 'em enny way; fur in the coves and eddies along a good many's mighty unwillin' to go; and then agin they're too willin' and shoot away with ye, as I've said, and shoot up on the banks, and then it's tug, tug, to git 'em back agin. Some on us hev to go on the banks keeping pace with the logs, up the ridges and down the ridges, and through the swamps and over the trees and stuns, heltery skeltery, licketty scramble, jest as we kin ketch it; sometimes makin' a short cut that's often a long one, crost a bend, takin' a bite o' suthin' through the day; dartin' in a tavern ef there should happen to be enny, and pitch suthin' to drink down our throats and a cracker or two, and out agin and follerin' along. Sometimes we folly all night, but gin'rally we don't. As a gin'ral thing we put up at night, and let the logs slide along and ef there comes a jam it's all the better. But a few times in my drivin' though I've druv all night, when the woods was so dark it rally seemed as ef you might cut the air into solid blocks; all the time 'twas rainin' too, that cold mizzlin' kind o' rain that feels like needles on yer face; you couldn't folly the stream nuther, a quarter o' the time on the bank, the brush was so thick; and ye could unly tell by the roarin o' the water and crashin' and wallopin' o' the logs where 'twas. Sometimes you'd hev to go a mild or so clearn round where the stream made a spread drownin' some swamp; and other times where 'twould run up some deep gully and we'd hev to swim crost and mebby feel our way over some tree felled from one bank to t'other, each side lookin' like a gret black gulf. I tell ye, we'd hev ter put hands and feet one crost tother mighty keerful goin' crost, treadin' like a painter or a bear, or fare wuss. And sometimes there'd come up a thunder storm and b-l-o-w, and the wind 'ud smash down the trees, whack, all round ye, and the thunder 'ud roll and crack so that 'twas onpossible to hear the stream roarin', and the rain 'ud fall hogsheads full. The unly thing pleasant about the thing then 'ud be the lightnin', fur that flashin' and glarin' all round, showed the trees, and they seemed company fur ye, and showed the way through 'em too. It offen cut so cluss crost your eyes as to cut the sight out on 'em a'most, and I've seen it strike, whizz, the big pines and hemlocks, so nigh to ye, 'twas next to scorchin' the hair on yer head.

" 'Twas a wild sight, too, and I don't know but skeery to see the stream a rollin' down through the black night and hear't moanin' jest as though 'twas lost in the woods. And the dark logs streamin' 'long and pitchin' through the rapids, seemed as ef there was an all fired set o' black things a fightin' t'gether."

"Was there nothing to enjoy in this kind of life?" I asked.

"Oh yes! I somehow enj'yed the whull on't; that is rayther. Part o' the time 'twas as pleasant as kin be. After workin' in the woods all day, to come back at night to a rousin' good fire, and the fellers all a jokin' and laughin' after supper, with now and then a good song; I tell ye, 'twas fust rate. Here's one o' the songs!" and he struck up, in a not unmusical voice, the following, timing the air with his foot:—

> Oh, it's lumb'rin in the forest, it's a lumb'rin we will go,
> When the winter winds is whistlin' and the woods is full of snow,
> When the winter winds is whistlin' and the air is bitter cold,
> We leave the life of menkind, for lumber life so bold.
>   Oh, it's lumb'rin' in the forest, it's a lumb'rin' we will go,
>   With our axes on our shoulders fur to lay the pine-wood low.

The deer is close a hidin' and the ice it holds the trout;
All Natur' fast is frozen, but we long to stir about;
The lumber lads is merry and the pine has ready pay,
So wife takes keer of cabin and we low the pinewood lay.
    Oh, it's lumb'rin' in the forest, &c.

Whack, whack from dawn till sundown we do lay our lusty blows,
And thund'rin' to the snow-banks deep, down, down the pinewood goes.
And when the day is ended, in the shanty all do meet,
And round the fire a roarin' all our songs and jokes repeat.
    Oh, it's lumb'rin' in the forest, &c.

"When the logs got down to the lakes, too," continued he, "and we ketched and pinned 'em t'gether—what we call cribbin' or boomin' on 'em—twas high old times agin. We boomed 'em tight all round with timber and made a big raft, then warped 'em through the lakes. That is, we'd sink an anchor thirty or forty rods ahead, and hev a rope twixt it and a windlass on the raft, and then we'd (twisting his arms round) warp up, warp up. When the weather was kinder warm, I never hev enj'yed enny thing more'n a sail this way down the Upper S'nac. The lake 'ud be as smooth as glass, not a riffle on't, except where some loon or other skimmed along, or a trout jumped up, or a gull or so dipped inter the water; and we'd go glidin' by the islands and the p'ints, and the sun 'ud burn softly and the wind make fannin' all over ye. You forgit all yer troubles a drivin' and wish you could git 'long so all yer life. And the moonshiny nights I've seen on the lakes too; when there 'peared to be a line o' gold dollars sparklin' half crost the water; and some places as white and shiny as the breast of a deer and others as black as a raven. 'Twas nice. Sometimes though the Upper S'nack 'ud be as ugly as p'isen. 'Twould be all black and white with the swells and foamin' and 'dashin', and the wind 'ud s-w-i-s-s-s-h down as ef 'twas a big blacksmith bellus. Wouldn't the raft dance? I tell yer, 'twould be lively times there! And then by the time we got inter the Gut by Bartlett's, mebby 'twould be calm agin.

" Then 'ud come lettin' the logs loose to shoot the rapids at Bartlett's.

"So you see the sort o' life the river drivers live. 'Tisn't a feather bed one, take it by and large, by a blamed sight! But I telled Will I'd shoot with him fur a pint jest about this time, and I must be stirrin'."

So saying, the boatman rose and sauntered out of the tent.

CHAPTER XI.

Camp Sketches.—Racket Falls Camp Left.—Down the Racket to Calkins.—
An onslaught of Musquitoes upon the Saranac Club.—Mart's imitations.

HM, m, m, m; hm, m, m, m, patter, patter, drip, drip.

We had our dinner in the tent, and I then stepped out to change the scene.

The nearer trees were looking dark through the misty air, and glimmering more and more indistinct, until they were completely shaded in. Over the hill in front ragged scuds were flitting, while white vapor rolled down its breast. The dripping forest, and the river, mezzotinted with the ceaseless drops, looked forlorn and desolate. The guides were in their tent, showing dimly from the gloom; four now in a game of cards on a flake of bark over their knees, and one cleaning his rifle. Corey was looking at the players, and Little Jess was repairing a rod.

Two of the hounds were before the tent, one snapping at the drops that splintered on his nose, and the other gazing at the forest with uplifted foot, and an ear-flap erect. A third went stalking solemnly around, occasionally lengthening himself back with protruded fore-feet and gaping lazily; while a fourth now rose to his fore-legs sweeping his tongue around the corners of his mouth, and now reared himself entirely to look sleepily about; then, after a turn or so, as if in search of his tail, crouching again with his head between his fore-paws for apparent slumber.

All these live dottings of the monotonous picture served but to amuse for a moment, and I re-entered the tent.

"Renning, your tongue is the longest, tell us a story!" said Bingham, stretching.

"I'm not much of a story-teller, boys, but——" commenced Ralph.

"In one sense," said Bingham.

"But," repeated the other, lighting a fresh cigar and disdaining to notice the insinuation, "I'll do what I can. About three years ago, I went up the west branch of Bog River to Mud Lake with a friend and a guide. It is the loneliest and gloomiest of rivers, and the same, or more, is true of the Lake.

"We reached the Lake about sunset. My friend and the guide took our boat to visit a cove some distance up, where the latter said he had on a former visit seen a moose. Left thus to myself I felt inexpressible loneliness stealing over me. I thought, should any accident befall my friend and the guide, how inevitably would I perish! To enhance the wildness of my position, I saw in the sand of the shore the huge tracks of a moose and panther.

"As I sat plunged in my reflections, I heard low deep sounds, apparently of anger, rising from a neighboring ravine. I fastened my eyes there, and saw an object just above the edge. It looked like the head of some wild beast. I placed my gun in readiness; the object rose higher; and now it seemed a human form which advanced toward me. I looked with astonishment. The form was that of an old man. His clothes were woven of pine fringes, his hair fell on the shoulders in large masses. It was composed of the grey moss which clings to the dead pines and hemlocks, and was surmounted by the antlers of a deer. A beard of moss flowed to his knees. His face and hands were scaly with lichen. His eyes were like the red balls of the wolf; tusks projected from his mouth like a panther's, and his nails were long and curved like the claws of an eagle. His gait was a long stride, and his feet, or rather hoofs, made clicking sounds like those of the moose.

"As he approached, I tried to move away. But some

power fastened me to the spot. I found I had to 'face the music.'

"'Aha!' said he, 'I've found you, have I!'

"As the remark could not well be controverted, I answered that I thought he had.

"'Do you know who I am?'

"I regretted most politely that I did not.

"'I am the Spirit of the Wilderness,' said he.

"I begged to be allowed to say, and would have risen had I been able, that I was very happy to see him.

"'I am the only survivor of a family that once covered all this State,' said he.

"'Ah!' said I, attempting a look of regret.

"'Here was our abode,' continued he, 'centuries upon centuries. The red men were our dependents. They lived happily for generations under our protection. The moose, the panther, the wolf, the bear, the deer, the beaver, also enjoyed our bounty. The winds were our breath; and, drinking in God's gift of rain and sunshine, we rendered Him our thanksgiving and praise in happy murmurings and songs. The birds bore our thoughts in merry syllables; the waters were our bands of brotherhood. Where are we now! The accursed white man, with his pitiless axe and devouring fire, has destroyed all but me. Here I have lived in such content as the fate of my poor family would allow. But these last years have brought a woeful change. My solitude has been outraged,' and his eyes began to gleam, 'by these detested whites. Parties of them from the cities, affecting the airs of hunters, invade my peace with unmeaning uproar, mountebank pranks, forlornest jokes, and most villanous rum. My eyes and ears are offended with them; my nostrils are sick of them. Therefore have I vowed vengeance;' and as he said this, he snapped his tusks together with a click that chilled my blood.

"'You,' added he, glaring more fiercely than ever, 'you are one of them!'

"I hastened to say that though constrained to admit I was white, I was merely passing through the region on very particular business, and all alone.

"'Business!' repeated he, and his eye grew fiercer; 'business! That word I hate. Are you a lawyer? Of all these people, a lawyer I most detest.'

"My heart (to use a slang but most appropriate phrase) sank into my boots. However, I said nothing. In fact, I could say nothing.

"'These lawyers,' continued he, 'are for ever nosing under titles and unsettling my boundaries; and then the axe comes crashing in. I hope you are not a lawyer,' fastening his great wild eye on me.

"I hastened to protest—that I—I—in fact that I was an artist.

"'I'm glad of it. These artists and poets, if they do no good, they do no hurt. They paint me in pictures and verses rather shabby sometimes, but I—on the whole—I like the craft. Yes, yes, I'm glad you're one of them, and not a lawyer. If you were'—and his tusks began to gnash again.

"I rejoiced at my escape. Politely proposing to spend the evening in my agreeable company, he advanced close and asked my name. I told him. He seemed about to seat himself. At this instant my unlucky fate intervened. As I whisked out my handkerchief to wipe away the drops of my excitement, a paper flew out with it, in red tape; a paper with the boldest writing on it—'Supreme Court. Bugg v. Rugg, R. Renning Attorney.'

"I grasped it, but too late; the fierce eye was on it.

"'Aha!' growled the Spirit, 'Renning, Attorney, is it? So you are a lawyer!' with a yell that rang like a loon's; and with flashing eyeballs he sprang at me. His claw was in my shoulder; and the next moment—I saw—my friend's good-humored phiz smirking full in mine.

"'Well, of all snoozers,' said he, 'you beat! I've been shaking the very boots off you to start you up.'

"Start me," said I. "Why—where's the Spirit of the Wilderness?"

"'Spirit of the pocket-bottle!' said my friend; 'here it is!' producing his flask of whiskey; 'and the next time I go to hunt up moose for the company, I hope you'll keep awake long enough at least to light a smudge for the mus-quitoes."

"So my friend has been humbugging us with a dream, has he," said Bingham. "This Spirit of his was unquestionably the spectre of his own sins; and as the rest of us must despair of telling a greater—h-e-m—than this, I move we play eucre."

As I did not play, I again left the tent.

The scene was now brown in the declining day. The sharp head of the woodchuck was alone seen in the gloom of the hollow stump; several small trout, left in the pan, were undulating in the water that had rained in it. The hill in front was blackening; the flashes of the rapids were getting dim; darkness was creeping into the white pines and turning into a mass the forest background. No symptoms of clearing. It seemed as if the rain would last for ever.

A hound stopped from grazing the ground with his nose, to shower the rain around him with a quick shake. He then gave a sniff as if trying to blow his nose, and another vigorous shake, and grazed the earth as before. Drive, with his neck raised into a crescent and his upper lip wrinkled above his teeth, watched the hill with an occasional low growl sharpened into a spiteful bark, while Pup, fastened to a log, had twisted himself into a cat's cradle, and was endeavoring in every wrong way to untwist himself, confounding his tail with his head, and his legs with one another.

The guides had ceased their game, and were now earnestly talking. As I approached I heard old Harvey say.

"I tell ye, Mart! it can't be done. No man ever went

up Settin' Pole Rapids alone in a boat. You never did in cr'ation."

"I know I did," said Mart doggedly.

"Onderstand me now," returned Harvey. "You kin go up part o' the way; but there's a p'int o' rock which no man *kin* git round. Now I tell ye so!"

"Well, *I* went round," said Mart, talking so earnestly as to catch his breath. "I went up to the p'int, and there I *did* hev a tussle. 'Twas licketty whang which should beat, I or the water, but I pulled and I strained! I tell ye didn't I work! Well, I did some. But I broke my oar in gittin' up."

"I tell ye 'tis *not* a thing to be done. Don't I know, and didn't I row a boat afore you was born. Now I tell ye you might as well try to row up old Whiteface, as to row round a sarten p'int there. But ef you didn't go up you come down onst. Ho! ho! ho! you and Cort, ho! ho! ho! licketty whip! I see the boat go round like a kitten chasin' her tail."

"What bad weather we're a hevin'," here interposed Will, "it's rained so much to-day it don't 'pear to know how to stop."

"This ere weather," returned Harvey, "is aggravatin'. I wish I could turn inter a trout, and then I wouldn't mind it. But while it's about it, why don't it rain a leetle whiskey as well as water. I think 'twould be a rael old hunderd idee."

I retreated again to the tent. As my companions were still engaged in "eucre" I seated myself by the entrance and watched the camp-fire blazing and crackling in the fast gathering darkness. The rain but sprinkled it into freshness. Now and then the pine tree near it spit a broad drop that stung a snappish ember, made a testy coal hiss, or a dot of warm ashes sound sullenly to its pat. I saw in the glowing depths a red deer drinking at a water-streak of ashes; and wasn't that Cort in his red hunting shirt seated on a crimson rock? And the smoke! now it was the dark topsail of the Flying Dutchman, and now Surtur with his flaming falchion moving to the last grand battle-field of Vigrid.

My picturings were at last destroyed by the simultaneous risings of my comrades from their game, and after an hour's glancings and flittings of talk we all retired to our hemlock beds for slumber.

The heavy eyes of the morning opened, still glazed with tears. But the rain soon dwindled into a watery transparency and then glimmered away. The blanket of mist broke into huge fragments with glaring white edges, as if the light were trying to drain through, and curls of scud grazed the trees, twining around the higher ledges. The outlines of the forest began to show with hair-like distinctness. The surface of the Racket below the falls was like oil, and the windless trees stood still as in a painting.

Tired of the landscape around the camp, we prepared to leave.

In an hour our tent was struck, our boats loaded, and all, except Harvey and myself, on the downward voyage to Tupper's Lake.

With his usual care, Harvey went over the camp to detect any article left behind. He shortly passed me toward the boat with a candle-end, several matches, a piece of twine and a tooth-pick taken from one of the smaller bones of a deer's leg in the cup of one hand, and a fork with one prong, a sugar-crusher whittled from pine, and a broken jack-knife thrust into the knots of his other; while a battered pewter spoon divided his mouth with a sooty unlighted pipe. I lingered for a moment to throw a farewell glance over the camp. A ghastly sunbeam glared across the silent scene late so full of color and motion. There were our beds of hemlock; there the thickets in which the venison had been sliced and the trout dressed; there the white pines whose murmurs had been to me so full of music; there the roots and stubs to which the ropes, drawing our tent to its shape, had been fastened; there was the stump of the marmot; there stood the acclivity where the owls had assured Harvey in his weather wisdom; and there the background forest with its meandering paths. The single thing left of all our property was the grinning deer's head.

The rapids were flashing over the rocks, and they seemed to say "farewell!" the murmuring pines breathed the same; the aspens trickled it as with tears.

As I passed the thicket at the head of the path leading down the headland to the river, I gave one more glance to the sylvan beauty of Racket Falls Camp, and the next moment was at the stern of the Bluebird. Harvey pushed her from the bank with his oar, and immediately we were following the other boats, which, however, were by this time out of sight.

A deep sound; a report of a gun, but distant.

"They've shot at suthin' forred there," said Harvey. "A deer most likely!"

We passed a little distance farther and another sound touched my ear. It was faint and quick, delicate as the tap of a ripple.

"Another gun," said Harvey, "but a long way off! That come from Folingsby's Pond, ten mile from here. It can't in course be one of our party, fur not even Mr. Bingham, quick-as-a-snap kind o' gen'leman as he is, couldn't ha' got there yit, ho, ho, ho! How fond he is o' tellin' how many deer he's killed or would a killed ef he'd hed a chance!"

It is surprising how far the report of a gun can be heard in the wilderness. The brittle sound flits across the ear from a distance almost incredible.

What with stopping to look over the "slews" for deer, gathering Indian Plumes, mohawk tassels, moose heads, and white water-lilies, and otherwise loitering, we did not reach the bend to the left or north-west, above Stony Creek, until sunset.

There was a splendid flush of color in the west, with clouds like blazing coals in a furnace.

"Too much red," said Harvey. "I'm a leetle afeard of to-morrow. Rain 'll be the order agin, I think; but it can't be helped."

The beautiful twilight shed its softness over the scene. On either bank the trees and herbage were drawn in the glassy river with the most delicate pencilling, forming a series of fairy paintings flecked with the gold, crimson, and purple of the zenith. From the trunk of the tree to the cut edges of its leaf, everything on the margin was seen as if the water was air. The ripplings generally of our way only made the emerald pictures undulate without breaking them. Occasionally, however, a deeper plunge of the oar fractured the beautiful tracery, but in a moment it was again joined as if by invisible fingers.

We had now arrived at the mouth of Stony Brook. Here Harvey pushed the stern of the boat in among the grasses of the bank, and I landed, took a seat in the smooth fork of the leaning water maple at the western edge, and watched him while he angled. Only one trout rewarded his trouble, which he threw into the bottom of the boat. Several white flashes at the end of his raised line, however, told the shiners or minnows were abroad. These elfin members of the fish tribe, with all their delicate, silver-scaled armor, only excited Harvey's contempt, and he either flirted them back into the stream with "dang the minnies," or kept them "for bait." Indeed, I had noticed early that Harvey was wanting in a sense of the beautiful, he regarding a trout as a trout, without reference to the golden bronze and rubies in which it glittered. I remarked about its beauty to him once. He had just cut off a portion of "ladies twist" with his dark jack-knife, and he answered, as with great gusto he placed the morsel into his mouth, that "'twas all well enough, but a trout 'ud be jest as good eatin' ef its color was like a tadpole's." As the remark was true enough, I said no more. So with a radiant wild flower to which I called his eye one day, so rich it shed a gleam on the water, and turned a passing water-fly into a gem. "Them things 'ud make right good greens b'iled," said he, "and muxed up with a leetle inion and vinegar they'd go good raw."

As for the tints of sky, cloud, and water, the purple films of distance, and the picturesque beauty of near prospects, they were entirely beneath his notice.

Forward we went again, over a surface gleaming with the colors of the wood-duck's back.

I looked at the trout in its splendid blazonry, and the golden-eyed water-lily in its creamy silver lying beside it, and thought with what little reference to man exists the greater part of the Deity's creation. Some things appear to be made for his use, but what myriads of others, grand and beautiful, have no connexion with him or his presence. The trout and the lily glitter generally in the solitude. The graceful deer, the forest waving in curves of matchless beauty, the billow splintering on lonely shores, the grandeur stretching from inaccessible peaks; all these ask not the eye of man to admire them. And yet he thinks the world made specially for him! instead of being but one of the myriad expressions of the Creator, one of the links in the infinite series of creation. All, from the constellations to the mote, are but portions of that mantle which the inscrutable I Am wraps around Him for His own purposes.

The tender tints tremble away into the soft pearl of the deepening twilight. Solitude and silence reign. No movement save our own. Even Harvey seems impressed with the quietude, for he is musing while he rows.

A distance of two miles from Stony Brook brought us to Calkins' clearing, our goal for the night. We found the boats of the company at the margin, and securing our own, after tasting the spring upon the bank, we ascended the rough clearing in the grey of the evening to the log hut that crowns it.

My comrades had found the hut alone, had taken possession, and were gathered near the door where two fires were blazing.

Log outhouses were each side the hut, with a cleared ridge in front sloping into a natural meadow on the winding Racket, and an upland in the rear. The whole was walled with forest, in some places touched red with an old burning.

I immediately found the fires were necessary to repel the musquitoes. In fact, if the whole clearing had been kindled it would scarce have sufficed.

Gaylor and Ralph stood by one fire, and Bingham and Coburn by the other. The first were performing a tragic pantomime; slapping their foreheads, beating their breasts, and almost tearing their hair. The last were in the comic spasms. Bingham's knees cringed as Coburn's shoulders hitched. Then Bingham's arms tossed wildly and Coburn's hands dashed still more wildly over his person wherever they could hit. Now Bingham shook his head as if to let his brains loose, and now Coburn struck up a perfect hysteric of motion as if every muscle and nerve had begun a dance of its own, and would end in running bodily away with him.

As for myself, preferring musquitoes alone to musquitoes and smoke, I struck down into the dark grey clearing. The evening was warm and close, and the thickening gloom had shaded away the outlines of bush, stump, and tree. The owls were shouting at the tops of their voices.

While sauntering along, I came upon Mart Moody shaping out a paddle. I watched his work; at last he looked up and spoke.

"Is that you, Mr. Smith? The woods as well as the flies is in full blast to-night. Did ye ever hear a painter sing out? H-e-c-h!" (giving a horrid scream.) "And here's the wolf" (with a howl so that Watch bounded forward with a yelp); "the deer" (imitating perfectly their heavy indescribable whistling); "and the bear" (with a snarl and growl that made me jump involuntarily backward); "but I guess you never heerd a moose beller," uttering a sharp roar that startled the woods into an echo.

"Why, Mart! you're an artist!" said I.

"There's a good many sounds in my throat," answered he complacently. "Here's the loon, and the raven and the eagle and the hawk," producing in succession the sounds of the several species he mentioned.

He then continued his work, while I strolled farther down into the glimmering meadow.

I fancied the sublimity of possessing what alone belongs to the Deity; an existence, the idea of which is given in the scriptural expression, "a thousand years are as one day." To see light leaving some immeasurably distant orb for this earth; its splendor moving on, on, on, through what would be to mortals centuries upon centuries; on, on, cleaving the startled darkness until it reaches its goal—to mark the formation of a world, the first throb of chaos, the mingling of the elements into the spinning orb, the withdrawal of those elements to their appropriate spheres and their elaboration into the perfect world—to note the march of events over our earth, the progress of the forest to the empire, decay drawing its grassy mantle over the latter; new empires rising and Time successively crushing them under his tread; while swarms upon swarms of life, human, animal and vegetable, glance and disappear—such is the sublime existence of God, and such the eternity of the past and the future under His eye;—all one immeasurable present!

What a Being! self-existent, self-sustained! His habitation that magnificent system of universes, in which our own cluster is only one of the myriad pillars and our world a tiny leaf of its capital. And yet amid all the wonders He has created, none is more wonderful than the human soul, boundless as eternity, yet enclosed with all its divine attributes in a frame fragile as the leaf that May calls into existence for October to waft into its grave. Grand thought! The loftiest archangel that smites the sunbeam with superior lustre has no more enduring existence than the lowliest beggar that dies in the winter storm unsheltered as the dog beside him, and nameless as the snow-flakes that stream around him in the blast.

And yet what an infinite distance between man and his Maker; between the Creator and the mightiest created! Yea, the stately suns that with systems for their diadems tread in gorgeous march through the countless ages along the illimitable spaces, approach no nearer the essence of the Father than the swarming animalcules that live and die in a single drop of water, approach in splendor and duration to the suns.

CHAPTER XII.

A Rainy Day on the Racket—Down to Folingsby's Brook.—Folingsby's Pond.—Bingham and the Ducks.—Captain Folingsby.

WE retired to rest at an early hour. Ralph and Gaylor occupied the lower room, Bingham, Coburn, and I ascended by a ladder to the loft, and the guides took sleeping apartments outside.

The lighted pine-knot which one of us held brought out in dark crimson relief the slanting roof, five feet at its highest and three at its lowest height; a row of bunks filling one half the floor and a pile of potatoes the other. A little window gleamed in the rear. A stifling air pervaded the loft and—what can I say of the musquitoes, except that they composed (almost) the very air itself.

We laid ourselves, however, upon the straw of the bunks, after demolishing the window panes and letting in a stream of fresh air, and tried to sleep.

In a few moments Coburn caracoled from the bunk and stampeded, followed, after a short series of ground and lofty tumblings on his mattress, by Bingham.

As for myself, thinking that as there was greater space outside, there was more room for the musquitoes, I armed myself with a kind of heroic despair and—let the fiends bite. They could not do so more than one night through, and I thought my blood might possibly stand that. "Tired nature" at last subsided into a kind of a trance—a sort of transparent sleep, in which I solemnly affirm I beheld a huge musquito stalk into the room droning like a buzz saw. Fastening his great glaring blood-thirsty globes on my unfortunate person, he made as if to plant his horrible pump on my face. I started up, and found the little square of the window grey in the daybreak.

There was a humming too on the roof as of a million musquitoes, as well as a dampness in the loft which told of rain. I arose and looked out. Sure enough there were the now familiar streaks glancing athwart the wall of forest and against stump, tree, bank, and hollow of the clearing. Another rainy day! I descended to the lower room, and there found my comrades and the guides.

After a hasty breakfast we decided, rather than loiter in that dreary clearing, to push on to where Folingsby's Brook entered the Racket, and there camp.

We embarked once more. I had donned my India rubber, and the thick tent blanket, and bade defiance to the storm.

Down we all swiftly flew, I catching glimpse through the misty air of the forward boats and occupants as we turned some bend; now of a stern with Gaylor leaning back; now of a broadside with Cort's flashing oar and Bingham bending to a rake of rain; now of Coburn huddling in the middle of his craft, and now of Renning dipping a vigorous paddle.

Past the bald hemlock flowing with moss like an old bearded prophet; past the mined elm, its top tilting to our ripple and raising dimples in the water; past the grey finger of the skeleton pine—finger pointing to the centuries that have rolled over the forest; past the water-maple's peristyle of pillars upholding the blended dome; past the ledge green with moss as an emerald; past the tongues of the banks thrust far into the channel, and the coves of hollowed foliage where the duck dimly seen had doubtless cast anchor for the day; past the old fir hardened into iron like the trees of Járnvid, and wreathed into green softness by the moss; past the trunk wrestling on the border with some strangling grapevine, a Laocoon of the wood; past the black sunken log where the ripples undulated; past the windy pebbles in the channel where the rain launched its fiercest lash, we swept along. On either hand frowned the aboriginal wilderness—a wilderness like that which walled Hudson as he tracked up his river; which darkened on Champlain as he coasted down his lake; where no axe but the one clearing space for the camp shanty had ever rung, no smoke had ever curled save that breathed by the camp fire; close-twined save at the beautiful green openings, grassy nests of the forest, tempting one to make there a home where existence should glide along in sylvan peace.

But little life was abroad. On the sandbank at the Three Corners a tall crane was standing as if in mute soliloquy over his prospect of a fish dinner, and at Wolf's Point by the Four Corners we saw the white brush of a deer glancing into a thicket. At "Buck Slew," where the bleaching skull of the enormous deer shot there by Harvey (he naming the slough from the circumstance), glistened from the alders, a mink leaped through the foliage.

Just after we had turned the Little Oxbow my eye was caught by another of those objects I have before mentioned; the enormous nest of a fishhawk in the antlers of a dead pine, cutting against a background of dark purple cloud.

The rocks of the Three Sisters looked grim in the grey air as we glided by, but The Emerald (the little grassy island close by) seemed in the polishing rain bright as the gem whence its name was taken.

At one of the spring brooks flowing into the river my comrades had stopped to try the trout. Having caught a number before we came, they started down with us, all checking progress at the mouth of another brook. Although success rewarded our efforts, we found fishing in the rain too much like the Chinese method of swimming under water to capture ducks, so we pushed onward.

The afternoon was advancing as we came abreast the wild meadow at our left or south bank of the Racket, where Folingsby's Brook entered.

The cheerful hack of the axe was echoing as we landed Corey and Little Jess had preceded the party, as usual, to select our camping spot, and had commenced clearing on a knoll west of the meadow, and at the mouth of the brook.

As if vexed at our coming escape, and to give it to us while it had us, the rain now fairly poured. But tree after tree fell before the guides; poles were planted; saplings shortened into stubs; and presently the tent was reared and secured by the looped and knotted ropes.

Meanwhile we "lookers on" sheltered ourselves as well as possible in the hollow trees, under jutting ledges and dense cedars, and in grottoes of hanging hemlocks.

A glorious fire shed a glow over the dripping scene, and we enjoyed its warmth and radiance until we could enter the tent, which we soon did. The ground covered with dead pine needles absorbing the rain, formed a comparatively dry floor to our little dwelling. The fire played over our variously tinted blankets, gleamed on our India rubber coats, powder flasks, and shot belts, hung along the slender tent rafters; upon the brass reels and rings of our rods, and along our rifles and fowling pieces; kindling bits of color and flashes of light all over our pleasant apartment.

The opened curtain of the front framed another picture. Stems seamed and smooth, dark, mottled and grey, columned a part of the view, with the newly prostrate trees heaping another. The falling axes of the guides glittered, and their red hunting shirts glowed in the firelight. Below the knoll a bright background was made of the rain-freshened meadow grass tinted with brilliant water weeds.

Just before sunset, following a shower which came trampling over the woods, river, and meadow at our front, and, beating our tent as with tiny flails, went roaring away in the rear, a gleam of fluid gold shot over the scene. The remaining drops were transmuted into a sparkling sheet flung athwart the dark landscape, like the silver veil over the brow of Mokannah, and a streak of tender blue opened above the western trees. Splendid tints flashed over the clouds; a cool breeze poured liquid balm around; each tree shook off its glancing gems, like a deer after a bath, while the whole landscape breathed the freshest fragrance.

Shortly, a jocund crew were we, around the usual table on the sylvan floor in front of the tent.

Lo, the treasures of that table!

Piles of trout, their crusted skin cracking open from the dark golden flesh; flakes of venison richly browned and swimming in ruddy juices; partridges showing their white dainty substance; ducks, their juicy breasts distilling red nectar; curls of crisp potato chippings, brittle biscuits, Indian cakes like sponges, and tea, a real cordial.

At dark Bingham took Cort and went on a night hunt down the river. The rest of us preferred remaining in camp.

I wandered a short distance into the woods. Overhead were broken streaks of sable sky, the stars seeming to cling to the tree tops and struggle through the higher branches. I could see a few black trunks close round me, but the rest were lost as in a dungeon. Ebon masses told the near thickets. Not a stir; not a breath. So dead the silence the Runic fetter of Gleipnir might have been woven from it. Spots of ghastly glare showed the phosphorescence of the decayed logs and stumps. There seemed at last a weird influence, a frowning horror in the murky depths. If phantoms had appeared I should scarcely have been startled.

From where I stood the mighty wilderness extended threescore miles unbroken either way, motes of cabins in specks of openings alone excepted.

At length I returned, and the gleam of the camp-fire, the movements of the guides around it, the tent, the cheerful voices of my companions within, all casting that social spell so congenial to our nature, restored the equilibrium of my spirits. The gloom dissolved; the feeling of isolation fled away; I was again one of the family of man.

In about two hours Bingham returned.

He had been unlucky as usual, the perverse deer keeping purposely from his rifle. "The fact is, gentlemen, they know the light of the jack just as well as Ralph here knows how to take a glass of punch, and no more can be said on the subject. Cort, make me a glass of punch!"

The morning arose fresh and radiant from her bath as did Aphrodite from the sea. The rose tints of dawn faded; the summits of the far hills warmed into purple; the tops of the trees brightened into gold. A little while and the sun was kindling the bushes, low rocks, and logs into yellow life, and then picking out the sprouts and dead leaves, until all was one broad illumination.

We were now to explore the beauty of Folingsby's Pond unknown to my comrades, and of course to me, but painted in strong colors by the guides.

We rowed one after another up the crooked brook or outlet, which flows in a north-westerly direction. At either hand was an expanse of wild meadow with wooded acclivities. The sunlight lay like a golden mantle on the meadow embroidered at the edges by the shadows of the hills.

The light tinged the adder's tongue into a deeper purple, and made a red intaglio of the Indian Plume fitting into some cranny of the bank.

The brook narrowed as we ascended, with thickets and broad tufts of wild grass in the channel, until it dwindled to a mere streak doubling and twisting like a water-snake striving to hide in the herbage of the meadow. Side cul-de-sacs enticed the boats, whence they were obliged to back once more into the channel, through which now and then they were forced by main strength over the sand and rushes having but a film of water upon them. The oars of the party had been abandoned almost from the first for the paddle, Harvey alone clinging to his until the blades more often slid over the borders than touched the water.

The stake driver rose awkwardly from her seat in the long, coarse grass of the bank, and fanned heavily away with a hoarse cry, the light touching her brown slender shape; that feathered buffoon, and peculiarly American bird, the blue jay, sent from the hills his peevish trumpetings, and the hawk sailed the blue as if he delighted in the freshness of the morning.

"Them stake-drivers 's a queer thing," said Harvey. "They make a noise like drivin' posts in wet ground. You hear it all over, and yit can't fix it to one spot."

At last, on turning a bend, a broad sheet of water burst upon us—Folingsby's Pond—expanding from the brook with a suddenness almost startling. It lies north-westerly, in an angular course with a succession of points either side of its five or six bays; is without an island, and has a length of three miles, with a breadth of two. Hilly forests slope to the water's edge unbroken by a clearing, and unstained by the red hues of fire or the grey of withered trees. Upon entrance, a headland rounding blunt to the lake like an eagle's beak arrests the eye with a rock like a huge duck in the water before it.

Harvey again betook himself to the oars, and, in the wake of the other boats, laid his course swiftly through the pond. At the head, where the shores are low and swampy, Renning and Gaylor, true to their instincts, began prying for trout around the mouth of the inlet that came crawling zigzag through the alders and swamp willows. Dropping here, flinging there, they teazed the lazy water for a half-hour in vain. Not a trout even the length of a finger rewarded them. At last Renning tried the fly. Skipping it over the broad parts, specking the sleepy pools with it, a little more time elapsed with evidently oozing patience on the part of the unlucky angler. Meanwhile Gaylor was working up the inlet, his grey coat glancing like a heron in and out of the water bushes.

A croak from a lazy bullfrog now and then sounded by a lily-pad, while the eager, brassy deer-fly buzzed around our ears and occasionally lighted with a tingle on our hands.

"Come, gentlemen!" at length said Bingham, addressing

Coburn and myself, the former of whom had squatted himself on a surly old log thrusting its nose from the dark mud of the margin; "aren't you tired of the antics of these two great fishermen. There's but little venison in the camp, and Cort says there's a good chance of a deer in Grassy Bay, around the next point. And you know, gentlemen" (presenting his piece as if to fire), "if my rifle covers a deer, it's good-bye to Mr. Deer. Come, Coburn, you look on that log more like a huge frog than a human being, wake up. Come, Smith! you can't snap twigs in the boat, thank fortune! so come along! We'll leave these two knights of the rod, whose ideas in this grand wilderness never soar above a trout, to the exciting pastime of whipping water-flags and catching old sunken roots, and we'll catch a deer, eh, Cort!"

We left Renning on a green bog where he was unable to stand still long enough to catch a trout from fear of sinking to his waist, and dancing in consequence from one leg to the other as if in a nest of snapping turtles, while Gaylor was crawling back round a mid-channel bush like an otter after its prey.

Rounding the point and reaching into the depths of the bay, we looked narrowly into the thickets of the shore for the tawny hues that tell the deer, but none were discovered.

"Shall I let Watch go?" said Harvey.

"I think not," said Coburn, interrupting Bingham, who was giving assent. "Our stay at the pond will be too short for that."

"We'll hev chances enough too at Simon's Slew and Tupper's Lake fur drivin', on second thoughts," said Harvey. "Mr. Runnin and Mr. Gaylor expecks to be back to camp afore sundown sarten, so as to try a brook down the river."

"That's always the way!" said Bingham, pettishly; "everything has to yield to trout in this party. A deer is no more thought of than a chipmunk. That's the reason I never kill—hem—that is—but by the powers, it's raining!"

Sure enough the golden scene had become grey. One of the prowling showers of the region had stolen upon us, and light, watery threads were glimmering against the broad breasts of the hemlocks and cedars, and athwart the dark cavities of the woods.

"It won't be much of a rain," said Bingham, covering the lock of his rifle with his coat; "and maybe it will rouse up the deer from the thickets."

At this instant a loud, mocking, taunting shout burst from the middle of the pond where the mist of the shower had already enclosed a narrow horizon.

"Uncle loon says diff'rent!" exclaimed Harvey.

"Confound him!" said Bingham, gasping his rifle; "where is he?"

"Round the p'int there!" answered Harvey.

"Give me a chance at him," said Bingham.

Another war whoop.

"I'll stop his yell," continued Bingham; "pull round, Harvey!"

Down came the rain like a cataract. The narrow circle of the pond bubbled and frothed like a kettle over a fire.

A clear, bold, ringing, clarion sound broke from the mist.

"Clear out!" said Bingham.

The burst of rain lasted until it had smitten us through and through, and then ceased as suddenly as it came. It stopped so quick that the middle drops didn't know it, but kept patting the water for several moments later.

The trees again struggled out from the near fog; the far wreaths grew transparent and melted. From a vanishing curl appeared the boats of Renning and Gaylor rapidly gliding towards the outlet.

"We're going back to camp!" hallooed Renning, making a speaking trumpet of his hand.

"I too," said Coburn to us. "This is rather poor sport. Push ahead, Phin!" and off he went.

At this instant the base of the wooded acclivity in front

blazed into splendid colors. Higher they rose; higher, higher; they bent; it seemed as if invisible spirits were forming an arch: downward the colors curved, down, down, until they linked themselves once more to the edge of the water.

"Well," exclaimed Bingham, "I never saw a rainbow grow before."

It had built itself before our very eyes, and now glowed there upon the background of the hill, beautiful as Bifrost before the portals of Valhalla.

It held its gleaming being, with a paler bow above it, longer than is wont, but at last the fainter arch died away; the superb colors of the other commenced slowly to dim, until dissolving gently, the bright messenger of returning sunshine vanished like some returning seraph from our view.

We were now abreast the blunt headland and rock, where the lymph was so clear I could see the white sticks at the deep bottom twisting like water-snakes.

"Suppose we follow the rest to camp," said Bingham. "I dont believe we'll find any deer, and there's nothing else I care for—Jupiter, see those ducks! a flock of them, by the living Mars! Pull, Cort, pull! and give me a shot! pull, pull! let me get any sort of a chance at them, and if you don't see slaughter I'm a donkey!" grasping the paddle and bending his tall form in deep, long plunges. "More speed, more speed, Cort! I say, Smith, we'll have some duck for supper, hey! Pull away, Cort, pull away! How the little devils scud! A mother and ten young ones! Pull, pull! Hurrah for ducks on Folingsby's Pond!"

"Ef you holler so, Mr. Bingham, now you've got so cluss, you wont git no ducks!" at last said poor Cort, panting with his exertions and his face streaming.

"Don't I know that," said Bingham, looking at his caps, and then aiming as the flock huddled close a short distance ahead. "Oh, confound them! there they go again!"

And go they did, the cluster breaking away like beads with the string broken, and all scouring over the grey surface.

Once more we approached, and once more away they scudded, making the water white as they went.

"They'll git off, Mr. Bingham, after all. They aint forty rod from shore."

"I know it; and how the little rogues skip," said Bingham. "There they go!" and the flock struck the margin and vanished into a thicket like a flash.

"You may git 'em yit, Mr. Bingham!" said Harvey, 'ef you'll land, and beat round a leetle. I kinder guess you'll find 'em under some log or bush. They aint gone fur, that's sarten!"

"Harvey, you're a trump!" said Bingham, making one stride to shore.

The rest of us remained in the boats. Now and then a snap or rustle in the woods told that Bingham was ferreting around. A minute or two succeeded. The near shout of a loon echoed; the flashing dragon-fly again threaded the water plants or darted in startling angles over the shallow; and the lake stretched away in dazzling whites and cool breezy darks, quiet as if nothing had ever disturbed it.

Another rustle and in a cleft of the foliage, a huge boot and a long leg appeared followed by what proved to be the whole of Bingham. Leaning his left hand on a hemlock, with his forehead ruffled up and his eyeballs distended, he peered around a moment and then glided silently away.

Bang, bang, and a terrible tumult in the water.

"By the powers! didn't I say so!" in Bingham's loudest tones. "Four, as I'm alive, four 'in one fell swoop,' or rather two, as I fired both barrels! I'd had the whole flock if I'd had another gun."

We pulled around a little rocky point, and there, in a beautiful covert of white sand, lay four white-breasted ashen-winged copperhead ducks.. The bright orange legs of one beside the grey ones of the rest showed the mother of the brood.

"I found them sitting in a row as close and cosy as you please; quite a family party," continued Bingham, while Cort threw them into the box, which was fashioned at the bow of the boat. "There they were quacking and putting their heads together as if in serious conversation over their escape. Cort, where's my flask?" entering the boat. "We'll all take a drink on these shots of mine, eh, Smith! here, drink my boy! a good shot, Smith! here, Harvey, take some! Cort, help yourself! a pret-ty good shot, eh, boys! and now I'm ready to follow to the camp! Go ahead, Cort!"

"Suppose we go around the pond first," said I. "It is a beautiful sheet of water."

"Very well! I'm up to any thing now! Go ahead Cort!"

We then took the circuit. We rounded the bays; brushed the herbage of the headlands and pierced the grottoes of the leaning trees. Now we caught glimpse of a duck skulking into the water-flags; and now we startled into the air a crane watching the water behind a point. Then, after loosening the echoes with three ringing cheers, we left the lovely pond, and threaded the twisted silver of the brook by sunset to the camp.

I afterwards gleaned some particulars of the mysterious personage who had given the pond its name, from those conversant with the traditions concerning him, and especially from one who was accidentally present at his death.

Captain Folingsby, as he was called, was a strange, melancholy man, of an age almost impossible to determine. From several indications he appeared to be in the meridian of life, but his hair was grey, and his frame, though massive and sinewy, was bowed.

He lived, forty years ago, in a shanty of thickest logs, built, as he stated, by his own hands, in the rear of the blunt headland. The whole region at that time had no residents, except here and there a red man, and was unknown save to the white hunter or trapper who straggled into it from the Lower Ausable or Lake Champlain.

No one knew when Folingsby came. A wandering trapper who visited the secluded waters (more secluded probably from the difficulty of ascending the shallow and winding brook) saw the shanty already erected. He was told of Folingsby's existence by an Indian whom he met at the mouth of the brook, and who had just seen, for the first time, the strange white man fishing in the pond.

Entrance into the shanty was only allowed to those driven thither by stress of weather. A lock of great strength and curious intricacy secured the massive door, and the one window was furnished with a thick ironwood shutter.

While at home Folingsby passed most of his time on the pond with his rod, or in the woods with his rifle. Sometimes he launched into the adjacent region, penetrating now and then to great distances.

The hunter at the head waters of the Upper Saranac saw him bearing his bark canoe over some carry, or skimming some water; the Indian trapper among the ponds of the St. Regis in search of the beaver, caught glimpses of him, rifle in hand, stalking through the surrounding forests.

Thus he bestowed his name on other sheets of water besides this pond—Folingsby's Clear Pond, near the head of the above lake, and Folingsby's Pond in the St. Regis woods.

A trapper, whose sable line ran by the pond, was weather-bound one day in Folingsby's cabin. The recluse talked but little, appearing to be generally sunk in gloomy meditation, and occasionally moving his lips as if in soliloquy. He showed, however, no want of hospitality; on the contrary, he produced his finest trout and venison for the trapper's repasts. The trapper said afterward in effect, that what most impressed him, was the lordly authority which diffused itself, as it were, from Folingsby's presence.

There was a grace and refinement too, in his movements and actions, especially at the meals, which made the rude trapper feel "as though" (in his own language) "he wasn't no man at all, but a kind o' half nigger all the time."

When the storm passed, the trapper left, Folingsby accepting his simple thanks with the condescending kindness of a king.

A year or two passed, when one October day a sportsman from a village on the eastern edge of the wilderness, visited the pond with an Ausable trapper, in search of fisher.

Passing the cabin they heard a loud voice talking rapidly, interrupted by hoarse screams. They broke in the door after great exertion, and found Folingsby stretched on his bed of bear-skins, and delirious with fever.

Unable to aid him, all they could do was to listen to his ravings, and restrain him in his occasional fits of insane strength.

His wild talk made them wonder and occasionally shudder. Sometimes he seemed addressing himself to high personages, Lord this and General that; sometimes to one he called Georgiana, and he would then break into mingled curses on her and on one whom he called villain and destroyer. His tones would, however, sometimes melt to tenderest music while mentioning her; but his mood would again change, and exclamations of "wretch" and "weak wicked creature" would flit through his ravings in accents of the most horrible hate.

Blood, blood, was then his theme, and from what the hearers could gather, his hands had been imbrued in the blood of both victim and destroyer.

Then he would fancy himself in battle, calling upon his men to follow him, and hurling scorn on all cowards who would desert their leader. His bearing at those times, the sportsman said, was bold and majestic, something as he supposed Washington's might have been in some great fight; Folingsby whirling his hand over his head as if waving a sword and striking out right and left.

He also muttered broken words about a chest, rolling his mad eye, and once or twice pointing his lean finger toward the stone fire-place, and he would then huddle up his bear-skins as if to conceal some object.

All through the day and night he raved, and at dawn he died, the name of Georgiana the last sound upon his lips.

The two wrapped him in his bear-skins and buried him in a neighboring dingle, planting a pair of rude stones at his grave.

They then explored the cabin. It was composed of two rooms, with loop-holes, the front one having the window. Nothing was seen in either, beside the bear-skin bed, but a rude bench or two, an arm-chair of roots, two or three rifles, with wooden angle-rods and their apparatus, axes, hunting-shirts, with other coarse clothing, and a few culinary utensils of the roughest description. The exclamations concerning the chest, however, stimulated farther search, and under a stone of the hearth they discovered in a cavity, a strong wooden box. Within, was a magnificent sword in a gold scabbard, with a gold hilt, sparkling in diamonds and impressed with something which, as well as I could gather from the description, was a coronet. There was also a brace of pistols, the stocks of rich, polished wood, mounted in silver, and inlaid with pearl, and stamped likewise with the coronet.

A scented dressing-case was also within, with gold and gemmed articles of toilet; a little cabinet of glossy and fragrant wood; a splendidly decorated uniform coat of the British scarlet, with gorgeous epaulets, and a gold laced chapeau.

At the very bottom was a package of letters. Some were signed Georgiana; were addressed to her dear Hubert, and filled with expressions of love, with details domestic and otherwise. The sportsman (who was an educated and intelligent man) was struck with some things in these letters, tending, as he thought, to throw a little light upon Folingsby. She mentioned in one, the arrival from the Peninsula of her Hubert's wounded friend, Lord ——, who brought her dear Hubert's letter; and that he spoke of owing his life in a certain battle to her brave Hubert. In another, she mentioned that Lord —— was residing near the castle. In another that the Earl, her Hubert's father, was confined to the castle from his failing health.

There was another letter of a subsequent date to the above, which appeared to be written by a high official of the British Government. It was addressed to Colonel, the Earl of ——, and in friendly and familiar terms, informed him of his approaching promotion for his distinguished gallantry in a certain battle; the sportsman thought the battle of Salamanca.

What became of the articles and letters the sportsman never definitely knew. They were replaced in the chest, together with the other articles, and transported by the two in their boat on their return course to the foot of the Lower Saranac, where they passed the night in the shanty of a hunter. In the morning the chest was missing. Whether the trapper or the hunter made away with it the sportsman could not ascertain. The former asserted it was the latter. The letters were most probably used for wadding, and the other articles doubtless changed into rifles, traps, powder, ball, and other necessaries of wilderness life in some of the cities, or large villages, to which the hunters and trappers occasionally made their way.

The strange circumstances that surrounded Folingsby invest him even to this day with mystery. The simple-minded woodmen visiting the pond still think his spirit inhabits it. In the misty days of Indian summer they imagine him glimmering in his boat off some point, or in some bay in pursuit of the trout, or gliding through some ravine of the hills in the track of the deer. In the sounds that echo over the calm sheet they hear his shout or the report of his rifle. During the moonlight nights they have fancied glimpses of his form, now crouching under a tree on the bank gazing at the shining expanse, now moving around the spot where his remains were buried, and now shooting with his canoe athwart the golden glitter of the moon-glade. In the wailing night winds of November they recognise, while seated around the camp-fire, his tones of mourning, and occasionally his wild shrieks as the blast swells through the forest.

A haunted place is Folingsby's Pond, and many the daring hunter or trapper who, laughing at every other peril, trembles as night environs him in its dreaded precincts.

CHAPTER XIII.

Down the Racket.—Old Ramrod.—Trout Fishing at Half-Way Brook.—A Water-Maple.—Cloud Pictures.—Woods in the Wind.—The Great Oxbow.—Ramrod's Shanty; and Chase by Indians.—A Talk on Fishing, with the Opinion of the Guides about it.—A Night Scene on the River.

OUR camp was astir as the morning colors were kindled on the hills of Folingsby's Pond. The day promised to be fine, and soon our tent was struck, Brook Meadow Camp deserted, and we afloat down the beautiful Racket.

Down we went over the glossy greens, the glittering whites of the river; down past elms and spruces and hemlocks and pines and water-maples and alders; down past sand-banks and gravel-beds, sunken logs and slanting trees; old withered upright trees and trees thrust midway into the channel where the water eddied and sparkled; down past lily-pads and water-grasses, leafy arcades and cloisters, colonnades and peeping nooks; down past glades and swamps and lichened ledges and dry ridges brown with the dropped needles of the pine:

> Down the winding woodland river,
>   Oh how swift we glide!
> Every tree and bush and blossom
>   Mirrored in the tide;
> Bright and blue the heaven above us
>   As—whose azure eye!
> Soft and sweet the wandering breezes
>   As—whose gentle sigh!
> White the cloudlet wreathing o'er us
>   As her spotless brow!
> Oh what king was e'er so joyous
>   As we roamers now!

> Ho, ho, we merrily go
> Down the winding sparkling flow!
> Down so cheerily,
> Never wearily,
> Ho, ho, we merrily go
> Down to the lovely lake below!
>
> "Mark the crane wide winnowing from us!
> Off the otter swims!
> Round her fortress sails the fish-hawk;
> Down the wood-duck skims!
> Glitters rich the golden lily,
> Glows the Indian Plume,
> On yon point a deer is drinking,
> Back he shrinks in gloom;
> Now the little sparkling rapid!
> Now the fairy cove!
> Here, the sunlight-mantled meadow!
> There, the sprinkled grove!
> Ho, ho, we merrily go
> Down the winding glittering flow!
> Down so cheerily!
> Never wearily!
> Ho, ho, we merrily go
> Down to the lovely lake below!"

"There was an old feller," said Harvey, breaking a half-hour's silence, and pointing to a little green opening between a couple of cedars, "that shantied out there some twenty years ago, who was old hunderd in the way o' huntin'. We used to call him Old Ramrod, and a cur'ous old critter he was too. When he fust come to the river he camped down on the Great Oxbow in a holler tree.

"But couldn't he handle a rifle? I tell ye! He could shoot inter a squirrel's eye! Why he al'ys cut off a patridge's head with a single ball; that wan't no kind of a trick. All in the way of shootin' was inkstand to 'im. And he wasn't nobody's fool at trappin'. He had the greatest lot o' traps I ever did see. Bear-traps and wolf-traps and painter-traps and otter's and beaver's and what not. And he'd named 'm all too. There was Clapper-jaw, and Sticktooth, and Whangdown, and Big Billy, and

Little Billy, and Bear's Misery, and Wolfclick and Bangup, and all sorts o' names. There wasn't no stream, nor slew, nor pond anywheres about this here part o' the country, but he knowed about as well as I know the S'nac Lakes and the Racket.

"He was about as big as a small sized moose that feller, and in the way o' wrastlin'—there's 'n orful sight o' deer tracks there; the bank's cut up with 'm—he could throw all that I ever heerd on; and when it come to fightin', w-a-a-l, he didn't sing psalms much when he was at that business. How he would strike! It 'peared to me that the very wind his fist made 'ud knock a common man down.

"There was another feller, too, about, that was an orful critter to fight. But he didn't hev no rule for fightin'. He'd claw and he'd bite, and he'd jump up and strike his heels right agin your breast, like 's not, jest like a hoss, and run 'twixt your legs, and all sorts o' ways. He was a stout feller, too, al*most* as stout as Old Ramrod; and young;— he wan't more'n twenty-five ef he was that.

"Well, one day, there was a shootin' match at the settlement at Harrietstown—one Christmas day, for five fat turkeys. Old Ramrod was there and this feller—let me see—what was his name? Snazy! no! Snar—Snowy! what the mischief! Snow, Snudgeon, Snack, Snew! oh, Potter was his name! we called him Foxtail 'case he al'ys wore a cap made o' that critter's fur, with the tail stuck up. Well, Foxtail had drinked consid'able and couldn't git no turkey. All he could do—see that bear track! what an all fired big one 'tis! there by them alders—he couldn't git no turkey. He was suthin' of a shot too, that is, when he was himself. When Foxtail was Foxtail he could shoot old hunderd, but there 'twas; that day he couldn't git no turkey. Well, what riled him most was that Old Ramrod got two out o' the five. In the fust place, the real truth on't was, he didn't like Old Ramrod a bit more'n a crow likes a raven, or a bluejee a hawk! 'caze why! he was jealous of Old Ramrod as a fightin' charackter; but he didn't do as the crow doos, keep away from the raven, but he jest up and stuck his blamed fool of a nose right inter Old Ramrod's face, jest as a passle o' bluejees will in a hawk's till the hawk jumps on one and gives 'im fits. But, as I was sayin', Old Ramrod got two turkeys out o' the five, and he'd a got 'm all I spose ef he'd a tried, but he was a gin'rous old sarpent, and didn't want I spose to grab all on 'm. Howsever, whether or no, this Foxtail, he got, as I said afore, r'iled, and so he ups and says to Old Ramrod, s'ze, 'Some folks feels mighty farse about turkeys.' 'Well, no,' says Old Ramrod, s'ze, 'not as I knows on!'

"'Well,' says Foxtail, 'I kin lick any man on these grounds, turkey or no turkey.' Old Ramrod didn't say nothin', but he tuk a chaw of tobaccy. Says Foxtail, s'ze, 'I don't ax no odds of no man! I kin lick an-y m-a-n on these grounds, 'tickally one what gits two turkeys out o' five in a shootin' match.' Old Ramrod began to cock his eye, and I could see he was gittin' kinder riz, but he didn't say nothin' yit. Says Foxtail agin, s'ze, 'Folks says there's an old critter called Ramrod about here that's some on turkeys, and thinks he kin lick all cr'ation; now I'm jest the chap for all the old Ramrods that kin be skeered up, and ef so be as the old critter wants an all fired lickin', I'm the b'y what kin do it, right square up to the handle, turkeys or no turkeys, hooray!' Didn't Old Ramrod jump! I tell ye he had his old deer-skin shirt off in the twinkle of a deer's tail in a brush heap, and the way he throwed down his wolf-skin cap wasn't slow, now I tell ye! Well, there he stood, and he drawed up his big old fists he did, and 'Come on,' s'ze, 'I'm hungry,' s'ze, 'after jest such leetle chaps,' s'ze, 'as you be!' He hadn't sunner said that 'an Foxtail (he had his coat and cap off too) run up and gin a jump to jam his heels inter Old Ramrod's breadbasket, but the old feller kitched hold on one o' his heels and gin a swing, and, lick-a-my-dod! didn't Foxtail turn over! I kinder consate he did! about a rod! and fell. I wonder he didn't break his consarned neck. Old Ramrod looked at 'im, as he lay down there all quirled up in a heap, as I've seen Watch look at a leetle cur dog, and, s'ze, 'Landlurd,' s'ze, 'gimme suthin' to drink,' s'ze, 'I'm dry!' Well, after a while, Foxtail got up with his shoulder out 'o j'int, and you may b'leeve he let Old Ramrod alone after that. But here we are at Half-Way Brook!"

This was one of the many streams emptying into the Racket, at the mouths of which, in the late summer, the trout gather.

My comrades were there busy at their fishing, and directly as we came up I saw the flash of a half-pound trout on Renning's line. The broad deep pool at the brook's mouth was already too crowded, so I selected a spot at the side of the bank where a streak of bubbles glided from a waterbreak and cast. My hook had scarcely touched the water before I felt the thrill of a trout's bite (very gentle in these waters), and up I whipped a half-pounder. Up glittered three more among my friends. Harvey cast in, and out came a fine speckled fellow of nearly the same size as mine. He commenced talking to the trout, as was his custom. "Now don't be too greedy! Be decent and we'll sarve ye all alike. We don't make no odds 'twixt ye! One's jeest as good as another. Leetle or big, it don't make no bit o' diff'rence! Unly come along! By goll! he's took my bait off as clean as a whistle! That was a chubb, I know! Yes!" jerking one up and swinging it with vast contempt into the river. "We might as well be goin' now; when these ere reptyles, and minnies, and sich vagabones venter out, you may be sure there aint much trout about."

Just as he caught the chubb, however, I had spied a dot of a pool under a sycamore root, where the bubbles of a little rapid had turned melting into a scale of froth. Casting my line into its centre, another half-pound trout swung into my hand, smooth and luscious, and up flashed another from the waterbreak on Gaylor's hook. After that, the busy tantalizing nibbles told us it was really as Harvey said, and, waging no war on the small populace of the river, and having in prospect two or three more tilts with the trout before we came to our camping-place, we desisted.

"There's a path from Half-Way Brook," said Harvey, as we started again. "It leads through the woods to the Upper S'nac, a mile above the Gut to Bartlett's."

"Are there many of these paths in the woods?"

"Not a dreffle sight. There's a passle o' lumber roads, but they're plain to see. In winter there's a grist o' roads made in the snow for lumb'rin. These paths though, what there is on 'm, is hard to hit. You might never find 'm, unless you stumbled on 'm, ef ye didn't know where to look."

We all landed for our lunch in a little wild-grass dingle, with a fringe of silver sand tasselled at the edge with arrowheads and rushes, mingled with Tyrian-dyed moose-heads and golden-globed lily blossoms.

Close to us was a splendid water-maple with thirty trunks. The gold and blacks beneath it made a floor of mosaic.

A kingfisher perched there before betaking himself to a dry overhanging limb at the margin, and gave a hoarse shout as if struggling with a bad cold caught from the damps of his business. A woodpecker followed him with a cracked laugh; then began a rat-tat like a drummer marking time, warming into a roll, and he then flew away.

The lunch being finished, I lay within the shadow of the tree, and gazed on the sky-pictures.

The blue was of that tender, transparent tint through which we seem to penetrate into unbounded depths, and over it the summer breeze wreathed its graceful cloud paintings. Now passed a turreted castle; now a pillared palace; then a fleet bore up; then came knights on snowy steeds; then a Spanish muleteer, an Arab on his camel, an Indian with his hatchet, a group of palm-trees; and then a superb gleaming Himmalayan peak.

At last my eyes ached with the lustrous images, and I bathed them in the soothing green below, watching the motions of the woods in the wind.

At a little distance an aspen shook as if to drop into pieces; then a pine waved its emerald plume. An oak next trembled, and a tremor ran through a massive fir-tree. Next a maple turned up the whites of its Argus eyes as the Meadow-Sweet kissed the blushing Indian-Plume; while the hemlock murmured through all its fringes at his loftiness forbidding a caress to the wild rose, which had opened her pink beauty directly beneath him.

The breeze, after its run through the woods, betook itself, like a deer, to the water. It skimmed away like a great water-fly; then, after throwing a dark, ruffled mantle over the surface, it leaped into a white cedar and flitted off through the pulsating forest.

I was at last aroused by a summons from Harvey, and hurrying to the boat, found my companions already in the stream.

Down again we went, checking our course at the mouths of two or three spring brooks for the speckled prey.

Passing a shingle weaver's camp, and threading the Rapids where a dozen rocks of differing sizes in the channel caused various currents and eddies, we came to the Great Oxbow.

This is a two-mile sweep of the river around a long point. Across its base, however, the portage is scarcely more than a score of paces.

We landed at the base, and drew the boat across, crushing the lush wood-plants into an emerald paste. Before launching again, we regaled ourselves on the whortleberries, whose blue, misty eyes glanced at us in every direction.

"Folks gin'rally say the Oxbow or the Great Oxbow; when they talk o' this place; but there's two Oxbows. T'other one is out there cluss to this; but it's a bad carry, and the boatmen don't never notice it," said Harvey.

"There's bin a mighty thrashin' 'mongst the bushes here," continued he, glancing round. "The bears 'as bin here, that's sarten—yes, yes—there's the tracks! But about

Old Ramrod, as I was a tellin' on ye," seating himself at the foot of a birch, I doing the same, "he made a good deal o' this place; he camped here for some years; and in his young days had lived here in a sort o' cave, or rather a holler in a big pine-tree, the biggest, 'cordin' to his tell, I ever see in these woods. You switched a thick cedar-bush a one side, and crawled inter a shelvin' place 'twixt the roots like a wood-chuck's hole, and there was a place in the body of the tree big enough to stand up in and walk a leetle about and lay down too, curled up, though, as a hound sleeps. Old Ramrod made two or three knot-holes in the tree bigger to give 'im air and light. They made good places to shoot from, too; and the St. Regis Injins bein' about the Racket in them days, these 'ere loopholes, as 'twere, stood him a good turn sometimes.

"He was a great Injin fighter, was Ramrod, for he had an idee the Injins had no business comin' on the Racket to hunt and fish, as they had their own waters all round the Upper S'nac. 'Twas treadin' on his toes, so he was down on 'em, and got up a fight whensumever he could, 'tickelly when there wasn't more 'n two or three agin 'im. He popped over all he could, and finally at last the Injins didn't never go on the Racket without expectin' a row with Old Ramrod or the Quick Wind, as they nicknamed 'im, 'caze he'd pounce so dreffle sudden on 'em with his rifle. The Injin for that name was Gollywolly; and I guess that word, by goll, that I use so much, comes from it. Whether or no, one day, he, that is Old Ramrod, had been up to Folin'sby's Pond, and had fell agin a rock, so as to break the lock of his rifle. Well, he started torts hum, and jest as he rounded the left-hand p'int o' the brook down inter the Racket, what did he see but an Injin canoe hauled up on the bank. He got at the same time a squint o' two Injins crooched up like a couple o' mud-turtles, or like a couple o' black squirrels, we'll say, crackin' hickory nuts. The Injins, though, was a smokin' through them queer kind o' things o' theirn—hatchets hollered out in the handle, with the bowl in the head. There they was, with their backs torts him. Well, he'd got 'fairly inter the Racket, and he was in hopes they wouldn't see 'im 't all, as two to one with rifles was too much odds for the old feller, farse as he was, when he hadn't got no rifle, or what was next to't, one that was broke. But jest as he was turnin' a bush, didn't they screech! Did you ever hear a war-whoop, Mr. Smith? it's so (clapping his hand to his mouth, and playing it with a rapid motion): hoo-oo-ooooooeee, hoo! And as they sung out, they started for their canoe in sich a hurry that they didn't never think o' their rifles. Old Ramrod see the whull consarn, and he put to 't. Didn't he make his dug-out spin! I tell *you!* But he unly got clear by the skin of his teeth; that is, by rushin' his canoe up, and dashin' crost with it to t'other side here (for the Injins didn't know this place, and kept straight on), and lickety splittin' it down'ards to Simon's Slew, where he hid a whull day in the bushes."

Again we were on our downward way, and the sky began to burn in the colors of the sunset. The clouds had long been streaming towards the west, and now reared their gorgeous architecture, gold, purple, and crimson, radiant as the angel-ladder that shone to the patriarch in his dream.

"A glorious day we'll have to-morrow, Harvey, for Tupper's Lake," remarked I.

Harvey shook his head.

"Too much deep red agin, Mr. Smith!" said he. "There's rain in that sundown; and hark! hear them two cranes flyin' along there. All that jabberin' says jeest as plain as the sky doos, 'rain tomorrer.' But here's our campin' place for the night, and there's our folks all landed."

The spot selected was a little green hollow on the right hand bank, with a spring sparkling from the roots of a birch along the dell's edge to the river.

Before the rose had faded from the shreds of the zenith-clouds, the grassy plat began to have a home-look; a blazing camp-fire reddening up our tent, and the crotched sticks whereon hung portions of venison, with a cluster or so of trout, ducks, and partridges. In the thickening dusk, by pine-knot torches, we took our supper, and after a smoke under the hazy stars, my comrades retired to the tent for eucre. I strolled to the river-bank, and found three of the guides, with their pine-torches, around the boats. It was a striking scene; the black walls of forest, the dark river dotted here and there with a star, relieved by pallid spaces caught on the sensitive surface from lighter portions of the sky, and flecked with the deep crimson of the torches under which a stone, a water-log, a ripple, a spot of lily-pads, a dipping bush, looked redly forth. The same dark-red lustre brought fitfully out a hunting-shirt, a bronzed face, a hand, an oar-blade, or the half hollow of a boat; the whole presenting a picture of strange, flitting effects, worthy Rembrandt.

I listened to the guides a moment.

"There's a trout as is a trout," said one, lifting a two-pounder. "This mouth o' his'n is open as wide as a school-mam's a singin' Coronation."

"I wonder ef we go to Tupper's Lake tomorrer?" asked a second. "I'm a kinder hungerin' after Redside or Grindstone Brook, I don't keer which."

"'Twould be news to us ef ye ever stopped hungerin' after anything," said the first. "But hang it! I've carried boat so much this summer, my neck's so hard a bear 'ud crack his jaw on't."

"Say skull, and we'd all b'leeve ye!" retorted the hungerer. "I'll leave it to the company ef there ever was a time yet that this chap wasn't more fond o' lettin' suthin' run through his neck than carryin' ennything on't!"

"Well, hooray, boys," exclaimed Harvey, "let's hurry up our work and make a sleep on't jest as soon as kin be. I'm consid'able tuckered out fur one, and I guess by tomorrer we'll all feel suthin' a-runnin' every where over us, ef I'm any judge when rain's a-comin'."

Entering the tent, I found my companions in a paroxysm of argument on one of the political questions of the day, Gaylor and Renning (as well as I could ascertain, from the hubbub) fighting off Bingham and Coburn. In a short time, Gaylor, having the weakest voice and the most modesty, and finding himself buried in the clamor, turned to me in a lowered tone, and then to Harvey (who had just made his appearance with an ejaculation of something about supper), finishing on him what he had to say in a sort of confidential aside. Renning soon after made a grumbling retreat, evidently crippled, and Bingham and Coburn had the field to themselves. Then in following up their victory they fell out between themselves, each at length pummelling the other with hard assertions, and each voice striving to soar above the other, until a shout from Harvey that supper was ready sliced the battle short off, and sent all to the waiting trout and venison, now as cool as the argument had been flaming.

As Harvey had once more predicted, rain came with the morning, confining us to the tent. In the desultory conversation that after a while occurred, we all caught at last upon the topic of fishing, Renning and Gaylor becoming exceedingly learned, and I thought rather tedious, in explaining the varieties of hooks and flies, and enlarging upon trolling, fishing at buoys, and what not. The guides seemed much interested in the discussion, listening with an air of great respect, while Renning, leaving Gaylor behind, with an occasional glance at them, contrasted, fluently and enthusiastically, but (the truth must be owned) somewhat pompously, the merits of the different hackle flies, and hooks, reels, baits, rods, and so forth, until Bingham involuntarily commenced a whistle, which he, however, bit off, and even the faithful Gaylor showed by the swelling of his features that he was struggling with an inward yawn. Still the guides lingered and listened, nodding their admiration to each other, and retreated only when Renning, fairly bothered with his own arguments, seemed hardly to know which fly, hook, reel, bait, or rod, he most preferred himself, and covered his confusion under the smoke of a fresh cigar.

Happening shortly after to pass along a thicket skirting the open tent of the guides, I became the involuntary depository of their reflections on Ralph's eloquence.

"Dang my parsnips," said one on his breast, tossing up his leg and putting a hemlock twig in his mouth, "ef I didn't swell all up, I was so full o' laugh at Mr. Runnin's topsy-turvy talk about fishin'. How he did go on about his black flies, and grey flies, and green flies. Ef he likes flies so much, I wish he'd all on 'em to himself in this ere quarter o' the country."

"Talkin' o' black flies," said another, "it's my idee ef he'd got unly about a dozen o' them nips that I had from the black divils last June in Simon's Slew, he wouldn't want to see no more o' that color."

"And as fur his reels, his plain and multiplyin', and Lord knows what all," said a third, "the unly reel I keer about is the Scotch reel, and the more multiplyin' that with a sarten schoolmam I knows on down at the settlement, the better for me!"

Here old Harvey broke in.

"I don't say there aint as nice men in the world as Mr. Runnin', but I do say there aint no nicer: he's old hunderd, that's a fact; and he's good enough fur fishin' in the streams and brooks round in the settlements—that is fur what I know—but, massy, b'ys, I raally thought I should split when I heerd him agoin' on about his reels, and his rods, and his flies, and grubs, and so on. It doos make me cackle to see these city fellers bring out to S'nac their rods, lookin' as ef slicked all over with 'lasses, and all shinin' with brass, and their brass reels that takes more trouble to handle than a dozen oars over a two mile carry. Them devilish reels is, after all, the wust things I knows on. They're al'ys a gittin' ketched some way in yer coat, jest when ye hook a big trout; or they go spinnin' out, jest when ye don't want 'em to, and ef ye hev a stop in 'em, the 'tarnal stop stops at the p'int where it shouldn't stop. But, howsever, this is the thing. About them shiny rods. Now, b'ys, I kin git a rod ennywheres in the woods, with a good plain hook, that 'll do all I want a rod to do, and I've fished more'n forty year in these ere wild waters; and as for flies, I'll take a worm, or mebby a bit o' minnie, and I'll go right after one that's bin fishin' with a fly and ketch jest twice as many as he did in the same spot. I don't keer how much he skitters here and skitters there, and all that. A worm's a worm in these ere waters. And then the rifles the gen'nlemen bring. Why, my darter Polly kin see to fix her hair in the stocks, and they're all finified off with silver. Now there's my old rifle Spitfire, that I've killed a hunderd deer with in about three weeks at Tupper's Lake in one season alone; I wouldn't give that rifle fur any one o' them kitteningoes they brings; and that, b'ys, is the whull matter!"

At noon it cleared. It was decided upon, however, as the camp spot was so pleasant, to stay where we were until the next morning.

"And as that's the case," said Bingham, "and we shall have a clear, pleasant night, I intend to start on a jack-hunt as far as the Rapids as soon as it's dark. Harvey, will you be paddler? Cort don't feel very well."

"Sarten!" answered the old boatman.

"Well, have your boat ready, and if there's a deer as far as we go on the river, I intend to make its acquaintance!"

But about sunset it thickened up once more, and shortly the rain threads began glimmering.

"Another rainy night on't," said Harvey sauntering up.

"Well," said Bingham, "truly may we say, in all sincerity, in these woods, 'The Lord reigneth.' But rain or no rain, I mean to float for deer to-night up the Racket. Be all ready, Harvey, so we can start at dark. The rain after all may stop soon."

The rain still fell. And it looked as though it wouldn't stop in a hurry.

Night came.

"Come, hurrah there!" said Bingham, slipping on his rough overcoat and clapping his rifle within it. "All ready, Harvey?"

"All ready, Mr. Bingham! Come, Mr. Smith!"

"What, is Smith going too? Well, hurrah, hurrah! the deuce take the rain! Come, Harvey, light your jack and push off! ought to be nearly to the Rapids by this time! Come, hurrah, hurrah," and off we pushed upon the rainy river.

The most intense darkness wrapt the scene, with a silence broken only by the humming on the leaves and sprinklings on the water.

Up we went, the Bluebird glancing her eye into the banks, but we saw nothing, heard nothing that told of deer. From a gloomy clearing on the left bank, came the asthmatic whine of an owl, and now and then the hoarse gulp of a frog. At last we reached the foot of the Rapids, with the shingle-weaver's camp just above. A single light like a star told where the woodman was weaving his shingles by his pine-knot torch. All else was solitude. Here Bingham and I landed, while Harvey pushed up through the Rapids to visit the camp. We kindled a bonfire with some old shavings on the bank, upon a broad rock at the foot of the Rapids. The glare flashed the black scenery into crimson life. Soon a shout sounded from the head of the Rapids, and amid the wild flaming light and a shower of red sparks, I saw Harvey descending in his boat and kneeling in Indian fashion. Darting hither and yon like a frighted bird; seeming at one time to be dashing on a rock, then swinging round in some eddy, the little Bluebird at length emerged from her perils, ready for her return flight to camp. Down the river again she sped, but as before we saw nothing. Once only there was a light, cautious, paddling tread in the water, but the gloom disclosed no living shape; black logs and blacker rocks alone met our view.

A little before midnight we returned to the camp. The rain was still falling, freshening into ruddier light the camp-fire, which sent up among the leaves long lines of golden lace work. Seated upon their stools around the tent, fronting the genial blaze, were my comrades, pretending to be lost in admiration of the glittering curls that were winding through the foliage, but really lost in the effects of a huge pitcher of punch.

Soon the rain ceased, and by the time we went to bed the stars were shining.

CHAPTER XIV.

Simon's Pond.—Harvey's Story of Old Sabele, the Indian.—Driving Deer.—
The Simon's Pond Pirate.—Tupper's Lake.—Night Sail on Lake.

MORNING arose calm, and mantled in light cloud. The sun-glow interfusing the delicate mist kindled it into a veil of pearl streaming over the brow of the day.

We had fallen so in love with our camp, and the softness of the weather was so luxurious, that we deferred our departure from hour to hour.

My comrades went to their eucre again, and I took a seat on a log near where the guides were "lying around loose."

"That chap that goes about peddlin' so much from t'other side o' Keene Mountain," said one, rolling from his breast to his back, and slouching his hat over his eyes, "let's me see, his name is—no matter, he's cross-eyed and chaws t'baccy some I tell ye! well, he was a tellin' round t'other day at Harrietstown, that he could kill more deer, ketch more trout, and row a boat better than enny guide about Baker's.

"'Why,' said I, 'you don't know as much as a yaller dog about enny o' them things you're a braggin' about.' He was a goin' to get mad, but he kinder thought better on't."

"Fools is fools," said Harvey, "and you can't make nothin' else on 'm. But I say, b'ys, let's hev a shootin' match!"

As he spoke, a ground squirrel darted upon a mossy log near, and lifting his brush, looked saucily at the guides. Will seized his rifle, and as the little striped clown of t underbrush turned, he fired, and the animal fell, minus a head. Tiny, chirpy titmouse next came hopping along, bending his brown turban to one side and the other; but as he paused under a buff hopple-sprout to peck at his raised foot, away went his turban, picked off by a bullet from Cort. Then Harvey glanced at a yellow bull's-eye of a knot bulging high on a pine-tree. Up went his piece to his left shoulder, and as the short, flat report rang in my ears, I saw a black spot in the middle of the bulge like a robin's eye.

"Wa-a-ll!" said the remaining guide, "I don't see no more chipmunks, or chickadees, or knots, and not even a respectable-sized devil's darnin'-needle on the stream to shoot at; but there's suthin' up there," pointing to a prematurely crimsoned leaf of the mercury plant, which wreathed a maple-stem, looking like a red dot on the soft grey of the sky, "that I rayther guess I'll drill a hole through."

So saying, he aimed, and the leaf vanished.

After dinner, we decided to start for Tupper's Lake (six or eight miles distant, and connected with the Racket), and there erect our camp for a week. A spot on the east shore, nearly opposite two islands called the Two Brothers, and about a mile from where we entered the lake, as explained to me by Renning, was the spot selected.

Everything being in readiness, we started, Corey and little Jess taking the lead in the store-boats. They were to precede us to the lake, to place the camp in readiness for our arrival, we having settled on a drive at Simon's Pond on our way thither.

Harvey and I took the lead of the party.

The river was smooth, and the colors upon it were all soft and velvety.

"Stetson's!" said Harvey, as we passed where a brook came in at the north bank, with a boat or two drawn up on the muddy margin. "There's his house and clearin'! There's quite a little settlement about here! half a dozen fam'lies, sarten! My son Sim's 'mongst 'em. 'Tisn't more 'n a mile right crost the woods to Racket Pond, below Tupper's Lake, and the Pond's eight miles from here. So you see what an onmassyful twistin' river the Racket is."

As we doubled a point we came upon a shanty, crouching, with its two gleams of windows, under a leaning fir, like a frog under a tilted lily-pad. A hunter sat upon a log, cleaning his rifle.

"Goin' to Tupper's Lake, I 'spose?" shouted he.

"Nothin' shorter," shouted Harvey, in return; "but I say! had enny sport at Simon's Slew, or on the pond, lately?"

"Killed two in the pond, jack-huntin', unly last night— a buck and a doe. They're mighty thick up there. Kicked the lily-pads clean up on eend."

"All right!" said Harvey; and we passed on.

We turned shortly into a little stream to the south, that spread, after a few rods, into a broad expanse.

"Simon's Pond!" ejaculated Harvey, and steered out upon its surface. All around us was a pavement of lily-pads, which bore fresh tokens of deer in the piled and upturned leaves.

We had taken the short cut into the pond, and had to await the other boats through the usual channel. After a while they appeared; and Watch and Sport were taken by Harvey into the woods for the drive. He soon returned, taking his seat at the prow, with the encouraging remark, that it wouldn't be long, he guessed, "afore we'd hear music."

The other boats dwindled off to their stations.

We were in a beautiful little nook; the Bluebird pinned to a log by Harvey's oar planted close to her side in the ooze of the shallow. A streak of white lilies, with spots of little, furzy pink blossoms, was just outside.

The snipe alighted and hopped, bowing in his grey coat and white waistcoat, along the wet stones, and the green bullfrog jumped with a croak on the black log, and lifting his yellow, speckled throat, stared at us with his great eye-jewels, as if he were carved from stone.

"I never telled ye about old Sabele, I bleeve!" said Harvey, after a while, but in a cautious tone. "He was an old Injin. I knowed 'im well. When I fust knowed 'im he was shantyin' where old Leo is campin' now, down on the Racket, jest above Racket Pond. He was as good a shot at a deer, and could ketch as big a lot o' trout as the next man, and he wa'n't no man's fool at trappin'; he was an orful old critter, though, when he got mad; but"— bending his ear suddenly, "I bleeve I heerd one o' the pups then—was as smart, actyve a man for his years as I've most ever seen, and as a gin'ral thing was purty good-natered. But when he got rum aboard, look out! Why, he'd dance and kick about, and keep his tommyhawk a-goin' and sssss-sing, he would, like a dozen bagpipes. 'Hah, hah slammerawhang, hooh!' he'd go, 'hah, hah, wah—hay' (cocking his ear, with eyes and mouth wide open), that must ha' bin one o' the dogs—Watch, I think. Well, he used to tell me some o' the terr'blest long yarns about what he did when he was a young man in Canady, in the last war. He fit fur us, he said, and he must ha' bin round some, 'cordin' to his tell. 'Sabele,' he used to say, ' put on de war-*paint*—all red on one side de face, and black on toder—den he dance de war *dance*, and hit de war *post* all down to no*ting*, and den he took de war trail;' that is, he went out for a gin'ral spree agin the British, a tomahawkin' and a sculpin—there's a blue jee agin'! what a squawkin' sarpent 'tis!—the wust way.

"He was livin' with his tribe on the 'Tawy River, and fell in love with a white gal—what a tattin' that plaguy woodpecker keeps up! I could hear the pups, though, for all that sharp rattlin'. There ain't no sound in natur' that joggles enny other sound to me. But as I was sayin' about old Sabele. This white gal was the darter of an old trapper that lived nigh the tribe. Now, as Old Sauko would hev it, there was two things agin Sabele and the gal; one was, it was agin the law o' the tribe fur to marry enny except Injins; and the other was, the old chief of the tribe wanted Sabele to marry his own darter; and as he was a bright, smart, actyve chap, and a great warryor (as the Injins calls their fightin' charackters), the old chief—let's see, what was his name?—well, I forgit it; but no matter, he forbid the match. But that didn't make not a mite o' diff'rence with their feelins—that is, Sabele and the gal— they hed sich an orful sight o' love aboard. So the old ₁chief, as ye may s'pose, didn't like it.

"But afore he did anything, he hed a talk with Sabele. Old Sabele has telled me this ere talk more'n twenty times; when he got *very* drunk he used to tell it, I tell yer, with all the hifilutens.

"Well the old chief, s'ze, to Sabele, s'ze, 'Wing o' the cloud,' s'ze, 'Eagle o' the sun!' the old—lem me see—was it oak? I disremember, but 'twas some old tree or other— the old—whatever 'twas—cedar, or white pine, or—maple fur what I know—is now—the idee was—a tott'rin' like— and 'll soon—the idee was—fall down—that is—the p'int on't was, that the old chief might soon die off, and then the Eagle—ef so be he behaved himself—would be head o' the tribe. 'But,' s'ze, 'listen,' s'ze! the 'Eagle,' s'ze, 'when he —kinder tries, you know, to fly right agin a blast o'wind —w-e-l-l—a harricane like—that's the idee—he's—the idee was—throwed back catwallopus right agin the rocks, where —as a body may say—he breaks all the bones in his body' —by goll! there's the pups, and in airnest too!" springing his locks. "The runway is by that little openin' there, cluss to that leanin' white cedar. Look out now, and you'll see suthin' in a few minutes. Watch and Sport's both a singin' like a row o' schoolmams at camp meetin'."

As he ceased, a distant guttural yet sweet and liquid ough, ough, ough, ouoo, ouoo, ouoo, ul-lul-ul, lul-ull-lull-loo touched my ear, rapidly swelling; nearer and nearer; then sinking, and floating away, then rising again; the music of different tones blending, separating, blending once more, and now coming closer and closer.

Harvey, with his rifle raised, and his whole appearance bristling with excitement, sat with his protruded eyes gleaming and fixed on the opening that was gauzed in a curl of sunny mist from the water.

Nearer, nearer, nearer swelled the music of the hounds. At last in the woods just beyond the cedar, a brown shape glanced, and the next moment a buck, with his antlers on his shoulders and his sharp face lifted, shot across the opening, his dark stretched-out frame appearing like a phantom darting through golden smoke. With one bound he leaped into the water. Harvey fired; the deer gave a convulsive spring and then sank.

"Deer sink this time o' year in the water jest like a stun ef they're shot dead," said Harvey, pulling up his oar and making the boat fly toward the spot where the deer had disappeared; "but this can't sink fur in this shaller. There 'tis," pushing aside the lily-pads.

The deer was lying on the bottom, not more than two feet from the surface.

"A three year old buck at least," added Harvey, striking the prongs of a boat-hook he always carried into the animal's neck, lifting his head above the water and dragging him into the boat.

"The dogs has turned," as a faint burst of cries came from another direction; "they must 'ave rousted up two deer. You shot the buck you know, Mr. Smith! This is a mason boat! You'll be rael old hunderd with 'm after this. They kinder think you can't shoot no deer no way; but this 'll make 'm feel thank ye mam all over torts yer! Ho, ho, ho! won't they look jealous—but by goll there's another deer in the pond—there—don't ye see a speck like a loon's head? Mr. Runnin's boat's closin' on't too. Mart's a goin' to tail it. Yes, by hokey he has, and Mr. Runnin's shootin'! We've got another deer," as the crack of a rifle echoed over the pond.

"So you've a deer too," said Renning as we approached; 'pretty well for an hour's work. Gaylor has taken up the dogs, and what say you all now to having a look at the pond!"

"Jess so!" answered Harvey, "that is ef so be Mr. Smith's agreeable, as I b'leeve he is, that is, I kinder consated you'd all hev a notion to take a cruise, and so"—

"Well, hurrah then!" said Renning, leading the way.

"There may be as nice men about," said Harvey, hitching his hat over his eyes, "as Mr. Runnin', but, as I've said afore, there aint no nicer. But don't you think, Mr. Smith, he's sometimes got a kind o' way of cuttin' crost folks when they're talkin'? Now I don't never stick my tongue in when I ought'n ter, and as you knows I haint no great shakes of a talker enny way; I al'ys 'ud a great sight ruther hear other folks talk than talk myself; but sometimes when I do say suthin' I somehow kinder like to say it through. But it's all right, so (croaking)

"'He went to the wars, alas, long years ago-o-o-o,
And I live but to see him unst more at Glencoe!'"

and so on!"

The shores were high and covered with forest. The water was clear as air, and in the soft afternoon light had in it a golden gleam like champagne. We skimmed rapidly to the head, landing on a ledge of grey rock for a lunch. We then entered the inlet leading, as Harvey informed me, into a small pond back of Mount Morris.

"There's the place for a jack-hunt," said he, as leaving the inlet we skirted a swampy meadow. "But I must tell ye of an old feller that lived on this pond some twenty years ago. I'll tell ye the rest about old Sabele tomorrer on Tupper's Lake. 'Tisn't old Simon that the pond's named after that I mean, but an old man, a hermit like, as I heerd a gen'leman call't, that was as lonesome in his way o' livin' a'most as an old loon. He was a cur'ous old critter, and I think a leetle out of his head. He was about the wust lookin' man I ever see. He had a scar from his eyebrow clearn down his cheek, and when he was in liquor and mad, for when he was in one he was t'other, that scar 'ud turn the color of a red huntin' shirt, and his eye looked as farse as a painter's. Some folks said he'd been a pirate, and I raally b'leeve he hed, for he'd talk the queerest when he'd rum aboard I ever heerd a decent man talk.

"'I've cut a man to pieces when I was down in Cuby fur a less thing 'n that,' said he one time when a chap gin him the lie in a shootin' match at Harrietstown, 'and dern me' (or suthin' wusser 'n that) 'ef I stand it now,' and with that he outs with his knife and makes a spring at him, and ye may bleeve there was a row there a leetle while. The old feller—his name was Kelsey—didn't use his knife though, fur a leetle chap by the name of—what was that feller's name agin? Doodle! no! well, he had a game leg, and we used to call him Hoppy. He was one o' them kind o' fellers that wasn't afeard, well, I might as well say it, of the divil; he come up and took him right by the elbow—he was as spry as a cat that feller—and afore old Kelsey knowed it, he had the knife away. Oh, but wa'n't old Kelsey mad, old Moose Kelsey, as we used to call 'im! He fairly roared, but twant no use, and finally at last he cooled down and took a drink.

"He wa'n't much of a hunter or fisherman, but he was an all fired trapper. At one time he'd a longer saple line than enny other man in all the S'nac region. It reached from this pond clearn up inter the St. Regis, massy knows how fur. More'n fifty mile though. I shantied with 'im a week, one fall, on Tupper's Lake ketchin' fur. We got all the rats we wanted, besides fisher and mink and saple; and we killed a good lot o' ven'son too. But I wouldn't a stayed with him a week longer fur all the fur and ven'son on the lake. Why he'd start out of a sound sleep right onto his feet with one jump, and y-e-ll; and his eyes 'ud glare, and sometimes he'd stagger and tottle back as ef he wanted to hide himself, and tremble he would jest like a fa'n when he's ketched, and he'd scream out, in a kind o' jerk, 'Go 'way, go 'way!' and at other times he'd jump forred and ketch the air and hev a fight all to himself with his knife. Sometimes he wouldn't sleep 't all, but walk up and down, up and down, all night. I got beat out at the end o' the week and put fur hum."

"What became of him, Harvey?"

"Well he died. He was found by a couple o' hunters dead under a tree nigh a wolf-trap o' his'n on the edge of the little pond, up there under Mount Morris. I never could fairly make out about 'im. After he died his shanty was sarched, and a cutlash and an old sailor's jacket, with an anchor on the sleeve, was found in a cubby hole, and an old scrap of a newspaper, printed I bleeve in New Orleans, that had a long account of a nest o' pirates that hed bin broken up in one o' the islands round Cuby. Some on 'm had bin hung and some put in a dungeon fur trial, and some o' these had broke out and run away. One in partic'lar was spoke of as bein' the farsest and bloodiest and most desprit of all, and a big reward was offered fur 'im. His parson was all in print, the cut of his face and height and all, and I tell ye, the newspaper and old Kelsey's looks 'greed like two mushrats. But here we are at the Racket agin, and now hooray for Tupper's Lake!"

Delighted at the prospect of so soon beholding a lake of whose beauty I had heard so much, I leaned back, after our turn to the left into the river again, and watched the gliding banks, anticipating the moment when we should open out into the lovely waters, and expecting it at every bend.

"I spoke o' Simon's Slew as bein' the spot where Old Ramrod hid away from the Injins," said Harvey. "We passed it a leetle while ago. It's on the opp'site side to Simon's Pond, and the all firedest place fur lily-pads I 'most ever see. You may bleeve there's jack-huntin' there. And talkin' o' huntin', I shot a mighty big buck jest by that jam o' floodwood in the river up there. He was 'most as big as the one I shot at Buckslew.

We had now reached a bend to the right. A low island covered with vegetation lay before, dividing the river into two narrow channels, while to the left, or south, stretched a path of water. Into this we turned. A few minutes passed, when suddenly a broad sheet of water expanded at our prow.

"Tupper's Lake!" said Harvey.

The view was surpassingly beautiful.

A green and gold sunset was burning in the west and gleaming on the water.

On each side the lake curved gracefully away; at the left in an unbroken line, and at the right blending to all appearance with a network of islands. In front were two other islands rounded as if by an architect, identical in shape and forming the gateway, as it were, to the inner view of points and headlands, crescent bays, island edges and liquid vistas that extended downward until closed by a mass of forest. Within this gateway glowed a golden film of light, while a depth of shadow purpled the water before it.

Over this splendid water picture we laid our course, leading the way diagonally to the left. As we skimmed along I heard again the bravura of the loon. The distant quaver came over the water from the direction of the grouped islands at the right, and I felt that something in keeping with the wild region was restored. Except the instance at Folingsby's Pond we had not heard the sound since we left the Saranac Lakes, broad expanses of water alone constituting the loon's haunt.

I turned to detect the speck of its head on the surface, but my eye only fell on the boats of the party skimming in our wake over the superb enamel of the water.

At length we touched the shore at a little cove, somewhat to the right of the south gateway-island, and running the bow up the sandy margin we awaited the coming of the other boats.

Corey had pitched our tent in a little opening at the edge

of the water, at the foot of the bank. The tent of the guides was beside it.

Here was to be the camp for our week upon the lake, and a pleasant spot it was.

In due time our traps were transferred from the boats (hauled in a row half way up the sand) to the tent; our rustic table was again erected under a cedar, and our evening meal of customary trout and venison prepared.

It was with a home feeling, after our roamings along the Racket, that we drew around the rude board in the sunset to discuss our wild delicacies.

Suddenly an unearthly scream rang through the forest. It came from directly over our heads; fierce, threatening, making our ears tingle.

"What the deuce is that?" said Bingham, his cheek bulging with a huge bite of trout, as he stared upward.

The guides laughed.

Another scream, more diabolical if possible than the first, echoed from the lower branch of the cedar, and I saw what I had taken to be a large knot take wing, and with a glide like thistledown perch on a stump near the table. Two round eyes like small moons gleamed in the light of our camp-fire, and we then saw it was an owl.

"Well, this is the strangest country I ever knew," said Bingham. "If you go on the water in the day you hear a yell like an Indian's in a war dance, and you are told it is a loon. You cruise through some tangled-up lily-pad hole that goes by the name of slew, in the night, and suddenly there'll burst out a sound like a strangled tornado, making you jump out of your skin almost, and the guide will say, 'How that deer whistles!' when it is as much like a whistle as a north-wester is like a piccolo flute. And now a company of Christians cannot enjoy a meal in their own camp, which I take to be their own castle" (here Bingham was evidently carrying the case to the jury) "without owls coming and screaming in the most disgraceful manner; just like a—a—a—a—in fact, as I may say, just like the devil. And, by the way, these owls have each more sounds in their throat than a military band with a company of cats and the north wind. They hiss and they whizz, they bark and they yell, they whine and they hoot, and they mew and they snarl; in fact, Mr. Harvey Moody, head guide of the Saranacs, can you tell me what sounds they don't make?"

During the excited Bingham's harangue, the owl had alighted nearer to the table, and now began to eye the provisions on it, as if wondering why, in the name of all that was polite, he was not invited to partake. So pert was his look, and so impudent his actions, that we all, Bingham (after his spasm of eloquence) included, burst into a laugh.

This pursuit of a supper under difficulties continued until Watch, thinking, probably, that the matter was "about played out," uncoiled himself from a hemlock root, and with his ear-flaps erected into a stately frown, and his tail ringed into severe determination, stalked, as if to stop this foolery at all hazards, towards his owlship, who, waiting till the hound was within a few feet of him, gave a spitting bark, ending in a caw of vast contempt, and glided spectre-like away.

The dark water now stretched before, with the black shapes of the islands massed within the gloom. Lines of faint light lay upon the surface from the few rays that lingered at the zenith, seeming to beckon me on; and the scene looked so dimly mysterious, I felt impelled to explore its shadowy recesses.

Calling Harvey, we pushed off, he taking the paddle. He drew it with a meek, regular sound, scarcely disturbing the divine quiet in which the scene was lapped. The water gurgled sweetly at the prow, and the air opened by our motion was balmy, and filled with the peculiar fragrance of the forest.

We ran up the shore, the woods assuming strange, fanciful shapes as we passed. Now a procession of kings streamed along with crowns of gold, and spangled with golden jewels. Now a fairy city of dark marble met my view, with sparkling casements. A dead pine on a bank before a ledge, and with a long, star-tipped arm, was Pallas before the Parthenon, with her spear-point gleaming in the everlasting lamp. Those withered trunks were Baalbeck in starlight; and the black object above on the boulder, with a speck of pallid light, some would have said it was a log, with a bit of phosphorescence, but it seemed to me a panther, with his gleaming eye on a slumbering hunter.

We left the shores and steered into the lake, and between the two islands in its centre. All was shadowy; dark trees mingled with dark rocks; alleys of black water studded with stars—all in the highest degree exciting to the fancy.

From the islands we glided into the broad space of jewelled black directly opposite the camp.

Breathing an air redolent of the balsamic odors of the pine and rich pungency of the cedar, I leaned back and gazed into the sweeping constellated heavens. I strove to pierce into the spangled depths, and to realize the grandeur of the upper spaces, whose infinitude crushes powerless the wings of the most soaring imagination.

Nothing gives a deeper feeling of solitude than floating over one of these wild lakes at night. The profound quiet, broken only by the loon's cry and some nightbird's plaint, which rather deepen than disturb it, and the darkness mystifying the surrounding woods, are full of mysterious promptings.

This feeling is also purifying. The colors are not those with which the day appeals to the sensuous within us; the sombre tone prevalent touches our deepest and holiest emotions. We lament past deficiencies and sins; we form wise and good plans and resolutions; we long to initiate a better and loftier future. Our highest affections are awakened; home and its loved ones; our friends, those on whom we are dependent, and who depend on us, crowd around. How the gloom is peopled! how the night overflows with dear forms and faces! The soul speaks, cleansed for the time from its impurities, as malaria is swept by the breath of autumn.

CHAPTER XV.

Tupper's Lake.—Old Sabele continued.—The Devil's Pulpit.—Its Legend.—
A Deer's Leap.—The Camp.—Trout Fishing.

THE frescoes of the dawn had not yet melted when I left the tent; but soon the tip of a white pine on the nearest island broke into rosy fire, and the dead grey brightened into a golden landscape of wood and water.

There was no stir yet in the tent. At length a red squirrel, twirling his brush like a housewife her dishcloth, cantered to the rear, where a corner had been left exposed, and threw within a chatter, as if in scorn at sluggards, and then scampered up a beech hard by. Out darted Bingham, rifle in hand, and sent a bullet after his squirrelship, visible in a high fork; but as only a twig fell instead of a squirrel, Bingham, catching my eye, turned around, red in the face, and picked a quarrel with Pup, on pretence that he had nipped his leg as he shot.

After an early breakfast we all separated; Gaylor and Renning to try the trout below Perciefield Falls which were about ten miles down the Racket; Bingham and Coburn to fish the buoys sparkling between the islands, and to explore the lake, and I to visit, with Harvey, the mouth of Redside Brook, a mile up, also for trout.

Tupper's Lake is about eight miles long, with an average width of two. Of its Indian names, Pas-kun-ga-meh signifies " a lake going out from the river," and Tsit-kan-i-a-ta-res-ko-wa, " the biggest lake." The former has reference to its connection with the Racket.

It forms an angle, and Mount Morris, or Tupper's Lake

Mountain, extends along its south and east sides at a distance from the water of three or four miles.

The lake lies north-east and south, is south-west of the Racket, and connected with it by two channels. The southern channel is the one by which we entered.

The northern, or "the outlet," leads to the "Indian Park," a tongue of land formed by a semicircular bend of the Racket on the one hand, and a little bay of the lake on the other. It flows for some distance between a rocky bluff of the Park to the north, and an island which divides it from the southern channel.

The north and west shores of the lake are hilly, Gull Pond Mountain extending along a portion of the course.

We coasted up the camp side of the lake to Redside Brook, and Harvey fastened the boat by its chain to a log.

There was a golden flutter of light on a ripple; the gleam of a white birch kindled the purple gloss of a pool; there was the emerald flash of the dragon-fly, and around the brown water-spider skated.

"Well," began Harvey, after we had settled to our fishing, "as I was tellin' on ye about old Sabele. When the old chief heerd o' the love scrape—I had a bite then—but I guess 'twas only a minnie—he had, as I was a sayin', quite a jaw with Sabele, a smoothin' on 'im down at fust by callin' 'im an Eagle and so on, which I don't think, fur myself, was enny great shakes of a name. I don't think half as much of an eagle as I do of a fish-hawk—one's honest and t'other aint! I can't give ye all the speech, but the long and short of it was it didn't do no good, and so the old chief was determined on suthin' else. So—aha, how de do, sir!" (jerking up a large trout, breaking its neck on the boat's edge, and casting it to the bottom), "so one day Sabele went—these deer-flies bite most as bad as mitchets this mornin'—he went to see his gal, and found the old trapper dyin'—hold 'im well up, Mr. Smith! taut line—not too taut, though, or he'll break away—jest so that he'll feel the bit. Give 'im line now! that's a two pounder, Mr.

Smith, I'll bet a saple skin agin a mushrat's—now reel in, and I'll ketch 'im by the gills—there!" breaking his neck also and throwing him below. "But, as I was a sayin', there was the old trapper dyin', and the gal dead, and the trapper telled Sabele that the old chief and another fightin' charackter of the tribe 'ad come to the shanty and 'ad tommyhawked and sculped 'm both. Wasn't Sabele mad? Wasn't he? I tell yer he could a chawed up a wolf-trap, 'cordin' to his tell! His heart was a bustin' too—massy alive, I b'leeve I've got the great grand'ther of all the trout in this ere part o' the country on my hook! sizz-whizz—don't ye wish yer could git off?—but yer can't, yer know. I'll tell ye the rest o' the story in a minute, Mr. Smith! There now, you hed to give up, didn't yer—though you aint so big as I thought you was" drawing in, then lifting an immense trout with a back like a leopard-skin by the gills, and joining him, with a broken neck, to the others. "Well, back Sabele went, lickety split, to the tribe, and was a goin' to let it right inter the old chief with his knife, but the rest on 'm wouldn't let 'im.

"Well, when Sabele found he couldn't let inter the old chief, he says to 'im, s'ze he,—I can't give it to yer as the old feller used ter, 'tickelly when he got drunk (which was, 'twixt you and me, nigh about all the time), for he'd go high up, I tell yer, and slash about, and make mouths, and strut he would, like a crow in a gutter—but the idee was, 'you'—that is, ef you, as a body may say, was dreffle mad, and wanted to tell a man he was a—I dunno as I know 'zack'ly how to say it—but ef you thought he was a great villyan, and scoundrel, and rascal, and mean feller, you'd say so, wouldn't ye? and mebby not say it scripter fashion nuther!—well this was the idee on't. Sabele said to the old chief, 'You con-demned old villyan! I've found yer out! You've killed the gal!'—Them wa'n't the words, Mr. Smith! but that was the idee, the p'int on't.

"'S'posen I did!' said the old sarpent, 'that's my business!'

"'Well, it's my business too!' says old Sabele—he was young Sabele then though—'tisn't the rael words, Mr. Smith, as I said afore, but the idee—'and I'm a goin' to let daylight through your dod darned old pictur-frame!' With that he rips out his knife agin, but they held him back tight by his coat-tails—no—not coat-tails, fur Injins don't wear none a bit more'n a frog, but they held 'im back, enny way. 'So,' s'ze, that is Sabele, s'ze, ' you want me to marry your darter! now, go to the'—that is, Sabele, s'ze—the idee was—go to t'other place with your darter, and I'll go to Texas—that is, there warn't no Texas—that is, Sabele didn't know nothin' about Texas, but that was the idee—and with that he turns on his heels and off he goes. At fust he felt so bad he thought he'd kill himself, but bless ye, Mr. Smith, this ere love business aint no killin' matter, after all, and life's kinder sweet—goll! cf there aint a rael old settler!" peering over the log.

Poised in the mottled depths above a sunken limb which was wriggling in the refraction of the restless water, was an immense trout undulating, fanning himself with his fins and "laying off" generally.

Harvey let his hook down cautiously by the fish, which gave a look at it, and then moved away from it like a mastiff from a puppy.

"Be off with yourself!" said Harvey, casting his line in another direction—" but as I was sayin' about Sabele—he'd heerd tell o' this wilderness region, and so he come down here to get a livin', and the fust I knowed of him he was a shantyin' on Long Island in the lake here. He used to trap and hunt and fish there, and then he went to the Injin Park at the outlet o' the lake, and then furder down to where I telled yer—where old Leo is now—we must go and see Leo when we git down there! he'll sell ye a nice pair o' moc'sins, and cheap too. Well, finally at last he—that is Sabele—got to be old and ragged, and went back to Canady and found all the tribe gone west; and come back, and was dreffle lonesome, and got the rheumatiz, and couldn't trap much, nur hunt nur fish fur that matter, and didn't git no money and couldn't git no rum caze he hadn't no fur, nur no ven'son, nur no trout, nur no nothin' to git rum with, and nobody 'ud give 'im any, and the older I grow the more I see that nobody don't give much to nobody enny way—and so when he found he couldn't git no rum he made up his mind he wouldn't live no longer, and got in his canoe and went singin' his death-song, as he called it. I s'pose you never heerd an Injin's death-song, Mr. Smith? I heerd Sabele one time, when he wasn't as drunk as common! oh, how he did d-r-o-n-e and draw-l-l-l it out, hoh-hoh-je-me-neddy-hoh-hoh-massy on us! hoh-hoh, 'lasses candy, and then he gin the warwhoop. Well, as I was sayin', he went floatin' down the Racket, and finally at last went whipperty fling over—there's a duck —a copperhead! I'll fetch him!" throwing down his rod, and the bird fell with Harvey's bullet directly through the green polish of his head. "This is fur your dinner, Mr. Smith!" rowing with alternate dips to where the bird was floating, and depositing him in the boat.

"But where was it he went over, Harvey?"

"Went over? why, he went whicketty clash over—I'm bound to hev that patridge too under that cedar bush—all these leetle things count in," firing, and stepping on shore he returned with the patridge minus a head.

"But, Harvey, I want to know where he went over?"

"He went over Pussyville Falls, and enny body that wants to go over them, may go and be darned, 'twont be me, this year at any rate; but spos'n we don't fish enny more, Mr. Smith—there don't appear to be many more bites, and as the mornin' is so pleasant I'll row ye round to the Devil's Pulpit."

"The Devil's Pulpit!"

"Yes! it's a high rock on Birch Island!"

"But why is it called so?"

"Well, they say the devil once got all the deer and fisher and saple and mink and rats and eagles and loons and trout and what not together to preach to 'm. He come from the top o' Mount Morris out there, and sailed up over the lake on two pine trees which he cut down with his claws. He telled 'm that in a short time the fishermen and hunters and trappers was a comin' and a goin' to hev a high old time with 'm all. And he laughed till all the sides o' the rock cracked. When he got through, he dug his heels inter the rock down'ards, ketched a two-year-old buck, blew on't and cooked it, took a brook trout weighin' about four pounds, sarved it the same, and then eat 'm both with about a dozen patridges, which he popped inter his mouth like dumplin's right afore 'm all. He then took and slung a couple o' the fattest deer over his shoulders, stuck a lake trout they say three foot long twixt his teeth, and baggin' about twenty black ducks, and kickin' the pine trees all to flinders, he skulled along with his tail through the lake till he got to the mountain, where he turned eend over eend and lit on top head-foremost and went down through like a streak o' lightnin'."

Harvey urged the boat slowly along, while I gazed at the rock lifting its stern front from the lake four score feet in height. Its length of three hundred feet was curved like an enormous half-moon bastion. There was a little cove at its lower extremity darkened by dense cedars. Thence the mass heaved rounding onward, with large boulders at its base, their summits plumed with evergreens. Mossy seams furrowed its black and grey sides from top to base. In the clefts of its enormous ledges—cracked and splintered and scaled with lichen—tottering pines had clutched their claw-like roots, and in nooks and on platforms, bushes had clustered and spruces planted their dark spear heads. The rock was also broken into several steep profiles, and its head was a smooth, iron-like precipice, rounding downwards to the lake. All along its summit dead pines stretched their jagged arms and reared their withered antlers.

"There was a deer jumped right from the top o' that

rock onst," said Harvey dipping a birch bark cup and drinking.

"From the top of that rock, Harvey?"

"'Twas a cur'ous thing, but 'twas so," replied Harvey. "'Twas one afternoon in August, jest afore sundown, Will and me and Cort was campin' on the lake on one o' the Two Brothers. There was two or three b'ys in the lake agin this ere Pulpit which we'd bin baitin' fur some time, and they'd got to be fust best places fur lake trout. Well, one day, about sundown, as I said afore, Will and Cort was there fishin' at the b'ys, one in one boat and one in another. Will was right under the Pulpit, and had jest ketched an all-fired big trout; well, 'cordin' to his tell, it must ha' bin a trout weighin' nigh about five pounds, and had a kinder riz up to rest himself, and was a lookin' right at the top 'o the rock. All on a sudden, an almighty big buck, with horns like a rockin'-chair, bust up to the top, and sprung, and fell kersplosh inter the lake. He put to 't, and both Will and Cort was struck so all up in a heap, that they let the deer git away. I al'ys thought the way the deer come to jump was, that some bear or painter was a runnin' the buck, and he didn't mebby know the spot, and come so sudden on't, he couldn't stop, or mebby he jumped slap dash enny way. There's one thing about it, a painter did take to the water a short time after that from Birch Island, and Will see 'im, and shot 'im. But talkin' o' bucks: there's Grindstone Bay out there to the left—a fust best place fur jack-huntin', and 'taint a very bad place fur trout where Grindstone Brook tumbles in."

We then coasted down the north-east shores, dipped into a little bay with a baldric of silver sand, next into Gull Pond Bay (so called by Harvey), and threaded the group of islands I noticed on my entrance upon the lake; the dark-green polish of the water-alleys and the intermingling shadows, full of sprinkled light. We then went into Mink Bay (which forms the lake side of the Park), and I began trolling, making the circuit of the spot of rock in the midst, like a mud-turtle, but I caught nothing. We then pushed into the outlet, and I cast beneath the grey beetling bluff. The water was deep and weedless, and under Harvey's quiet rowing I soon secured a lake trout, of two pounds or more.

Its thick frame, with its grey and yellow spots, contrasted unfavorably with the more slender shape of red spangled brown and golden bronze shown by his gorgeous cousin of the brook.

We then turned and made for the camp, in the low afternoon light. Reaching it, we found all the party returned. A back shanty for a kitchen had been built. A deep square pit had been dug as a cellar, wherein our stores were deposited, and covered by a flake or two of spruce bark. A rude table had been planted under a cedar, with cross pieces on forked sticks for seats. Cross poles, on which to hang powder flasks, bullet-pouches, and the like, also stood at various points.

In the centre stood the tents, with the usual camp fire in front. A path led up the ridge (as I discovered) to a spring.

The beautiful spot was alive with culinary operations; the old trees listening to the song of gridiron and saucepan instead of bird and ripple.

I took a seat in a green root, twisted like an arm-chair, and looked around. My attention was caught by Pup. He dashed from a thicket to the fire, stopping so quick as to cant his hind legs up. There he gazed, with one ear pointed, as if for a stab, until a tiny rocket discharged by the flame wheeled him short round, with a yell like a loon. He then trotted sidewise to a bush, with a sniff at a stone, and a blow of his breath like a pshaw. At the bush he barked himself for a few moments off all his legs. He then stole toward the camp-kettle, hung by a sapling over the fire, and in whose twitching froth potatoes were bobbing, stretching his neck so far as to uncurl his tail, till a glance from Corey shrank him into half his size, and he sneaked off limpsy.

Never did a hungry set enjoy a dinner more. The pure air of the woods, the exercise, and—I know not what, keeps you on a sort of famished look-out all the time. The very exercise of eating, too, seems to give you fresh appetite. And without meaning to turn informer on my comrades, or tell tales out of school, I must say that Bingham's stomach, in the woods, gave me a nearer idea of the bottomless pit than any other thing, human or divine, I have met in my travels.

After our meal we all betook ourselves to pipes and comfort. One lolled against an upright of the tent, another on a camp stool or in a dry brown hollow, or on a bank of moss; while one lay flat on his back, with his boots planted against a tree, as if determined on pushing it out of his way. Our talk was light and lazy. The sunlight spread broad and dreamy upon the grass; here, sprinkled itself away among the leaves, there, struck aisles into the forest. The little birds touched upon the trees, and there was the occasional bark of a squirrel. Before us stretched the glittering white and sombre grey of the slumbering lake.

One of our party at length seized an axe and laid vigorous but rather ineffectual blows on a pine, which the Anak seemed to scorn, for he did not show even a tremor. And no wonder, for if the axe fell twice in the same cut it was by accident, and as I turned to look at a beam of light like a ladder against a cedar, my friend was tugging with a face of scarlet and frown of fury at his axe, having by a desperate blow buried it in the soft wood to the eye.

The islands and headlands threw long eastward masses of shade upon the lake; the sunset sky was one glitter of light, and the water broke into a glory of color.

Nothing delighted me more during our sojourn at the lake than the daily variety of its looks. Not a fragment of cloud, not a flying hue, but found on its delicate texture an immediate image. Tints not detectable in the atmosphere kindled its surface. Thus, every moment almost, its appearance changed. Now it smiled in tenderest azure, then a little airbreath lighted upon it and a gleam of silver ripple cut athwart; next some impalpable shade turned it into purple. Now it was grey glass, then a vagrant wind fanned up flitting darks all over. Again, a blue and golden calm; then the surface blackened, and intermittent foam broke out like the gleam of fireflies; the tumult followed once more by softest quiet and divinest hues.

As the light just after sunset is most propitious to the angler, the whole party now embarked for the mouth of Redside Brook, a little distance above. This spot is the most famous for trout of all the cold spring brooks that enter the lake, and fine sport was anticipated. Nor were we disappointed.

We moored to the logs and bushes, and shortly trout in numbers were gleaming and leaping on the bottom of our boats. Toward the last, Renning tried a white night-fly, thinking he might strike a larger fish than with worm or minnow. He touched the water just where a log peered out from a lair of grasses. Whew! wasn't that a bite! Off the fish darts like a bullet; down he dives as if the pricking in the throat could be doctored in that fashion; up he comes again, finding little consolation down below; then he launches out and spins around. He darts toward a log, but Renning turns him off; how skilfully he plays him! how he gives him rope to hang himself more certainly at last! mark the countenance of the angler so grave, and the whole demeanor so collected and self-reliant! He reels in and reels out, keeping the fish "taut up to the rein." But now the prey's motions are slower—he makes one more desperate lunge for the lily-pads, one more dart toward the pool under the hanging lid of the sedgy bank; but he is wearied and drowning; so Renning pulls him carefully toward him. There is a flap or two in the water, and a faint outpull; at length something glitters under the surface near the boat. Mart seizes the landing-net; dips quickly, and in a trice a three pound trout is captured.

After this Waterloo of our Napoleon, we rowed back in

the dusk toward the camp. Is a bear crouching in yon nook? or is it a cedar bush on the edge of the water? If I had not known that Bingham was ahead in his boat, I should certainly say this lank shape was his with rifle resting against a rock for a shot. But no, it is merely a broken trunk with its crooked elbow leaning upon a ledge. If we were at Mud Lake, I should take that object for a moose looking at us with staring eyes. Too—hoo too—woo-o-o-o-o —psha! it is an owl in a low, broad water-maple.

"It is rather singular we don't encounter panthers," said Gaylor, after we had returned to camp. "I've been here four times, yet I've never seen one alive yet."

"'Tisn't offen they are seen," said Cort. "I've hunted and fished round here all my life, yit I've never seen many on 'm. There's quite a passle, take it by and large, but they keep back in the woods and rocky places where people don't go. There's a good many more on 'm in Maine, 'cordin' to the lumber fellers. Deer and trout is as plenty as here too, and moose a plaguy sight plentier; fur I tell yer what 'tis, gen'lemen, it's one thing to talk about moose and t'other thing to git 'm. But they say out there on the— lets me see," putting his finger on his forehead, "there's a nob in't, or a nub—no, nob; what the plague is that name"—

"Androscoggin," said Bingham.

"No, no, there's a nob in't, I know."

"Well, they call mountains knobs, sometimes," said Bingham; "and all Maine is nothing but mountain. As a fellow once said in my hearing, you're scarcely half way down one before you're going up another."

"Cort means Penobscot, probably," suggested Gaylor.

"That's it," said Cort quickly, "the Nobscot! well, they say there's an all-fired grist on 'm, that is, moose, up there, and"—

"Come, come, Cort!" broke in Bingham, "we know all about that. Suppose you moose up a little punch. I haven't had any in two days! I shall forget the taste of it."

And the obedient Cort immediately set about his brewing.

CHAPTER XVI.

Bingham kills a Deer in the Lake.—The Indian Park.—Leo, the Indian.—
The Loon.—Showers on the Lake.—In Camp.

In the morning we all decided upon a drive. Watch and Sport were accordingly let loose, and we took our several stations on the lake for the expected deer—Harvey and I in the little Bluebird, as usual. We crossed the lake, and fastened to a bush in a small cove.

The spot at first was lonely and quiet. At length sights and sounds began to steal out. The grey wheel of the gnats revolved up and down with its fine hum of motion; the water-spider skipped along; the sparkling waterbreak made its purl heard; while a squadron of musquitoes, charging from a cover of rushes, filled the air with their fine sultry trumpets, and plied their lances, till I thought every pore held a needle.

"Don't mind the flies, Mr. Smith," remarked Harvey, crushing a phalanx between his hands, "and they won't trouble ye half so much. I wouldn't glad the little varmints so much as to notice 'm. Ef they will bite, let 'm bite and be derned. But I consated I heard Watch," bending his ear, "I didn't, though."

I had for a little time been observing a spruce perfectly drenched in a broad fall of light. This illumined spot shaped itself at length to a cathedral window. There it glowed with its lancet arches, its mullions, its trefoil, all its bold and delicate traceries, and all a-blaze with jewelled hues. Those hues streamed from off the shoulders of saints, and melted through the pinions of angels in vivid reds, greens, and yellows; they stained the aisle below, and sprinkled the roof with gem-like rain.

"About trollin'," Harvey drawled out at this moment, causing my window to vanish, "'taint every feller kin troll that thinks he kin. Trollin' is trollin', and it ain't nothin' else. 'Taint fishin for brook-trout, nur deep fishin' at the b'ys, though every fool that comes out here thinks ef he can't do nothin' else he kin troll. Hark!—no, it's nothin'! About trollin', splice your two hooks back to back, and stick yer minnies from mouth to tail, so as to hev 'em wobble in the water; hev your oarsman row slow; keep clear o' the weeds (weeds is the deuce and all in trollin'); drop your line as keerful and quiet as a painter walks; then draw in and out, in and out; and ef ye don't ketch yer trout, there ain't no trout about there to ketch."

A half hour glided away, I watching the glint of the light on the water, and looking at the forest, and Harvey whistling and humming to himself.

Suddenly he started.

"There's the deer, by golly! there in the water!" unchaining the boat and seizing the oars, while I snatched the paddle; "it's strange we didn't hear the hounds!"

At this moment a boat appeared, making swiftly for the deer. It contained Bingham and Cort, the former paddling with all his might, and the latter rising and falling to his rapid oars.

"Now for a chase," said Harvey; "that buck's as good as gone, though, with our two boats after 'im."

The scene was the open water opposite the camp.

The buck made for the west Brother Island, straining every nerve, and driving swiftly through the water.

Our boat was nearer the island than Bingham's, and we tried our utmost to head the deer off; for, once there, Birch and Long Islands—the three divided only by alleys of water —would lead him too far down the lake for us to hope anything in his pursuit.

We succeeded, and the buck turned again to the open space.

Bingham, by this time, had also approached, and I could see he was in a frenzy of excitement.

"Pull away, Cort!" shouted he, "pull away! We must have that deer! Jupiter, what horns! Don't let Smith get in before us! Pull as though you were drawing your legs through your mouth! Hurrah!"

The deer, wild with terror, was plying every sinew, leaping half way out of the lake in his desperation; the water furrowing from his shoulders, his nose in the air, and his eyes almost bursting from his head with his exertions and fright.

Both boats were now within a rod of the striving, panting, snorting animal.

"Hurrah, Cort!" yelled Bingham, dipping his paddle to the eye, "one or two more pulls, and then tail him; and if I don't give that deer"——

The boat shot up as he spoke, and Cort, leaving his oars, lunged to seize the brush of the deer. Quick as thought the latter eluded him, turned, dived completely under the boat, and rose on the other side. This brought the deer closer to us, and Harvey, throwing aside his oars, made a dash on his part to tail the animal. The frenzied creature once more dived, but was again forced to rise.

"Cort, it's very strange you can't tail that deer," at last said Bingham. "He's either made of quicksilver, or both you and Harvey there are as lazy as Deacon Haskell's preaching, and you can take a drink between every word he says. Now at him again!"

The deer had again struck out, but Cort shot up, and this time he grasped the brush, while the animal, snorting loudly, redoubled his frantic efforts at escape.

Bingham aimed within a foot or two of the deer's graceful head. I caught the wild gleam of the dilated eye; the report then rang, the head fell, and a tremor shook the tawny frame. Cort's keen knife next flashed at the victim's throat, and his strong arms lifted and deposited him in the boat.

"That's the way! hurrah for our side!" exclaimed Bingham. "The best way, after all, to shoot a deer, is to tail him. If I could have had all the deer tailed, I've shot at in these slippery woods, I could start a victualler's shop in the settlements, eh, Smith!" and off he and Cort pulled toward the camp, while Harvey and I steered toward the Indian Park.

We entered the outlet; at our left rose the cliff, its ledges breaking out of the clinging foliage, and turning with its afternoon shadow the belt of water into ebony, and darkening the long low island between the two channels. Soon we reached the Park. It wore a sweet, pastoral look in the lowering light, the glowing atmosphere softening the lights into golden down, and the shades into transparent purple.

A single log cabin, unoccupied and ruined, stood in the Park, with an old haystack at one corner, and a beautiful birch tree at the other.

Beneath the slanting radiance, the weather-stained hues of the hut were turned into a rich tawny, the russet of the stack gleamed in golden brown, and the tree, together with a black cherry beside it, seemed burning in amber flame.

Up the Racket Mount Morris met the eye, mingled and smoothed into one misty blue. In the middle distance the river, divided by its midchannel island, came flowing through two branches into the board basin which fronted and flanked the Park.

"There's iron up there," said Harvey, nodding at the wooded ridge that rose above the Park. "Folks don't know much about it, but I'm a blacksmith you know, and keep my eye out for sich things. If you'd like ter, I'll show ye some blocks on't," and drawing the Bluebird's bow on shore, the old woodman led the way across the pleasant grassy plat, scattered with trees and thickets, and showing traces of old cultivation, into the forest covering the swell of the ground. We had risen nearly to the summit, when Harvey picked from the rocky earth a fragment of black, sparkling ore, which I found to be a specimen of magnetic iron, rich and very heavy.*

"There's plenty more all round here. See there, and there, and there," continued he, pointing about. "But let's go on, I want to show yer where this p'int begins."

Crossing the summit and descending, we came to a small wild meadow, the neck of the peninsula, where the river came with one bold bend, toward the little bay belonging to the lake.

"It looks jest as ef," said Harvey, "old Tupper had put out his little finger, and the Racket was comin' to take it, and the woods had stepped up and dropt a green handkercher 'twixt, and gone on agin to drop another one at the eend."

Returning to the boat, we found drawn up by it, a canoe or dug-out, smoothly hollowed from a birch log, with a beautifully shaped paddle athwart it. Immediately an Indian, with a rifle, and followed by two dogs, appeared from the woods nearest the lake.

"Goll, ef here aint old Leo!" said Harvey. "Why, Leo, how de do!"

"How do, how do!" answered the Indian, in a low, guttural accent, smiling and holding out his hand.

"Been a huntin'!" asked Harvey, shaking it.

"Yese, oh yese!"

"Kill enny thing?"

"Nah, nah, oh hang, nah!"

"See enny thing?"

"Yese, yese, oh yese! See a-a-a—yu-yaw-gwin—a-a—vat you call eet?"

"I dunno. How should I?" said Harvey.

"He goes so, bo-o-o-m—m—m," striking his sides with his elbows.

* This specimen I subsequently found to contain ninety per cent. of iron.

"Bullfrog!" said Harvey.

"Taun, taun, nah, nah, oh hang, nah—he fly."

"Flies and goes boom," said Harvey, thoughtfully. "Well, a crow goes boom, or quaw, which is the same thing. Was it a crow, a black thing that goes quaw, quaw?"

"Nah, nah, oh hang! n-a-a-h!" said the Indian. "Dare, dare!" as one of the dogs roused a bird at the edge of the woods.

"Oh, a patridge! Well, what else did you see?"

"Quaah—he go so," jerking his head, "and says qu-a-a-h."

"That's a crow, I know."

"Nah, nah, nah black thing! Nah crow."

"Well, what the old mischief is't then?"

"Go so—oh goo' mannee," rapping on his rifle-stock.

"Woodpecker! why didn't you say so—what else?"

"Dyaweh, oh so mooch!" placing his hands about a foot apart.

"I should think a body 'ud die away all to pieces, to talk to this old wild goose of an Injin. I git everything so muxed up in my head tryin' to find out what he means, I can't remember nairy thing when I talk to him nor which from t'other. What the Old Sanko is dieaway?" tartly.

"Down dare," said the Indian, pointing to the water.

"Well, what d'ye mean? Trout, muskrats, mink?"——

"Yese, yese!" interrupted the Indian.

"Oh, mink, hay! Where is yer fur? I should like to see it. But 'taint the right time o' year, Leo, to ketch fur, you must know that."

"Nah, nah! oh hang, n-a-a-h," and Leo threw aside a cedar branch in the stern of the canoe and showed a string of trout on a birch twig.

"Oh, trout! I don't think there's much die-away on them onless ye eat enough to kill a hoss!"

"Yese, yese! trou, trou, so mannee!" holding up the string, which was really a fine one.

13

"Very good, Leo! a good nice bunch on 'em. Them's good dogs o' yourn too," looking at the gaunt, tawny, wiry, wild-looking animals. "Rael wolf-dogs, Mr. Smith! swift as lightnin' and savage as a mad moose. That's a good rifle you've got to boot!" taking the weapon and examining it critically.

I looked at the two as they stood together, both representatives of a class unknown to cultured life; the old, bronzed hunter and trapper, and the wild red man, united by their habits and modes of life, and both so perfectly in keeping with the scenes where I saw them—the natural meadow—the primeval woods—the lonely lake—the log hut—the wolf-dogs—all so different from the objects to which I had been accustomed. I could hardly realize that I was scarce two-score leagues from populous and polished cities, and I revelled in the charm of the contrast before me.

"Well, Mr. Smith!" said Harvey, handing the Indian his rifle, "we might as well be goin'. Good-by, Leo! I'm comin' to see ye! Down there yit, I s'pose!" pointing down the Racket.

"Yese, yese," said the Indian, laughing as if the old trapper had uttered a good joke.

"Good-bye!"

"Goo-bye!" and whistling to his dogs, that were revolving in a snapping and gurgling ball on the bank, the old Indian shoved off. Harvey did the same, and we glided toward the left-hand channel of the river, on our way to the camp.

The Indian, paddling on his knees in the middle of his canoe, turned the Park and went down the Racket, mousing along the banks, his hunting-shirt as he descended dwindling to a red spot, which glanced in and out the thickets and hollows of the shores in the low sunshine like a jack-light, until an elbow of the stream shut it entirely from view.

Coasting along the mid-channel island of the river we

turned to the right, and entered the lake through the south channel. The waters were kindled in the sunset; the top of Gull Pond Mountain was in a glow, and the islands of the Two Brothers had assumed the golden softness peculiar to the hour. The great star of the camp-fire was filling the nook with ruddy light, giving it, with the tinged tents and shanty, and figures moving about in the flitting flame, a picturesque as well as a genial look. As we approached we heard Bingham, just returned from a partridge hunt, as I discovered, detailing to his comrades at the highest pitch of his loud voice his exploit of the buck.

The last lustre of the sunset was pouring into the camp. The hounds were gliding about all in a glitter; a rod and rifle were pointing keen glances over a stump, and Bingham's buck, not yet dressed, was lying at a root sleeked over with light.

The sunshine was peeping into the bushes, and striving to force its way into the forest. Although it made a high-rooted birch glow like a vast lamp hung upon the bank, it but edged the adjoining cedars.

Pup again caught my eye. He was roaming about, lifting one ear and then the other, looking at the tree-tops, cantering and stopping short to bite off a fly, then twirling into a heap only to untwirl, see that the ring of his tail was perfect on his hollow back, and peer under the bushes. At length he stopped before a hollow tree with a hole at its root, and the play opened. Now he started back to his haunches; then launched forward, streaming out in yells; then bounded with all his feet from the ground back again, and then dashed his pointed nose beneath the beech to jerk it quickly away. Occasionally during these manœuvres a grey paw, or slim whiskered snout, would dart out in the direction of the dog. At last Pup buried his head and shoulders under the tree, with one hind leg after the other quivering in mid-air. This was immediately succeeded by his hasty retreat with a hideous yell and a dismal whine, his nose one gore of blood. Bending it to the earth, he rubbed it with his fore paw as if it were a nuisance to be rid of, glancing continually at the bush with a rueful air. At last Watch, who had been to all appearance sleeping between his paws, rose as though his patience was exhausted and he was resolved to see what all this racket was about, and marched with a severe dignity and a not-to-be-baffled look to the bush. Pup had contented himself with peeping in at the basement, but Watch magisterially, with arched neck and lifted tail, looked in at the window. As he did so, he pealed his slogan, and rushing into the citadel, reappeared, shaking a kicking, spitting, snarling woodchuck by its neck. After a short struggle, the battle ended in the death of the woodchuck, which was taken by one of the guides, who forthwith skinning and dressing it and stretching the white, delicate frame on a pronged stick, proceeded to broil it for dinner.

The evening wrapped around us sultry and close. The camp-fire died down, and as the darkness gathered there was a fine show of summer lightning. The tents flashed in and out—the shanty and trees stepped forward and back—a dog gleamed forth—a gun—a human form stood out and vanished; and amid this black and red dance I retired to my bed of hemlock feathers and was soon asleep.

I was awakened by a violent shake.

"Come, Smith, wake up. It's about daylight, and if you sleep any longer what brains you have will evaporate. I can almost see them melt now."

"What do you want, Bingham?" said I.

"I want lake-trout. Harvey says we can't have a better time; and if I don't make those buoys out there suffer, you may say, when you get back home, I didn't kill that buck. So, hurrah! Smith, get up, and go with Harvey and me."

I accordingly rose, and in a few minutes we were gliding toward the first buoy.

"The guides take a great deal of pains to bait these buoys," continued Bingham. "According to Harvey, you can hardly go amiss of one of these fish with worm-bait. Diet of Worms, eh? But ph-e-w, how close it is. I wish we had brought Renning out with us just as we left him. The tornado he raises with that nose of his would shake up the air a little, at all events. But here we are at the buoy. Now, Harvey, my line—hurrah!"

"Hurra-a-a-h!"

"Hey!" said Bingham, seizing his rifle (he carried it wherever he went). "Where is he, Harvey?" staring around.

"There!" said Harvey.

"Good-bye, Mr. Loon," exclaimed Bingham, firing.

"Psh-a-a-ah," said the loon, ducking under.

"He's a dead loon," said Bingham.

"Wait," said Harvey.

"Hurrah!"

"There he is," said Harvey.

"The deuce take his impu"—

"Hurr-a-a a-h!"

"Head up like a soger," said Harvey.

"Let us get a little closer," said Bingham, fidgeting. "I didn't have a good chance that time."

"Pshah psha—pish, pish—p-s-h-a-w-w-w! Hurrah! hurrah! hurrah!" shouted the loon, burying himself nearly to his head. "Hurrah," rising again to his shape.

"Now's your chance," grins Harvey.

"Hurr"—bang. No loon there.

"We'll see him floating on his back in a moment," said Bingham, confidently.

"Hurrah." The sound rings proudly, but more distant. The loon's neck specks the water near the east Brother.

"Psha-w-w-w, psha-w-w-w; hurrah, hurrah, hurrah-eee," and with this final challenge the loon disappeared.

Bingham tried to look unconcerned, but only succeeded in looking brazen. He turned once more to his line and threw it. For ten minutes he played it up and down, according to the approved mode.

"Where the plague have the trout gone to, Harvey!" said he at length, crossly.

"One has gone onter my hook," said Harvey; "and from Mr. Smith's line, I guess another is on his'n."

"There's none gone on mine, that's certain," looking fixedly at the fine specimen that Harvey raised and secured. "On the whole, I think breakfast must be on by this time. At all events it ought to be, judging from certain interior feelings I have; so let us go back to camp." And back we went.

After breakfast we again divided. Gaylor and Renning went with Mart to fish in Grindstone Brook; Bingham and Coburn with Cort and Sport, up the lake for a drive; while Harvey and I visited the outlet bluff again, to troll the deep waters at its base. Will and Phin went to Simon's Pond with Drive, also for deer. Corey and Jess remained to take care of the camp.

Not proving fortunate in trolling we decided to return to camp, particularly since what air there was proclaimed rain. After proceeding nearly across the lake, I saw a cloud in the west drop its gauzy ladder to the rim of the horizon. Reaching the camp I entered the tent, and watched the coming of the shower.

The forest outlines on Gull Pond Mountain mingled greyly, then the whole mass was swallowed. Over the darkening lake the dense mist moved, devouring the prospect. The pyramid of a cedar on the farthest of the Two Brothers melted; a group of jagged, scorched hemlocks died away; a skeleton pine, rearing the nest of a fish-hawk, like a skull, glided back, and the whole island vanished. The nearer Brother was next in a misty mingle, and then with a rush the shower was upon us. The prospect was limited to a white half circle of water, with dim images of rocks and trees around me. The camp, so soft and pleasant in the sunset of the day before, became in a moment reeking with wet. The hounds, however, enjoyed it hugely. Pup, having washed his face from the blood, was as frolicsome as a boy in the snow. He lapped the pools, snapped at the drops and shook them into sprinkles from his coat, while the sober Watch, having endured quite philosophically the liquid beating on the wind side of a thicket, settled himself by the camp fire, thrust out his paws as if to dry them, and blinked at the rain.

At length the halloo of a loon sounded from the mist, and out he glided; the rain ceased; to the wand of a sunbeam, the misty curtain lifted, and there was the instantaneous glitter of a diamond scene. In another half-hour, however, a new shower came, swallowing the lake in its mist from the south, and changing again into jewel-work under the sun.

For the next two or three hours, there was a quick interweaving of rain and sunlight. The former would streak the scene; then blue eyes would open in the sky. The arcades of the forest would glow, darken, be masked in the shower, and flash again into gold.

Things continued so until past noon, when the clouds blended themselves into one smooth leaden mantle, and a rain set in, which, from its obstinate look and pertinacious pour, threatened to last a week. There was such a sulky pig-headed air about the storm, a determination to give the whole scene "the devil" (according to Bingham) this time, that I began to find a legion of devils flitting about my spirits. At the expiration of some three or four hours, however, I was most agreeably disappointed. The lead-color above whitened, then broke into large fragments, while a splendid gathering of clouds at the west commenced to kindle, as if under a strong wind, for a gorgeous sunset. And gorgeous it was—peaks of gold, ridges of crimson, waves of purple, filling the west and firing the lake.

Emerging from a path lying on the water, like a crimson column, a returning boat appeared, which a nearer view showed to contain Bingham and Cort.

"Phew!" said the former, taking two strides from the stern to an old green log at the margin. "Ph-e-e-w! if ever there was a poor devil glad to get back here, I am. This watching a runway in the rain, with no run on the way but the rain, which run away like the deuce, especially my way, and was most confoundedly in the way, till I wished I was out of the way, is about the meanest thing in my experience, especially when the pocket-bottle gives out, as mine did. It was literally—

> 'Water, water every where,
> Nor any drop to drink.'

Cort, make me a glass of punch."

This harangue, delivered with the greatest volubility and in the most stentorian sounds, made the woods echo; and after the delivery, the excited orator took a seat on a stump, with an eye on the glass which the long-suffering Cort was hastening to manufacture.

"We had better luck," said Renning (he and Gaylor had reached the camp from an opposite direction, while Bingham was roaring); and he placed a basket brimmed with glittering trout on a log. "There are thirty pounds there, at least! Good game trout, too; none less than half a pound, and from that up to two, and in one or two instances, three."

"Never was the old adage about a fool and luck more strikingly verified than in an instance happening on Tupper's Lake on a certain day in the present month of August," said Bingham. "I've about made up my mind to abandon shooting and take to fishing. Any blockhead can fish, but it takes the wits of ten Yankee pedlars, and the patience of twenty Jobs, to do the shooting. I've about made up my mind now there are no deer in the woods."

"I didn't catch the trout at Tupper's Lake," said Renning. "We found poor sport at Grindstone Brook, so we went down to Setting Pole Rapids."

"Who said you did catch them at Tupper's Lake?" returned Bingham. "I appeal to the company if my respected comrade here doesn't show a marvellous alacrity in applying to himself the adage mentioned. I think it a remarkable, if not painful, instance of self-consciousness. Ah, Cort, this glass is fit for Jove!"

"I knowed a feller by the name o' Joe," said honest Cort, "that was the best hand at makin' a glass o' punch I ever see. And when he made it, he could drink it, too, and without winkin'. Good gracious, how that feller could liquor up! He druv the river for a livin', and was the best hand about here. He was called Driver Joe. I've seen 'm drive logs"——

"I wish I could see you drive musquitoes," interrupted Bingham. "Every drop of rain to-day has hatched a family of them, and hungry-mad at that," threshing about. "Coburn, your skin is thicker than mine, something like sole-leather, I take it, from the looks—do come here and let them settle on you. You will this way do more good than you've done to-day, for I believe the deer went by on your runway, where you doubtless were asleep, while I, awake and watchful, saw nothing. But there's one thing about it, Coburn; I hope Renning and Gaylor won't celebrate their luck to-night with one of their confounded choruses! I can stand anything mortal, but when it comes to sounds so utterly diabolical, I yield—eh, Smith?" and Bingham, after scenting a pinch of pulverized tobacco (he had forsworn all other use of the weed), began examining his gunlock.

Deep in the evening, while I was watching the stars glittering through the black trees, Will and Mart appeared with a doe they had shot at Grindstone Bay. The moment Sport and Pup saw each other, they rushed into one embrace, rolling over and over with yelps and harmless bites; and it was not until Will threw each a slice from the venison which was already dressing by the light of the camp-fire, that they separated, attacking the slices, tooth and nail, and wheeling their eye-balls round, as if every stick and stone were in wait to wrest their morsels from them.

CHAPTER XVII.

Thunder-storms.—Lightning Island.—Thoughts at the Indian Pass.—A high Wind.—Captain Bill Snyder.—Night Sail in the Wind.—Cove at the Devil's Pulpit.—Mist on the Water.—Harvey's Indian Story.

ALTHOUGH clear, the succeeding morning was warmer and closer than the last. There was a brooding calm after the first freshness of the dawn had vanished, which hung like a weight upon the frame and spirits.

The trees dozed in the languid light; the hazy islands looked drowsy; and the opposite hills seemed half dissolved in the warm, dreamy mist.

After an hour's sport at Redside Brook, we were driven back by the sultriness of the air, and the sun which beat like a great burning-glass upon the lake.

The morning was passed in the camp—all seeking the most comfortable positions. Bingham's long legs were sprawling in everybody's way, until he adopted the expedient of lying on his back and crossing them, with his toe in the air like the tip of a balsam fir. The hounds moved sluggishly, or coiled themselves at the apertures of the thickets, where the slightest air could draw, with their tongues lolling from their mouths, and their tawny forms streaked like sweat. The delicate-stemmed maple-leaf did not show a glimpse of its pearly lining; and even the wild poplar, that quakes if a raven fan it, gave scarce a flutter. From the edges of the forest came the snappish bark of the ground-squirrel slinking under the shady logs and roots, as if in complaint of the heat. Over its floor, too, ran a slight rustle, as though the dead leaves were also restless and were striving to turn over. Across the glass of the lake, quavered with startling distinctness, and wakening a thousand echoes, the cry of the loon; now it was the despairing shout of some drowning wretch, and now the triumphant whoop of an Indian warrior on the trail of his foe.

About noon, the hot, filmy sky became broken at the south-west by glaring white vapor tinged with copper.

At length two crags of cloud rapidly rose over the shoulders of Gull Pound Mountain. Up they moved above the darkened summit, deepening as they came, till they frowned black as the ravens on the shoulders of Woden.

As they approached, they joined into a mass, with streaks of vivid red darting through its heart, as if it were cracking open in the terrible flame behind it.

The lake blackened; glances of lightning quivered over it, and volumes of thunder unrolled their jarring lengths. The swells danced; the quick white-caps flashed; the woods of the Two Brothers tossed to and fro, in the outburst of the wind; then a blinding glare, a quick, ringing, splitting bolt, as if the heart of the forest had been cleft; and the rain tumbled. All now was one wild turmoil of howling winds and writhing trees, and driving rain sheets, and the hoarse dash of the foaming lake.

At length, through the driving scud, a large object suddenly broke, which we saw was an eagle borne struggling on the wind. One wing was evidently injured. On he came, swooping and tumbling, and, wafted over the tops of the trees, was lost in the rainy mist behind.

The fierce mountain storm soon passed, and the afternoon was quiet and beautiful.

Corey and Harvey being bound for Stetson's, to replenish some of our stores, I accompanied them.

When half way up, however, an angry black and red sunset glared through the woods upon us, threatening trouble.

We obtained our meal, milk and maple sugar, and started on our return. Corey was at the oars and Harvey at the paddle, and we skimmed through a gloom which (although the eagle eyes of the guides pierced it) was to me like a cavern's. Except the sounds of our way, the ear of Heimdall could not have detected a whisper in the woods or on the water.

Suddenly the black sky opened in a quick, fierce glance of lightning, displaying enormous clouds, hanging low over the forest and water. A growl of thunder succeeded. Then came another glare, redder, fiercer, and a peal was launched that made the ear ring.

The storm now burst. The lightning kindled an almost stationary blaze in the clouds, and there was nearly one grand continuous roll of thunder. The rain streamed upon us, while the roaring of the woods told that the wind had spread its pinions. Steadily onward we went, however, to the torch of the lightning, the trees, rocks, windings of the banks, and spaces of water glaring out in the fierce crimson, until, leaving the kindled and blackened vista of the river, we emerged upon the wrathful lake. We had not danced far over the wild swells and through the tinged rain, when a blue, forked flash left the ragged zenith. It fell upon the top of a towering pine, on the East Brother Island, like the hammer of Thor on the forehead of Thrym. The top burst into flame, casting a scarlet track upon the lake and flooding our boat with a passing glare.

But now the logs of the shore, the tents, the trees, the very streak of water-lilies edging the shallow, the red picture of the camp painted by the lightning, gleamed into view, and, in a few moments, we had safely moored the Bluebird, and entered the shelter of the tent.

The stars were soon shining from between the parted clouds, but the pine tree still burned, and by the light of this gigantic candle I sank into my dreams.

Fresh and breezy, rose the following morning; the sky was a delicious blue, against which the trees waved their tops joyously, the leaves fluttering and flashing, while the fragrance of the woods was delightful. The eagle sailed up the stream of the wind, dipping his wings either side, and the loon glided below, his brindled shape clearly cut against the crystal air.

The deep black shadows were drawn in hair lines in the sunlight, while the million ripples of the lake bore each a star upon its front.

The whole party, except Corey and Jess, Harvey and myself, left for a drive. The first two busied themselves in drying some venison, while the old guide and I launched on the lake toward the buoys.

"The wind was consid'ble heavy at one time yisterday," said Harvey, "but I've knowed it blow a good deal harder on these waters round. There was a man blowed clean off a raft on the lower lake, one spring. 'Twas a river-driver, Sassy Dick we called him, and the sassiest kite, next to a loon, I ever come crost. Well, he was on a dozen logs, comin' down the lake, and when he got within a mile or so of the outlet, a gust come and took him clean off his legs inter the lake. He was a fust best swimmer, and kept up nice, though the swells was orful, and after a little while he made out to git onter the raft agin, that was catwollopin' about in the lake, and went a swashin' along till he got inter the S'nac river.

"That pine too was a good deal of a sight," continued he. "I see another tree, onst, struck jest about as cluss. 'Twas in an island in the Lower S'nac, not fur from Martin's. It's called Lightnin' Island, by some. The tree was cut round like a corkscrew, and as deep as my finger. I see 't done. I was comin' from Bartlett's one afternoon in J'ly, and h-o-t 'twas—why it raally 'peared to me as ef the water 'd bile! Well, all on a sudden, as I was rowin' 'long, a do-zin' like, the lake turned as black as a loon's bill, and jest as I come abreast o' the island, massy, didn't there come a flash! Why I thought my eyes was scorched right out; and 'twas follered right along by a crack. Goll, ef it didn't seem to split me right in two! It struck that tree. But spos'n we don't try the b'ys this mornin', but see if we can't git some trout at Grindstone Brook."

We went tap, tap, tapping across the lake to Grindstone Bay, where the brook tumbles down the rocky stairs of the bank, and in an hour filled our basket with large and handsome trout.

"There's a little pond up there," said Harvey, pointing to the northwest, "and follerin' a brook along the same p'int o' compass brings you to Gull Pond. The outlet o' the Pond jines the Racket twixt Settin' Pole Rapids and Fish Hawk Rapids, nigh the head o' Fish Hawk. But what say ye to a short tramp in the woods torts the little pond?"

The emerald, gold-dotted light of the forest was grateful after the glare on the lake; and the fresh, cool air was so invigorating I seemed to step on springs.

We entered a vista whose carpet was woven deeply of moss.

These vistas strike the eye with beautiful effect, wearied with the endless entanglement of the woods. Streaks of light dart athwart, mottling their floors and kindling the bushes at their margins. Sometimes a rill bickers through, murmuring a continuous music mingled with the songs of perching and glancing birds. They are spots for dreams, where the tricksy wood-sprites might hold their moonlight revels. The deer feeds there; they are haunted by the ground-squirrel and rabbit; and there the black-cat steals at night to cheat of its bait the hunter's trap lurking in the mossy cavern of the hemlock's roots for the mink or sable, while the fallen trunk stretches within, under its pall of moss, like some old Sachem of the Forest.

We came after a while to a small dark sheet of water. The dense verdure crowded to the very edge, except where two or three little bays pierced inward, showing bits of gleaming sand. As we gazed, a deer appeared wading around a curve of the nearest bay, cropping the water-lilies right and left. He came on, sinking lower and lower in the deepening water, until he opened into the pond and struck boldly out, his antlered head and plying shoulders alone visible. He crossed the sheet, leaving a track of silver, bounded into the bushes, shaking glittering spray around him, and vanished.

At length we retraced our way to the boat.

At the camp we found the party returned from their drive, with a fine doe. We had a pleasant dinner in the sunset, and as the broad yellows and blacks began to shrink into stripes and patches over the land and water, we rowed to Redside Brook for an hour of twilight angling.

On our return the auroral splendors—the weird valkyrior of the Scandinavian Runes—arose. Up sprang these wild riders of the North, urging their rainbow-steeds far up the steeps; wielding their battle-axes, darting their spears, and waving their banners in the magic tournament of the dark-blue field above.

A moaning wind was in the forest when I awoke. A sombre sky greeted us; the lake looked grey and mournful.

I sat beside our tent and listened to the wind. A desolate wail thrilled through the wood, that plunged me into the deepest sadness. But once only, and that since, have my thoughts been so sorrowful. Then I was under the grand battlements of the Indian Pass. Weary with wandering through the woods, I halted a little distance from the Pass, in the dim twilight of a cloudy day, to bivouac for the night. At my side whispered the ripples of a little stream, and to accompany my frugal meal, it furnished me a draught from its cold goblet of crystal. Before me towered that stupendous wall, the north barrier of the Pass, second only in sublimity to Niagara. Then also a wailing wind went through the forest. Night came on apace. As I gazed upon the rock, soaring and looming in the darkness, the wind seemed to say, "Poor, fleeting mortal, what are thou to this work of untold ages! Does it not rebuke thee with its grandeur, and crush thee with the frowning of its strength? And if a mere rock, a grain brushed from the Almighty's hand, thus awes thee into nothing, how darest thou claim immortal life, the loftiest attribute of that Almighty!" And a more bitter mockery seemed to deepen in the wind.

"Thou pratest of a soul! Thou, to arrogate what is denied this stately pile! thou, perishing as the flower it nourishes in its clefts! Away with thy presumptuous folly! Know this and tremble—to thee and thy wretched race, the end cometh with the grave!".

I shuddered to the core of my heart. I felt utterly abandoned and desolate. The after life that sheds its smile upon the dark trouble of this, was it indeed a fantasy?

While I thus mused, a cloud overshadowed the rock and blotted it from my sight. But above me beamed a star lone through a rift in the cloudy mantle. A mere point it shone, and yet so pure, so brilliant, my nature rose expanding as I gazed. The wind no longer spoke; music instead seemed lengthening from the star.

"Fear not, and be not sorrowful," my heart thus interpreted the cadence; "thou bearest a light within that shall shine when I, counting my life by centuries, have for ever vanished. Though perishing as the flower, thou art eternal as God. Let the consciousness of this sublime truth rest ever upon thee, and may it prove thy felicity and not thy curse!"

The earth was my bed that night, with the swinging pine for canopy; and through the forest tore and raved the chilly wind, but a happy glow was at my heart, and my slumber was balmy and sweet.

And often now, the memory of that night rises soft and clear, and the shadows that oppress me flee away.

The clouds looked wilder, the wind strengthened, the lake grew darker. Swelling more and more, the blast swooped through the rocking forest. Far away would sound a deep roar, increasing rapidly into trampling thunder; the gust would then burst over head with the shock of a mighty billow, and sweep furiously down the foaming lake.

At the forest edge, the white pine streamed out crazily, the maple was in convulsions, and the aspen seemed as if it would fracture itself into atoms.

Nor did the lowly tribes of the forest floor escape the searching wind. The adder's-tongue hissed to the trembling, shrinking Indian Plume; the sword-grass and arrowhead exchanged quick passes, and the bulrush beat with its brown war-club the purple helmet of the moosehead.

At length, I summoned Harvey, and as the wind had somewhat lessened, we launched the little Bluebird upon the lake, Watch leaping in at Harvey's call as we left the shore.

Up we went. The white-caps gleamed and the dash of the tossing swells filled our ears. We landed at last off the foot of Long Island, in a little cove on the west shore of the lake. It was a wild, tangled, jagged spot; dead pines slanting from the foliage, streaming with grey moss; firs bending outward; cedars pointing straight to the water, and a multitude of dry twigs, steeped in moss, tangled all about. Old trees lay in the water, which last was clustered broadly with water lilies. Lighting a fire, we passed the afternoon gazing at the swells rolling and frothing over the lake; at the trees bending and writhing to the wind, and in listening to the volume of sound poured by it through the woods. Various tones made up that sound; howls, like a giant in agony; shrieks, like a score of perishing victims; unearthly, mocking voices, as if from a legion of maniacs, sinking occasionally to one lingering cry, like a wail over a lost soul.

Deep, dead, prolonged shocks of sound would also frequently echo—the fall of great trees overturned by the wind.

Amid all this tumult, my ear was caught by strange, wild tones, that issued from a neighboring ridge. Now shrill screams, then jarring screeches; they made my blood run cold.

"In the name of wonder, Harvey, what sounds are these?

If the Saranac Indians were here now, I should think they were torturing some one at the stake."

Harvey laughed, and leading the way a little up the ridge, pointed to where one pine leaned, from the loosening of its roots, against another, and was swayed to and fro by the gusts.

"Talkin' of Injins," said Harvey, "when I fust come to the S'nac with father, there was nobody else about there but Injins. I used to meet 'm on the lakes fishin' in their bark canoes, and trappin' about the streams, and huntin' everywheres. They was great hands to still-hunt and good shots too. There was a tribe on Bear Island in the Lower S'nac, and one Injin—come here, Watch! what are yer hazin' and nosin' about fur! we don't want ter roust out no deer now! come here and stay here, or there'll be a yellin' in the woods enough to wake up dead folks!—one Injin, a young feller, killed another of the same tribe. He ran away down here to Tupper's Lake, but he was ketched, and the chief killed 'im with his tommyhawk. I was trappin' on Mink Island when the others fetched 'im back.

"There was old Captain Bill Snyder, he was o' that tribe. He lived around here until about fifteen years sin', huntin', fishin' and trappin', to the last. One day I met 'im though, jest—there's a hawk bin sailin' over that fire-slash for the last five minutes; I shouldn't much wonder ef there was a dead deer, or mebby a sick fa'n in the deer-weeds there; or mebby it's only a woodchuck—well, 'twas jest this side o' the Middle Falls, 'twixt Round Lake and the Lower S'nac, all painted up, and an eagle's feather in his sculp-lock.

"He hadn't nothin' on but a strip o' wolf-skin round his body. He'd got to be then about ninety. Well, I axed 'im where—a trout jumped up then by that lily-blow, a good un, a two-pounder I should jedge—where he was goin' fixed up so, and he said in his way, 'Down dare,' p'intin' hereaway. 'Ole Injin on war path; nebber come back. Goo' bye! Too ole; don't want to live no more—goo' bye!'

"He never was heerd on agin, that is, for sartin. Joe Platter, or Hunter Joe, as they called 'm, who was shantyin' at that time on the Injin Park out there, huntin' by Little Wolf Pond, about a month after, come upon a couple o' wolves, snarlin' and fightin' over a passle o' bones in a little holler o' rocks. He shot one, and that skeered away t'other, and he picked up a feather that he showed me, and 'twas 'zactly like the one I saw on Cap'n Bill's head; but there was no knowin' to a sartenty what did happen to the old chap."

The wild and troubled sunset came, and the drear twilight. The wind, which had been increasing since our landing so as to render dangerous an attempt to return, began to lull at the folding in of the darkness.

Although the night was black with the great clouds that rolled over the sky like stormy billows, and the roar of the lake still hoarse and threatening, Harvey at last decided on returning to the camp.

True, with a fire and under the boat, we might have passed the night somewhat comfortably; but there was a dash of wild romance to me in wrestling with the fierce lake; besides, Harvey's word in all wood matters was law.

We embarked, and over the black rolling water we went, against the swells, Harvey at the oars, and I at the paddle. Harvey had lighted his jack, and the ghastly foam glistened as it flew about us, and I felt the sprinkles of the spray, raked off by the wind. Still onward we danced through the darkness, and Harvey's blithesome whistle blended with the wind.

At length, a low roar in the distance caught my ear; rapidly it approached; Harvey ceased his careless whistle and braced himself to his oars.

"It's comin', Mr. Smith, look out!" said he, dipping his oars deep, and lifting himself from his seat as he pulled.

"What, Harvey?"

"The gust o' wind. It 'ill make the Bluebird jump, but I consate she'll hold her own. We shan't go fur, though, afore I'll try shelter. It's too squally a night to be out."

On came the gust. It struck us; the little Bluebird staggered as if hit by a blow, and swung off; two black walls of water foamed beside us, and the air was, for a moment, filled with flying spray.

The next, her head rose up a steep swell, and onward we darted, rising and sinking, the howl of the wind mingling with the dash of the rollers.

Suddenly a black, towering mass burst out of the gloom.

"The Devil's Pulpit," said Harvey. "I guess I'll try the cove."

There was a loud wash of waves for a moment, and a glimpse of climbing foam. The boat seemed about to be dashed against the beetling precipice, that looked as if a portion of the murky darkness had become solid, when we glided instantaneously into smooth water.

"Here we are!" said Harvey, "snug as in the Harrietstown mill-pond. We'll hev a fire in the rocks here in a jiffy, and make ourselves as comfortable as we kin. We've got the jack to see by, and" (rummaging in the box at the bow) "here's crackers, and goll! if there aint a couple o' ducks here too! The b'ys must have shot 'm, put 'm in the box here and forgot it. But they'll do for our supper."

So saying he paddled the boat between a labyrinth of old logs in the water next the margin, landed on a rock, followed by myself and Watch, drew the boat on the edge of the gravel, and then separating the jack from its handle flashed the light around. We were at the threshold of a large fissure in a rock, with a cedar slanting over, and dense foliage on either side. Soon Harvey had a fire blazing in front, and a bed of hemlock boughs on the floor of the nook, over which, dividing it into two equal portions, a dead trunk had fallen.

All without was tumult, all within, peace.

Rage, cruel wind! in vain thy wrath!
  The shelter of this isle I share!
No more to-night the billowy path
  My swift but fragile bark will dare.
I hear the blast in roaring flight,
  I hear the surge in angry shock,
But feel the camp-fire's generous light
  Flooding with joy my nook of rock.

Soft radiance bathes the slumbering hound;
  It flits athwart my stalwart guide
Who, on his couch, a rest hath found;
  I also soon will seek his side.
Hark! was not that the panther's scream
  'Borne from yon rock upon the blast?
But ruddier leaps my camp-fire's gleam,
  And livelier joy around is cast.

Rage, cruel wind! my little bark
  Trembled as down thy fury fell!
Wild foam flew glancing through the dark
  Death seemed to ride on every swell:
Without, the blackness blinds my view;
  Billow and forest blend their roar;
Within, falls quiet's blessed dew;
  Come, slumber, spread thy pinion o'er!

The wind had ceased as I looked out from my nook at sunrise, but the lake was lost in mist. Soon, however, a broad beam of the sun cleft it, and the light wind caused it to rise. How beautiful was that rising! Silver billows rolled over the lake; spotless pinions waved above. Now gleamed the walls and summits of a city, now an enormous forest moved slowly by, and now a grove of pearl. The masses vanished, leaving fragments to work their magic. Was that the white canoe of Hi-a-wont-ha stealing into yon winding cove? See that white eagle clinging to the pine! And so the mist went curling up, until its flakes all melted upon the rich blue of the summer heaven.

As we floated toward the camp, Harvey told me of a wizard shape, a white spectre, that on misty mornings the hunters had been accustomed to see around and upon the lake.

Now it glanced through the forest, now it trod the water. It climbed the hill, it threaded the gully; it was a panther in the tree or a wolf on the rock; a deer in the grass; a fisherman at the brook or a hunter in the glen.

"As for me," said Harvey in conclusion, "I al'ys telled the consarned fools twant nothin' but a piece o' mist, but most on 'm wouldn't bleeve but they see some one o' them things, 'tick'ally them that had bin out all night with whiskey in the boat. Them last 'ud stick to 't so fur as to say sometimes that each man on 'm not unly see one painter and deer and what not, but, goll, ef they wouldn't say they see two."

Reaching the camp in time to take breakfast with the others, we again embarked upon the lake, all scattering as usual to different points for fishing or hunting. The day's beauty was just fitted for exploration and the enjoyment of leisure and freedom.

"How many islands belong to this lake, Harvey?" asked I, as we approached the Two Brothers.

"Forty-two," he answered. "Some on 'm hev names, but the most part don't. There's the two afore us; and next up'ards is Birch and Long Island, and the two Norway Islands next, and then Jinkins's Island, and another at the head."

"Folks gin'rally say," he continued, "that Tupper's Lake is the handsomest piece o' water in the whull region, but to my thinkin' the Upper S'nac is. The head on't is the beautifulest I ever set eyes on. Standin' on a little rocky island called Goose Island, where I've camped many's the time, there's water round ye four miles broad, with unly one more island nigh, a leetle round rock that looks like a snappin' turkle's back. But still, Tupper's Lake 's nice, 'tick'ally the head on't that we'll see on our way to Mud Lake."

We landed on the west Brother, leaving the Bluebird with a knot of white lilies touching her waist like a bouquet. We lay in the warm, brown hollows, sprinkled with light through the network of giant hemlocks; glanced out upon the water, that shot here and there a keen glance; watched those feathered mice, the ground-birds, leaping along and bending their dusky red turbans this way and that over the decayed leaves; and listened to the squall of the blue-jay and the rat-tat-tat of the woodpecker.

Island after island tucked away in the north-western part of the lake, we visited, inhaling the fresh odors of the water, laving our arms and brows in its balmy softness and enjoying the shady coolness and speckled light.

At length we glided through the outlet, and along the beautiful basin that opened before the green sandal of the Indian Park.

"A tribe o' S'nac Injins lived on the Park there, onst upon a time," said Harvey, dipping softly alternate oars. "Old Sabele telled me a story about 'm one day that I'll tell ye, ef you'd like to hear it. Don't ye feel dry? (producing a pocket bottle from the box at the bow, swallowing a large draught and following it with a sip or two of water, in his hand, from the boatside.) This lake water's so warm, it want's suthin' to take the sun out on't. But as I was sayin', this tribe was a part o' the one that lived on the Injin Carryin' Place. They had a quarrel, and so this part came down here, and the other stayed up there. Well, things went on so bad that they wouldn't speak when they came crost one another; and every now and then the big bugs 'mong 'm, when they happened to bunk up agin each other on the Racket or round, would hev a fight with their sculpin'-knives and tommyhawks, as politicianers 'mong us white folks, whenever they come t'gether on 'lection day, pitch in and give one another lickety-whack. Well (this talkin' makes me kinder dry), bimeby there was queer doin's noticed around and about the Park, or rayther he was fust seen at Simon's Slew, not that 'twas Simon's Slew then; I don't know 't 'ad enny name then, onless 'twas some Injin name; and I'll tell ye what 'tis, Mr. Smith, there's more inkstand in some o' them

Injin names than one 'ud s'pose them kinder haythen sort o' people, as a body may say, knowed. Now, there's a good many of these Injin names about"——

"But about the story, Harvey?"

"Oh, lets me see! I've got so many things to think on! How fur had I got?"

"Mercy knows; but you were saying that he (whoever that may be) was first seen at Simon's Slew."

"He—why that was the young Injin b'longin' to the Injin Carry tribe that came a-sparkin' the gal that b'longed to the Injin Park tribe. His name was—well, I never kin think o' names, but it meant in Injin, The Big Wind what Howls. I'll call him Howl fur short. The gal's name was Hop-so-me-turvy, or some sich name; but I'll call her Hopsy. I knowed a gal when I was a young man by that name, that jest was—wa-a-l, I won't say there hasn't bin as nice gals as Hopsy, but I will say there haint bin no nicer. Oh, that gal!—why don't you take suthin' too, Mr. Smith? this whiskey is fust best!—couldn't she dance! and wasn't she a hoss at singin'! We had singin' school at Harrietstown onst a week, and a chap—an all-fired good singer, too —he was a school-teacher by the name of—well, I bleeve I'll forgit my own name one o' these days. He was a Yankee, that chap, and I kinder consate he'd been a peddler. I calkilate he could do the thing up in the way o' singin about as well as enny a-goin', that is, in my 'pinion. I don't want nobody to s'pose I want folks to bleeve that 'caze I say so 'tis so. I've as good right to my 'pinion as ennybody has to his'n; and my 'pinion is, that that chap was about as good a singer as"——

"But the story, Harvey, the story."

"Oh, yes, sarten. You don't remember where I left off, do ye?"

"You were speaking of Hopsy, the Indian girl."

"Yes, yes. She and Howl got 'quainted somehow on the Racket; he skeered off a wolf, I bleeve, that was a-goin', or Hopsy consated was a-goin' (but 'twant no sich thing: there aint no wolf on the Racket, nur nowhere else, that a human critter couldn't skeer off, onless he was al-mighty hungry) to make mince-meat on her. 'T all events, they got a hankerin' after each other, as b'ys and gals will; and as 'twouldn't do for 'm to keep comp'ny afore folks, as both tribes 'ud a bin in their hair then, they got t'gether behind their backs, as 'twere, that is, around and about the Injin Park, when they thought nobody wasn't seein' on 'm.

"This love business, Mr. Smith, is a cur'ous thing. Some love one thing, some another, some half a dozen things ter onst. Now, I love tobaccy, and trout, and ven'son, and inions; and I tell yer, Mr. Smith, what's old hunderd in the way of eatin'—it's two things—a moose's lip and a beaver's tail. Ef you ever happen to light on 'm, and don't say they're the best eatin' you ever had, you may say right to my face I'm a fool. But talkin' about this love: there's a good many people loves rum, and I don't think it bad, sometimes, myself—won't ye take a l-e-e-tle suthin'? it'll do yer good, this hot day!—but, as I was sayin', as a gin'ral thing, young folks loves one another, and these two did to death a'most; and so, as I was a sayin', they'd come t'gether when they cackilated no one was a-lookin'.

"But there was somebody, though: a feller b'longin' to the same tribe she did, that had a hank'rin' after her too, and was consarnedly put out that she didn't take to him. Well, whether he kinder consated there was another feller —that stake-driver looks kinder sassy in that slash there, and I've a great mind ter—off with ye, ef ye must go— another feller that she liked better, or whether he'd seen 'm t'gether when he was a snoopin' around, I most forgit what Sabele said about it. 'T all events, he got all-fired jealous, and went a-snoopin' and a-sneakin' round—what was his name?—well, I'll call him Snoop-round—and he found out the place where they used to come t'gether on moonshiny nights, and all kinds o' nights, for that matter. Well, I forgot to say that Hopsy was darter to the chief or boss of the Injin Park consarn, and Howl was son to the boss up there at the Carry. Well, now, Mr. Smith, I'll tell ye what 'tis—won't ye raally take another drink? it's rael old hunderd, this whiskey. Well, as I was sayin', there's mighty mean men in this world! men that 'ud kill a doe with a fa'n by her side, jest as lives as not, and a leetle liver, ef they'd a notion they could make a little suthin' by't; and what's jest as bad, that 'ud kill half a dozen deer, mebby, when they didn't want more 'n one, ef they did that, and the consekens is, there they lay for the painters and wolves to feed on. I've seen a good deal of sich kind o' business in my life. Onst, at Big Wolf Pond, I"——

"But the story, Harvey! You were telling how jealous the young Indian was."

"Oh yes. He got so jealous, he up and telled the old man, that is, the old Boss, the old Boss I mean that had Hopsy fur a darter. Let's see—his name now! wasn't it Linkumdoddy? No! that's in the chorius of a song Will Johnson sings. What was it?—well I'll call 'm Linkumdoddy, or, I guess, Linkum fur short. As I was sayin'-let's me see, what was I sayin'?—oh! about Snoop-round tellin' the old man! Wasn't the old feller riled? I tell ye, he'd horns down and mane up! He was a terrible farse old critter, and he up and telled Snoopy to take two or three with 'im, and crooch in amboosh, and when Howl and Hopsy was t'gether, to pounce on Howl like a hawk on a June bug, and haul 'im right up to the old Boss. The next thing old Linkum did, says he to Hopsy, 'Darter o' the S'nacs,' s'ze, 'the Pine o' the clouds,' 's'ze, 'bends his head,' s'ze—I can't give it to ye in the hifalutin way old Sabele used'ter, but the idee on't was that he, the Poppy, that is old Linkum, was a mighty big bug, in his own consate, enny way, and was 'shamed that he had a darter that could make sich a fool of herself as to keep comp'ny with a feller b'longin' to t'other tribe, and that as fur 'lowin' it he'd see her—that is as much as to say—that is, ef a feller wanted me to do a thing I wouldn't do no way, I'd say I'd see 'im dod darned to darnation fust and then I wouldn't.

"But somehow or the other—you know what gals is, Mr. Smith—she didn't mind her daddy; and I consate she wasn't old hunderd there, fur ef I tell my darter not to keep comp'ny with a young feller fur reasons best knowed to myself'and after that she doos—why 'taint my fault but hern, and ef I ketch the young feller around and about, I'll twist 'im out of his boots, and as fur her, why—well, no matter—but mas-sy I wouldn't do nothin' like what old Linkum did. He must a bin a terr'ble farse, cross-grained, cruel, bloodthirsty old sarpent, as you'll see, Mr. Smith. Well, things went on so a week, or mebby eight days—by golly, I consated that black stump in that bush was a bear, the leaves was a kinder over it so!—when Snoop-round, who'd bin a-sneakin' round and about all that time with two or three others jest as mean as he was, finally at last ketched Howl when he and the gal was a-walkin' and a-castin' sheep's eyes fust on one another and then on the moon, and a-goin' this way and that way, and a-mincin' and a-smilin', and he praps sayin' to Hopsy that she was a leetle the nicest gal in all c'ration, and she was a swallerin' it all whull, but holdin' her head down and pretendin' not to like it, but L-o-r-d bless yer, Mr. Smith, she did—all wimming doos. Well, they was a goin' over all that aire when little Snoopy pounced with the others that was as a body may say jest like two, and I dunno but three tin pans on one dog's tail, my Watch ef yer a mind ter, and I don't bleeve that four tin pans 'ud be more'n a flea-bite to him ef he was after a deer. How he would lickety-spang over the ruts and things, and how the pans 'ud fly, hey! I remember one time I was on a runway and I could see up the side of a ridge as plain as the ruff of a house. Bimeby the deer come like old Sanko, and a leetle after 'im come Watch, and I *tell* yer, he went so fast 'twas as much as I could do to see 'im. Now, do you bleeve that five or even six, and I dunno but I'll say ten, I *will* say *ten* tin pans 'ud a stopped him! By the 'tarnal Jehosiphat, *no!* Watch is leetle the grittiest dog"——

"You had got as far as the courting in the story, Harvey."

"Oh—yes—yes—a—a—had I? let me see—what did happen then! They courted so of'en that I disremember the partic'lar p'int on't. That was the trouble twixt that Snoopy and—oh, I remember now! Well, Snoop-round and his tin pans as 'twere, not as they was tin pans raally, but unly as you might tie one and mebby half-a-dozen to Watch——"

"So the Indian and his friends I suppose lay in wait, that is, lay in ambush for Howl and Hopsy——"

"That's it—jest it. Did I ever tell it to you afore? No! well it's strannge you should a guessed so cluss. But, as I was sayin', Snoop-round and his tin pans, as I call 'em, tuk Howl (but he fit like a wounded bull-moose; still it didn't do no good—how kin a body fight three to one?) and he tuk Hopsy too. 'Aha!' says he (this is about the idee on't), 'What will yer poppy say to this, Miss Hopsy?' 'Jest mind yer own business you great, big, mean feller you,' said Hopsy ('t all events that was the upshot on't), fur I tell ye, Mr. Smith, she was mad; and I don't blame her a bit; 'twas an orful mean trick in that Snoopy; still what kin ye expect from sich kind o' chaps! There's a feller now they call Catamount Pete ('caze he telled sich a rousin' lie one time about a catamount he bragged on he killed); he's about the meanest scamp when he gits riled agin a feller! There's no let up to 'im, enny way. Well, the p'int on't was, they fetched 'im—I raaly consated I heerd a mink then, but I guess I didn't—they fetched 'im afore old Linkum. That aire Howl must a bin consid'ble of a young feller fur an Injin 't all events, fur when he come afore the old Boss, he kinder straightened himself up as ef he said, 'What's the meanin' 'n all this! Why hevent I as much right to spark a gal as enny body else?' But the old Boss spoke up so kinder quick he hadn't time to say nothin' much enny way. 'Prepare to die!' sez the old critter. 'Prepare to die!' jest as quick, he kinder tumbled it out. 'W-a-a-l,' says Howl (this is the idee on't, Mr. Smith! I can't give ye the rael Injin touch—old Sabele did that, and he would wobble his arms and twist about, and roll his eyes, and look farse, and yell, he would, tellin' on't, tick'ally this part you could a heerd 'im a mile). Says Howl, ' Ef I must die, I must, but I want ter see Hopsy agin afore I do.'

Didn't the old feller skip and jump! I tell yer! 'You *shell* see Hopsy,' sez he, 'and in a way you won't like to, no how. Here,' sez he to his folks round, 'you jest tie up this chap to the tree there, and you, Hopsy, you, come here!' Hopsy came up a-tremblin', and they tied the young feller to the tree, and here old Sabele used to spread himself. I remember a leetle on't. 'Wind what Howls,' sez old Linkum, ' when Natur is all blossoms, but kinder dies away to a whisper, when the tornader's about' (meanin', Sabele said, that Howl was a tarnal great feller when 'twas all fair weather—a fair-weather Christian as 'twere—but was a kind o' sneak when enny misfortin' was about to happen), ' sing yer death-song with a loud voice of you kin, which I don't bleeve; fur why? Linkum don't see a waryer tied up to that aire tree, but a woman,' and here old Sabele used to ketch his breath and his eye bulged out as big as, w-a-a-l—as big as a twenty-five cent piece, 'and he shell die by the hand of a woman. Here, Hopsy,' said the old sarpent, ' take the hatchet and strike it inter the head of the coward!'

"Hopsy she scrooched right down to her pa's feet (as I heerd a young lady tellin' another, one time, in my boat on the Lower S'nac. She was tellin' a story about a pa, as she said, comin' down on his darter's lovyer a good deal like this; twas pa here and pa there—I thought I'd hev to snicker right out), and she cries and she begs, but massy, Mr. Smith, twant no use; Pop had made up his mind, and that was the eend on't. Well, when Hopsy found all her snifflin' and carryins-on didn't do no good, and that she'd got to take the hatchet enny way, she riz up, and finally at last she grabbed it. All this time Snoop-round was lookin' on and a-grinnin' and a-larfin' at the twist things had took. 'Twas rael nuts to him. Well, as I was sayin', Hopsy, when she found she couldn't do no better, she grabbed the hatchet and she gin a screech and —I do wonder what all that snarlin' and spittin' means out there! it sounds to me like a fisher in a trap—I'll go and see! but I guess I wont—'taint none o' my business. The fisher aint mine, an 'taint in season ef 'twas. I wonder a'most there should be enny trap there so airly; but it may be an old one—and she gin a spring clearn up to where Snoop-round stood a-grinnin', his mouth stretched from ear to ear, and—shuck! didn't that aire hatchet go inter that aire skull o' his'n. It must a struck fire! I've no notion but 'twas hard enough; sich mean, off-ox folks's skulls aly's is. And didn't he yell? He throwed up his arms and fell jest like a log, and was dead in half a minute. And what d' yer spose come next? Kin ye tell, Mr. Smith? Kin ye guess? Well, I'll tell ye. 'Twas the stranngest thing in the world. But Sabele telled me he'd swear to it on a stack o' Bibles, or that was the idee on't. Jest as Snoop-round gin his last gasp there was an orful skreekin' and howlin' in the bushes, and about twenty of the fightin' charackters of the Carry Tribe bust in, took Hopsy and the young feller—young Howl I mean—off, and what's more, they took the old Boss himself, fur a big part o' his fightin' charackters was away moose huntin' on Bog River, where we're a-goin', though he bit and scratched and fit off jest like the very old Scratch. The way the Carry folks come to bust in was, that the old daddy on the Carry kinder got oneasy about his son stayin' away so long, and hustled 'm off to see what the upshot was. Well, to make a long story short, the Carry daddy he made as ef he sot all the store in the world by the Injin Park daddy and old Linkum, he finally at last consated he couldn't do no better than to let Howl hev Hopsy, and so, as the old song says, they lived in peace and died in a pot o' grease! And now s'pose'n we twist round these islands here twixt Mink Bay and Gull Pond Bay a leetle, afore we go to camp."

We accordingly wound through the island channels, with the rich, birchy perfume of the woods extracted by the afternoon sun scenting the air, and with little suns and dancing meteors and steely sprinklings and broad dazzling lights on the water, until they gave place to the topaz and ruby of the sunset, and they in turn yielded to the sober tints of twilight.

At last we laid our course for the camp. We found our comrades and the guides there; a deer and "no end to the trout," testifying to the success of their day's sport.

CHAPTER XVIII.

The Sabbath.—Preaching at the Indian Park.—The Pool.—The Sky.—Politics.—The Constitution.

THE next day was the Sabbath. The sky was robed in bright blue and gold, with an embroidery of pearl. The lake was breathless. Not a leaf fluttered in the forest. As I viewed the scene's repose, I thought how beautiful is the fancy that the day's sanctity in the Christian mind finds sympathy in the visible universe—that, at this time, Nature stills her throbbing pulses, the tree waves with more tranquil grace, the bird sings with softer tone, the water lapses in a calmer ripple. Poets, whose hearts are filled with love of Nature, have delighted so to depict this day, and the thought spreads tranquillity in turn over the heart. And thus does soul transfigure Nature, and Nature sanctify the soul. What images crowd the fancy, too, in gazing upon Nature's grandeur or beauty! What serene joys of thought, what pure, sweet, lofty sentiments are her offspring!

All the beautiful mythology of the olden time is born of her.

> "The intelligible forms of ancient poets,
> The fair humanities of old religion,
> The Power, the Beauty, and the Majesty,
> That had their haunts in dale, or piny mountain,
> Or forest, by slow stream, or pebbly spring,
> Or chasms and watery depths!"

To the tree, did the antique fancy give the dryad; and the naiad to the stream. On the cloudy peak, with its gleaming levin, it seated the thunder-bearing Zeus; from the glancing light, it created the golden-sandalled Hermes; and Aphrodite from the grace of the breaking wave.

And though "Pan is dead" with the deifying faith that worshipped him, still fancy finds moral emblems in the various forms of Nature. In the rose's blush, we see love's own hue; and purity in the whiteness of the lily. In the flow of the majestic river, we recognise strong resolve, calm in its very depth, and moving toward a determined end. In the bursting torrent we see impetuosity of spirit; in the tangled glen, the heart dark with evil passions; and self-reliance looks calmly forth in the steadfast and towering mountain. Indeed, these myths of the old civilization typify each a sentiment or truth. May we not behold in Jason and the Golden Fleece, the type of a daring spirit in search of some rare secret of Nature, bearing from far and unknown coasts of speculation some sterling thought? Porphyrion, is he not the emblem of Will assaulting Fate, and recoiling from the rock of its immutability? Prometheus, the symbol of a grand soul crucified on the bleak and barren crag of untoward circumstance, and while conscious of the sacred fires of genius and all-embracing love, feeling but the vulture of inexorable fate gnawing at his heart? Ixion clasping the cloud, is it not Ambition grasping worldly fame? Sisyphus, Toil struggling upward, unrewarded, to die in despair at last?

About ten o'clock, Phin, who had rowed as far as the Indian Park, returned with the tidings that a travelling preacher, on his way down the Racket to Potsdam, intended to hold forth an hour hence. We all, accordingly, embarked, and on reaching the Park, found two or three black-bearded woodmen from the vicinity, in red hunting-shirts and clean check collars, waiting for the promised service. The two boats in which they had arrived were placed upon the bank, bottom upwards, under the birch tree, near the water's edge, and formed seats.

Soon, other boats appeared gliding down the Racket, and one through the outlet, which I found afterward was from the head of the lake, eight miles distant. These were filled with men, women, and children, in their best and gayest attire. Together, we numbered some twenty-five or thirty.

The scene from a mound, a little back in the Park, presented a lively and beautiful picture. In the foreground was the meadow, deep in its wild grass, dappled with sun and shadow. Next was the spot of worship, the bank and boats chequered with the different dresses of the group. The middle distance gleamed with the silver lights and purple darks of the river, over to the sunny greens of its midchannel island and shores. A soaring background of downy tints, reared by Mount Morris, closed the picture.

The preacher was a long, lank personage, with an apple of a head perched on a stick of a body. He stepped from the log hut to the front, and began the service, by reading a hymn with a nasal drawl, and stumbling over the longest words.

An old fellow, with features buried in an ambush of wrinkles, then sounded the pitch; joined in a keen falsetto by one whom I took to be his wife, an old lady whose sour face seemed sharpened on the grindstone of a rather quick temper, and who appeared to have run so pertinaciously after her work as to run all the flesh off her bones.

The first then opened upon the air in a thick bass, as though the rugged tones were too big for his throat, and as one of the guides said afterwards, " a-kinder scraped as they come up."

The air was carried by the wife, whose shrill tones seemed momentarily threatening to sharpen into the termagant pitch of home. In fact, she appeared angry with the tune, from the beginning, and no wonder, for it crawled over the words like a mud-turtle over stones.

The two had the air mainly to themselves, portions of the congregation occasionally breaking in with discordant blots of sound. All these gave up after a while, with the exception of a wiry-looking chap, eager in his expression as though ready at any time to jump out of his skin, and a bouncing girl, whose dot of a nose perked up from between two red worsted cheeks; both of whom busily engaged themselves in snapping at the tune, without catching it, all the way through. Next them, however, stood a brawny, check-shirted fellow, smelling awfully of whiskey, who, with a pertinacity worthy to behold, clung to his singing, evidently without knowing the tune, and belched out his muddled tones in the loudest manner, carrying havoc as he went.

The performers had opened their lips for the seventh verse (three more to come), when the preacher (or "Deacon"), probably and naturally supposing the tune bid fair to last the time of service out, broke in upon it with the invitation to prayer, leaving the singers to close their mouths as quick as they could over their half-strangled notes.

The prayer was a compound of fierce joy at the certainty of so great a portion of the human race being doomed to destruction, with the exception of "the elect," and a self-hugging complacency that the said elect, of which he plainly intimated he was one, were to be the inheritors of so certain a happiness.

At the conclusion of the prayer, he gave out another hymn, and as if he wished to be spared the excruciation of the former music, opened on a tune himself with great power, if little melody, elevating his chin at the high notes, and dipping it into the pool of his loose white cravat at the lower, like a duck drinking.

He was alone in his music, the old couple probably not knowing the air, and the rest restrained by respect from trying, as at first, to catch it on the wing.

The sermon was a repetition of the ideas in the prayer, spread thin, the worthy plainly considering himself on the most intimate terms with the Deity, and dealing out life and death with the air of a principal.

At the conclusion of the service, the motley company departed, the Deacon drawing paddle down the Racket, toward his destination, with a companion at the oars, while we returned to camp.

After dinner, I rowed myself in the afternoon glow to a point on Birch Island, just below the Devil's Pulpit, to enjoy the seclusion and quiet.

I fastened my boat to a log, and in the idleness of the moment noted the slight effects around me. By the water's edge was a pile of rocks shaped like a cromlech, and near it an oak with a crescent of light clipping its shadowed stem, like the golden knife of a Druid severing the sacred mistletoe for the rites of his ancient and mysterious faith.

In the forest there was a flitting of light and shade, and a tremble of branches in the low wind, with an occasional glance of a bird through the fretted vaults.

A pool lay near, sheltered by a stooping birch, and a small rapid.

In its airlike depth was a trout, moving around restlessly, scenting a lily stem; pondering over a mossy rock; darting toward the surface; steadying himself by the occasional flutter of his fins; staring with huge eyes all about; waving his tail, like a deer grazing, and working his mouth as if chewing a cud. By and by, a miller came close to the glass of the surface, quivering with admiration at the image of his silver coat. His spasm of self-love was short, for the trout, lurking in the ambush of a stone, like a bandit in his cave, darted forth, gave a nip, and the luckless miller vanished.

Then came a shiner that sent a silver flash through all the pool. Now he poised himself, head downward, as if to lunge through the ooze; then stood on his tail and gaped. At last, he turned himself into a wheel and gyrated away. He was succeeded by a gleam of gold, cast by a sunfish, that flattened himself on his side, and lay there, until a bullhead blundered along, and turned one of his horns on him, when the sunfish whisked himself away.

At this juncture there was a plump, and then a sudden darkening of the crystal inclosure, through which I saw the dim shape of a muskrat, who scampered across the bottom, and then rose by a sedge on a dot of grass, with its flag half-way up its staff.

First, his ratship pulled the stem of a yellow lily as if to ring the bell; then he nibbled the gold of the blossom; then he skimmed to the edge of the bank, with two furrows like a wedge pencilled from his shoulders, and cut with his needle teeth the barb of an arrowhead, and towed it in his mouth to his burrow, where he vanished. In a moment, however, his blunt, whiskered face and glittering specks of eyes were thrust forth again in my direction, thinking, I suppose, what a queer thing that log was, when an involuntary motion on my part caused him to disappear in the winking of an eye.

I then leaned back at the boat's stern, and gazed into the noontide heavens. As I viewed the overwhelming arch, springing so magnificently from the horizon, robed in an azure so rich and tender, and gleaming with its silver clouds, I thought how little appreciated, comparatively, is this most wonderful, beautiful, and majestic of all the Creator's handiwork.

The brightest and loveliest hues dwell within its concave, as do the blackest and most threatening. There beams the rainbow, born of gold and precious gems; and there glares the lightning from the scowling cloud. There fans the breeze on downy pinion, and there whirls the dread tornado. Within it, echo the sweetest sounds as well as the most awful. There the lark warbles to the ear of the morning, and there the thunder hurls its crashing terrors. We talk of the vastness of ocean, the desert, the forest, the prairie; but what is the horizon presented by each to the mighty sweep of that canopy we have but to raise our eyes at any moment to behold? There it arches, ever present, whether blinded with its grey, rainy mantle, rolling in cloudy surges, smiling in blue loveliness, or kindled by the sunset and the dawn. There in the highest degree is the sublimity of magnitude and the beauty of softness. And not only are the tenderest and most delicate objects, the transparent film, the twining mist, the spangling snow and the curling cloud, found there, but it is the home of the glorious sun, his gentle sister of the silver brow, and the far-away constellations. And what sway it holds over us! Be it sombre, we grow mournful; be it bright, our heart leaps up " and is glad."

We look upward when in sorrow; into the sky have departed the loved and lost; there prayer is wafted; there soars the released spirit; there dwells God.

We fall into raptures beneath the dome of St. Peter's, at the beauty, the grandeur there seen; we revel in its streaming sunlights; we bend to the almost crushing sense of its immensity; and yet we never fasten an eye for one half hour on the sky's dome, its loveliness, its majesty, its illuminated glories, its boundless sweep. All, too, to be had in a moment, without crossing stormy wave or mountain peak; all its beautiful and stately changes, its glory of rising and of setting tints. If by some magic the sky could be shut off, and then be opened upon us for a price, we would make the welkin ring with voice of admiration and wonder.

We gaze at the summer ocean in its heaving slumber! What is its smoothness and quiet to the boundless expanse above, with the cloud-sails gliding over, and the fairy barks at anchor? View this same ocean in a storm, with its watery cliffs and chasms, and dashing its fierce foam in the black brow of the tempest; the sight is not grander or more fearful than a sky of battling thunder-storms. Its roar; why, the crashing bolt, the unchained blast, the trampling hailstones, roll out sounds more dread and wrathful!

We thrill with the sublimity of Mont Blanc and Chimborazo, the grand range of Alp and Himmalaya—mighty crags, clutching the upper air with icy fingers; but behold the cloud-ridges, pile upon pile, lowering in a mighty frown over one half the heavens, and plunging leagues on leagues of earth in shadow! We bow before the grandeur of Niagara, where seas plunge upon the globe's heart in reverberating thunders; but glance merely at some cataract of stormy vapor dashing down the sky-slope! Niagara, to it, is a mere cascade!

We linger days on the beamy lights, the velvet shades of the old masters: of Domenichino, of Cimabuë, of Giorgione, of Titian, of Tintoretto and Claude, whose names glitter with the magic tints of Italy, and ring with the golden richness of her music. The colors born of that one painter, the atmosphere, flash disdain upon the tame blazonry of their mimic hues. Even the divine frescoes of Raphael must yield to the common tints of dawn and twilight. And the architecture of Angelo, of Brunelleschi and Giotto—they have cast a spell to which Time is powerless; but look upward, in your walk, or from your desk, your study, your plough, even while your hands are busy, and there is architecture, with pillars and arches and colonnades and towers, not tiring the eye in their sameness, but changing even as you look, resting on foundations of living sapphire, and flushed with flitting tints that transcend even the divinest dreams of those mighty masters, the "great heirs of Time."

Returning to the camp, I found my comrades darting furious gestures through a cloud of words, amid which flitted the cant political expressions of the day, with the word "Constitution" particularly conspicuous.

Politics, next to business, occupy us Americans almost exclusively. We elevate, consequently, our political leaders into national idols. The press supplies the pedestal on which they are reared to the altitude of giants. We abuse them, it is true, but upon the principle of the Chinese, who, though they cuff their josses, never cease to regard them as gods.

Thus we ascribe to these political heroes of ours all

kinds of qualities not their own, and crown them with our honors, as barbarous nations stud storks and ostriches with jewels, and then bow to them in worship.

I had been so frequently worried by this political talk of my comrades, that I hastened to bury myself from the din in the tent of the guides. Outside I found them collected, listening with great attention, and, as the talkers probably supposed, with a due impression of their superior wisdom.

I might have supposed so too, had I not, an hour afterward, heard one of them say to another, and, in my opinion, summing the whole matter up most sensibly:

"The gen'lemen set a good deal of store by the cons'tootion, but for my part, I think it's the best plan fur each one to take keer of the cons'tootion what b'longs to 'im. It's more'n most on us kin do, with all our lookin' out. I say, let all this talk about presarvin' the cons'tootion, and standin' by the cons'tootion, jest go to the dogs, and we'll go to snoozin', that is, as sun as we take a drink round—b'ys, what say ye?"

CHAPTER XIX.

Sail up Tupper's Lake.—Jenkins' Clearing.—The Shanty of the Spring.—Bog River Falls.—Head of the Lake.—Up Bog River.—Leo.—Track of the Moose.—Roar of the Moose.—Mud Lake.—Death of the Moose.

MONDAY I had fixed upon for my excursion up Bog River to Mud Lake, in search of moose.

This river is composed of two branches; runs, after their union, northerly, a couple of rods wide, and tumbles into Tupper's Lake at its southern extremity or head, by a winding, foaming cascade over two rocky terraces, about thirty feet in height.

The branches unite two miles from the lake, and westerly up the northern branch fourteen miles lies the lake to which I was bound.

Understanding the trip was difficult, I engaged Phin to accompany Harvey as an assistant. We were to be gone two days. Meanwhile, my comrades were to continue the camp at Tupper's Lake, or, if they moved, were to leave word on bark or paper, woods-fashion, as to their whereabout.

The morning was passed in preparation.

Deep in the afternoon we left Camp Cedar (so christened by Renning), in the Bluebird, with Phin at the oars; I, upon my folded blanket, in the middle, with a back-board; Harvey at the stern, with his paddle; and Watch curled up at the bow.

The lake was all blue and silver, with scarce air enough to bend the streak from Harvey's pipe.

Onward we went, the opening vistas and changing shores offering continually new water-scenes.

Leaving the Devil's Pulpit at our back, we glided along the mile's length of Long Island, and turned, opposite its head, and a small rocky point of the shore, into the south limb of the lake.

"Bog River Falls!" exclaimed Harvey, pointing to what appeared a sloping plate of pearl amid the rounded shores at the head of the lake, three miles distant. "About a mile furder you'll hear the roar. In the spring, when there's high water, the falls gits up consid'ble young thunder. The foam splashes over ugly. I've seen mighty big trees dashin' and quirlin' and crashin' over the rocks, as though lightnin' 'ad sent 'em; and then a deer 'ud come rollin' and strugglin', and be pitched down'ards, like a duck's feather in a ripple. The deer 'ud be dead enough, though, when it got to the bottom."

Large masses of light and shade, cast by the shores and islands in the low sun, lay along the water. Beautiful little sunset pictures gleamed out as we went; a mossy rock; a tiny dingle; a brook rapid; a colonnade of trees; an arbor of linked branches; a pool under a bank, like a peeping eye; a half-whelmed trunk, with water sparkling round it; an islet of watergrass; or a bit of marsh, where tiger-lilies curled their spotted pennons among the spears of the rushes.

Opposite the two Norway Islands (on the lower of which the tall, slender Norway pine was thinly towering), as well as a little above the upper, we cast successfully at the mouths of three trout brooks that crept into coves upon the east side. We then crossed the lake, passing a small island like a leafy dome, and entered a beautiful bay, at the head of which, in a small clearing, stood a log-hut, with several outhouses. On the left a wild mountain frowned against the sunset sky.

"Jenkins, who has the choppin' up there, is the unly one who lives on the lake," said Harvey.

"How near, or rather how far off are his neighbors?" asked I. (A neighbor in wood parlance is any one within fifty miles.)

"On along the Racket they're rather nigh," answered Harvey, as we continued up towards the next point, "that is about eight or nine miles off. But up over that way," pointing to the mountain, "on to Potsdam about forty miles, I guess 'twould be puzzlin' to find as many as ye could count up on one hand."

"Isn't that rather solitary for him, Harvey?"

"What?"

"Solitary, lonely!"

"Oh, lonesome! Why bless ye, no! In his boat, with enny kind o' rowin', 'twill take 'im unly about two hours to go to the Racket, where there's lots o' people. There's some five or six fam'lies stringin' along mebby ten or twelve miles. I call it rather crowded, that is, ef a man raally takes to the woods. Now I don't live in the woods 't all. There's a big settlement round me, some five or six housen that I kin count up right off. Fust" (counting on his fingers) "there's the school-house; then there's a barn; then father's in the holler; then there's a brother o' mine furder on; then Cort's at the S'nac Pond; then there's Col. Baker's, and Miller his son-in-law; and as fur Harrietstown, there's a settlement there sartenly of a dozen housen, without reckonin' the sawmill. It's a durned sight too thick fur me round. But I've of'en wondered how you folks git along in the city. I should raally s'pose you'd git kinder tangled up 'mong so many people there. Ef I lived there I'd hardly know my legs from another man's without chalkin' on 'm. But what d'ye say fur campin'? There's a fust best place inside this p'int."

We accordingly landed at the spot indicated, a dry smooth knoll, where we found a large bark shanty, with the front open to the lake. In a little hollow adjoining was a spring, about six feet in diameter, boiling clear as dew and cold as snow from a deep floor of pearly sand.

We landed, put our "traps" in the shanty, kindled our camp-fire to repel the charges of a fierce corps of musquitoes, and cut our hemlock mattresses for the night.

It was now just after the sunsetting. A blush was painted on the lake, below a streak of golden purple with a white star trembling at its edge.

Beyond, the dome-island (which Harvey called Deer Island) seemed moored in mid-air, while the background of the sky was filled with the mass of Mount Morris.

At the right, or south of the latter, frowning over Bog River, a little above the falls that I could see sparkling down the bank, were two mountain tops, which I christened the Hawksnest and the Panther, the former from its hollowed outline, and the latter from a fancied resemblance to the head of the animal named.

Everywhere around the water, and upon the islands (except the clearing of Jenkins) swept the woods, darkening now in the twilight.

Merry was our meal in the eye of the star, and we fell asleep with the camp-fire drenching our shanty in pleasant light.

The dawn's first grey was tinging the darkness as I awoke at Harvey's summons for our start.

The lake showed its broad neutral tint in the front, with the dim shores on either hand, and the islands beyond swollen against a black background.

The east momentarily warmed, while in the strengthening grey of the zenith the stars were melting like sparks in ashes.

After breakfast we pushed out in the fresh, cool (almost chilly) air, diagonally toward the falls, whose voice was loud in the stillness.

We ran up to the rocks, where the cascade, dashing and twisting in severed channels between log, thicket and rock, rushed in a broad mass of foam down a sloping ledge into the lake, pushing its dancing waters far beyond. At its spinning foot we threw our lines and soon secured a goodly number of fine trout.

Harvey and Phin then clambered with the boat and "traps" up the steep bank of the carry around the falls. I lingered behind to gaze once more down the broad vista of the lake, with its jutting points and the dome-island in the distance, until the view was closed by the high background of Long Island. At the right heaved up the broad blue breast of Mount Morris, which, owing to the angular form of the lake, is equally conspicuous at its foot as at its head.

After I had stamped on my memory this enchanting waterview, I followed my guides, turning aside as I went up to glance at the dark log-fragments of the old military road laid through the wilderness, from the Mohawk valley to the St. Lawrence, in the war of 1812.

Blotting the grey engravings on the surface, up Bog River we swiftly glided.

The grey light gave place to the soft glow preceding the sunrise. Rosy clouds smiled overhead, and in the east the umber of a long cloud burned into tawny gold.

Suddenly a high pine brightened and stood transfigured.

Even so, thought I, is woman glorified by the divine fancy of poets. She owes the recognition of her charms to those children of the passionate heart and glowing brain. They kindle the aureole that crowns her brow.

"Apollo was pitching his darts"

thick and fast into the trees, which flashed gold at every blow, as we reached the fork of the river. Up the right, or westerly branch (as before noted), lay our path with an immediate carry.

I asked Harvey whither led the other branch.

"To Little Tupper's Lake, six miles," answered the old woodman, as he and Phin prepared to shoulder the boat with its luggage, "and the nicest lookin' lake, next to Big Tupper's, and al'ys exceptin' the Upper S'nac, that there is about here. There's three carries two miles in all, to git there."

"Where then do you go?"

"A carry of about thirty rod 'll bring ye from there inter Rock Pond, about two miles long. Then a carry of two miles takes ye inter Bottle Pond, one mile long. A carry then of about sixty rods brings ye inter Carey Pond, half a mile long. Then a carry of eighty rod 'll take ye to Sutton Pond, a mile long. Then a carry of half a mile brings ye to Little Forked Lake, two or three miles long. You then run up inter Big Forked Lake, eight miles long, and then a carry of half a mile brings ye inter Racket Lake, and crossing it you git by a carry of a mile inter the Eight Lakes, and down them inter the middle branch o' Moose River, clearn down inter John Brown's Tract. Or you kin turn down Big Forked Lake inter Long Lake, and so inter the Racket River and come to this very spot agin, and, except at Racket Falls, and them below, not stir out of yer boat, makin' a rael twist-round."

A mile's tramp brought us again to the stream, and after another mile we reached the third carry a score of rods across. An equal number on the stream bore us to "Winding Falls," forcing us to the fourth carry. The fifth lay a half mile farther, and after three more portages respectively of forty, thirty, and eighty rods, we entered a pond.

"The Lower Pond," said Harvey, "and after a good dry carry on t'other side, and the last one too, we hev four more ponds to cross and we're at Mud Lake."

Crossing, we struck the carry, which was about fifty rods over, and entered the river again, ascending it half a mile to a small winding lily-pad pond. Three miles more of river brought us to the third pond of the same size as the first or "Lower," with high banks, and crossing it the river again received us.

All along we had found the same scenery; close ranks of firs and cedars on either side, throwing their sharpened shadows across so that we seemed floating over their transverse tops; and green openings, with a rear wall of forest. The trees above named, however, bristling in masses, or scattered in the parks, formed the prevailing feature of this grim and sluggish, or dashing and foaming river, yielding it its lonely and funereal aspect. In every direction, also, dead pines and hemlocks thrust up their pallid, rough raggedness, dripping with grey moss, and frequently clutching in their raised talons the huge nest of the fish-hawk.

Suddenly around one of the bends, an Indian in his canoe came rapidly towards us. He was on his knees paddling in the middle of his craft, which was of birch bark, expanded at the sides, with ends sharp and rising like a crescent.

"Why, here's old Leo, agin!" exclaimed Harvey. "Why Leo, is that you? Where on airth you come from, eh?"

"Conutie, dat ees, up dere, over dere—Ookostah Conutie, vat you call eet—Ingleese?" said the Indian, ceasing to paddle, and allowing his bubble to float up.

"Cost her, what!" asked Harvey.

"Taun—nah—nah! Ookostah Conutie, vere nindunhe—dat ees—vere moose go, down dere, up dere, over dere—fool of—uh—uh—what dis!" dipping at a lily-pad, but missing it, and bringing his paddle up dripping.

"Water!" said Harvey.

"Nah, nah!" shaking his head impatiently, "nah, nah, oh hang, nah!"

"I don't know no other name but water for't. Consarn his old picter!"

"Nah, nah—vater not a beet—dis, dis," tearing up a lily-leaf this time with his paddle.

"Oh, you mean lily-pad! Why couldn't ye say so at onst! Plague take the old feller! Forty l'yers couldn't understand him. Well, what of the lily-pads? You've been up in 'm, eh!"

"Yese, yese, up dere—over dere, vere moose go."

"You mean Mud Lake, I guess."

"Nyuh! yese, yese! Muddee Lake, oh yese! No see no moose. Up dere squaut (holding up one finger after another), ticknee, shagh"——

"Sha, sure enough! What do you mean, Leo?"

"Mean, mean, what dat?"

"How many days were ye up there?"

"Squaut, ticknee"——

"Don't understand, Leo!"

"No onderstand! what fur no understand?"

"'Case I don't," sharply, "what d'ye mean by squat?"

"So mannee," holding up a finger.

"So many, what?"

"So mannee what!—nah—nah—nah—so mannee day—squaut, ticknee, shagh day" (raising three fingers).

"Oh, three days!"

"Yese, yese, tree day—oh hang!"

"What shoot there?"

"Vat shoot dere? Shoot naagah; dat ees, vat you call eet?—o-h yese, plantee, plantee!"

"Nagur, nagur! nigger, you mean. I shouldn't s'pose you'd a shot niggers there. There aint none, nur white people nuther, fur that matter."

"Neeger, neeger! vat dat?"

"Why niggers, black niggers! people what's black! Bless the Injin, can't he onderstand nothin'?"

"Neegers—black—dat ees jenshtau—nah, nah, n-a-h—oh hang!"

"Well, what is't then?"

"Go so, go so!" motioning with arms and body, as if bounding along. "Head so," pointing his hands either side.

"O-o-o-h! you mean deer."

"Oh hang, yese—deer, deer—oh yese, plantee, plantee!" throwing off a blanket, and showing a large pile of dried venison.

"Good, Leo, you've done well. But d'ye raally say you didn't see no moose?"

"Moose! oh hang! nah, nah, vat you tink; you git moose! nah, nah!" shaking his head violently, "you, nah, git moose nudder. I git nah moose, you git nah moose—oh hang, nah, nah!"

"Well, I dunno as we shell. We'll try hard for't, though. But we're summat in a hurry, so good bye, Leo!"

"Goo bye!" and off the canoe shot to the Indian's quick dexterous paddle, and in a moment he was hidden behind a turn.

"Ahead is the last pond," said Harvey, "and then comes the river agin, and the confoundedest, crookedest consarn 'tis too, that I've seen in these woods, not even leavin' out Folingsby's Brook, and Little Wolf Brook, and to go twistin' through the last makes the boat wriggle like an eel!"

We landed at the entrance of the pond for a lunch. In a few moments my guides had lighted a fire, over which the trout we had taken at the falls were soon hissing, impaled on the forked sticks.

The sky, notwithstanding the brightness of the morning, was now overcast, and threatening rain.

Against this lowering background rose, here and there, a tall withered pine above the general foliage, in one of which was an eagle's nest, like a Doric column with its capital.

We had just finished our meal, and Harvey was flowing out in a story about "Wrastlin' Will, who lived nigh the Ausable Forks," when suddenly he stopped.

"Look there, Mr. Smith," said he, "aint that moosey lookin'?"

I glanced around, but saw nothing.

"Here, Mr. Smith," turning aside a leaf of brake. There, was a track stamped in the black ooze of the bank, much larger and more rounded than a deer's, nevertheless long and somewhat pointed.

"Is that a moose-track, Harvey?"

"'Taint nothin' else, and not an hour old, nuther," answered he.

"I'm in fur that moose," said Phin, starting from a log where he had been seated with his rifle between his knees, and moving rapidly toward a thicket. "That's the dod blamedst big moose what's a goin', and I'm after 'im enny way."

"Stop, Phin," said his father, "the moose aint behind that aire bush, no how. Don't you see the track's p'inted torts the water. See there where he's fed," glancing towards the lily-pads, all torn and tilted, near the margin. "Let's be goin' though; moose don't stay long in one place, and we may git a shot afore we know't."

Closely examining the wooded hills, we crossed the pond, and once more entered the river.

It was, indeed, a watery cork-screw, narrow, with broad, grassy intervals.

We had wound through about two miles, and Harvey was again in the midst of a story about a "black fox he'd shot at Loon Lake onst," when he suddenly exclaimed, "Hark!" at the same time stopping his paddle and raising his hand, while Phin rested on his oars, and erected his head like a listening hound.

After a silence of several moments, I was about to inquire what was the matter, when there came a distant bellow, sharp, ringing, and, notwithstanding the distance, startling.

"It's from Mud Lake, sarten," said Harvey, dipping his paddle deep, while Phin did the same with his oars. "That's moose all over, and a rael bull-moose, too. Hooray! won't we hev some fun bimeby! and it's

"'Too-rool-loo-rool, loo-rool-loddy!'

Let's make the Bluebird sing through the water, Phin. I raally feel as ef we're goin' to hev a moose's lip fur supper to-night—hey, Mr. Smith?"

I answered cheerfully, and then resigned myself to my thoughts. There was something solemn and exciting in thus winding through the innermost heart of this immense wilderness, with the stern voice of the rare animal in whose search we had come still ringing in my ears. The wild, dark stream, the awful solitude—all rendered the scene deeply inthralling.

Proceeding some distance, we now reached a pavement of lily-pads, extending from bank to bank. Pushing through these, a gloomy sheet of water at length spread before us.

"Mud Lake," said Harvey, in a low voice. "Don't make no noise! Praps a moose may be right agin us—who knows!"

I didn't, and kept perfectly quiet, gazing at the scene.

The sheet appeared to be about two miles long, by a mile in width, with low shores of broad marsh, closed in by a thick barrier of firs and spruces. At the left, as we entered, was a high point or bluff, forming a small bay.

Lily-pads covered the lake, except toward the head, where was a space of dark water.

Over the whole brooded an air of utter loneliness, which, aided by the dull, heavy sky, rested with a depressing weight upon my spirits.

"'Tis a lonesome kind o' place, as I telled ye!" said Harvey, in a whisper, ceasing to paddle, as did Phin to row, "that is, as fur as menkind goes, but not deer," pointing to where the broad margin was cut up by the sharp, delicate feet of these creatures. "And yes, by golly, see there! there's a dozen tracks or more of moose. It's goin' to be a good night for floatin'. But come, Phin, make a smudge while I git out some sticks fur a fire, or Mr. Smith 'll be eat up sun with the flies; and after that we'll bush up a shanty, fur it may rain in the night."

The smudge was indeed grateful, for every inch of my face and hands seemed to hold a musquito and a midge added. But I comforted myself philosophically with the reflection, while I was thus being set on fire by the infernal insects, that the terrible black fly, which draws blood with every sting, was not also marauding. The golden days of June are dimmed by his horrors, but the sun of mid-July gives him his general quietus, although he does not entirely disappear until the other little winged pests of the forest vanish.

"I've met with 'm," said Harvey, in answer to my question, "all 'long till cold weather, with the other flies."

"Where on earth do they come from, Harvey?" I asked, pantomiming wildly in the air.

"The black flies hatches in rapids and swift water, and also in yaller lily blossoms; the mitchets in fir and spruce trees, and the musquiters in swamps. But the Old Sanko unly knows what the critters hatch at all fur;" and Harvey commenced, with Phin, making the camp.

I sat on an old stump and watched the two. A few hacks of Harvey's axe brought down a maple, from which he detached the limbs. He then divided the trunk into suitable logs, splitting them for the camp-fire, which, with the aid of dry sticks strewed around, was soon merrily blazing. Meanwhile, Phin had levelled a small hemlock, and stripped its branches, from which he cut with his wood-knife the fringes for our beds. While one then planted in front of a smooth-faced rock two crotched poles, with a cross-stick, the other girdled a couple of spruces, and by inserting his axe, stripped lengths of the bark for the sides and roof. In a brief time the shanty was completed.

"Qui-r-r-r-r-r!" said Harvey, lighting his pipe by the camp-fire, after he and Phin had removed the blankets and other needful articles from the boat to the shanty, and seating himself to prepare the jack, "how them tree-toads squawk! They're queer things, Mr. Smith. You can't tell, half the time, where the noise they make comes from. You may be lookin' right at the critters, that is, ef you look sharp, fur it's unpos'ble a'most to see 'm; and there's another thing; they look jest like a big wart on a limb, or a spot o' moss or a knob on the bark, as much as one wild pigeon's like another. But as I was sayin', ef so be you look right at 'm, the squirkin' they make don't seem to come from them, but some other place."

The air rang with the hollow notes the little minstrels piped, while the deep gulp, or rather smothered roar, of a bull-frog now and then sounded, which seemed to jar the log it came from.

All was now ready for our night-hunt after the moose hoped for, notwithstanding honest Leo's disappointment, and we embarked.

The jack, in the intense, quiet darkness, shed a bright light on all objects within its range.

Phin managed the paddle with the same noiseless skill I had so often admired, while Harvey sat under the jack, in an attitude of intense watchfulness, with his double-barrelled rifle on his knees. Watch, to prevent mistakes, had been chained to a post of the shanty.

On the little Bluebird stole, close to the shore.

Once or twice Harvey lifted a warning hand, or motioned, but, after a moment's gazing, or bend of his ear aside, he relapsed again into his passive attitude.

"I'll tell ye what 'tis, Mr. Smith!" at last he said, but in a low whisper, "old Leo I bleeve has skeered all the moose off, and deer too. We've bin 'most half round the lake, and here's the clear part o' the water, and nothin' seen or heerd. But we may hev luck yet, after gittin' past this bank. A leetle clusser to the edge, Phin!"

We passed through the clear space, struck the pads again, and went rustling on.

Opposite, I saw the camp-fire like a red speck on the blackness, but it was soon lost.

We had now reached the inner side of the point or bluff, near our starting point. Suddenly we heard a paddling in the water. Harvey thrust his head forward; a quick deep snort sounded; he motioned to the right, then to the left, the boat obeying closely; then came the click of the gunlocks.

At the same time I saw two large orbs of pallid flame, and the darkness gathered around them into a mass which rose higher and higher, and loomed nearer, till a huge black hulk stood before the jack, and hanging over it a large head, with blazing eyeballs, surmounted by what appeared to be an enormous half circle.

Harvey gave a quick backward gesture, the boat drew to the rear about a rod, and then two sharp reports rang, so close together as to be nearly blended. A violent splashing followed, with several terrific snorts, and thick, heavy blows of breath, and I heard Harvey exclaim,

"He's got it, he's down! that's a dead moose! up with the boat, Phin," whipping out his wood-knife, "but slow, slow; they're an awful critter if they're unly wounded. I rather hev an idee, though, he's got enough on't."

The boat glided cautiously up, the mass did not stir, and Harvey, bending low, made a quick motion with his knife.

"Dead as a smoked trout," said Harvey, with an exultant laugh, "and his throat cut to boot. Now fur gittin' 'im round the p'int to the shanty. He's a big critter, and aint to be handled like a mushrat, but I guess we kin with hard strainin'. This is great luck, Mr. Smith! It'll be hang with old Leo all the time when he hears on't.

"We wont dress 'im till mornin', Phin," continued he, as we landed the carcass, "and as this luck's rael old hunderd s'posen we take a drink all round. What d'ye say, Mr. Smith? Come, Watch, stop yer yelpin' and whinin'. You seem to be mighty farse to git at a dead moose, pup, but be still, or I'll make yer yell fur suthin', and it's

'Lighted with canneon the wilderness blazed.'

My 'specks to ye, Mr. Smith!"

The savage lake; the bark shanty; the blazing camp-fire, the black forest, all presented an impressive picture. Heightening it was the mass near me; that of an animal uncommon even in this wild region, its existence scarce believed in by the denizens of our cities, and fast disappearing from these dark haunts, to live but in the traditions of the hunter's fireside. My two guides also had their place in my solitary musing. Seated in careless attitudes by the camp-fire, the flame tinging their bronzed features and rude garb, they represented a class indigenous to the region. With eye, ear, every sense sharpened to intensity, full of forest resources, self-reliant and brave, they seemed a portion of the forest, like the deer and the panther.

Again I asked myself if man is happier for all his culture and refinement! living a life whose air is thick with human sighs, and whose path is thronged with weary footsteps. And yet in all this misery, may there not be design? May not the All-Wise Father be leading man through purifying trial to the height predestined ere the fall? Progression is His law. The bud becomes a flower, the chrysalis a butterfly, "this mortal puts on immortality." I cling to the hope that humanity, with all its burden of woe, is moving in the right direction; falling back here, but advancing there; the long line reeling and plunging along but onward, till in the future ages it may struggle up into the unclouded sunlight of Truth. Oh blessed Millennium! dream and hope of Prophet and Apostle! when will your splendors dawn! when will the earthly happiness man sighs and toils for, descend upon the earth!

The falling asunder of a log in the camp-fire woke me from my reverie. The wind had risen and was moaning in the forest like the wail of a broken heart, and rain was beginning to fall like tears. I retreated into the shanty, whither my guides had preceded me, and in listening to the increasing wind which soon roared through the forest, like the rumble of distant breakers, I fell asleep.

CHAPTER XX.

Back to Tupper's Lake.—Night Sail down the Lake.—The Echo.—Deserted Camp.—Message, woods fashion.—Tupper's Lake left.—Down the Racket. Indian Camp.—The Water-lily.—Legend of its Origin.—The Mink.—News of the Party.—The Eagle-nest.—Through Racket Pond.—The Island.—The Irish Clearing.—Captain Peter's Rocks.—Camp at Setting-Pole Rapids.

THE morning arose clear and inspiriting. The guides had dressed and quartered the moose, and at the early breakfast taken on the inner sheet of fresh, fragrant spruce bark, I first tasted that wildwood, delicate luxury, a moose's lip.

We then embarked upon our return course; I taking a farewell glance at Mud Lake, as it hid its sombre loneliness from the radiance of the morning, like sorrow from the gladness of the world. At sunset we hailed once more the plunging waters of Bog River Falls.

We angled in the upper pool and in the tossing waters at the foot of the cascade, with the soft, pleasant light from the west sprinkled over the scene; and in a brief half-hour we caught sufficient trout for our supper and breakfast at Camp Cedar. Harvey and Phin then stretched themselves on the bank at the lowest plunge (for their labor on the carries with the moose and boat both had been severe), while I explored the beautiful falls—the several channels braiding the rocks as they dashed to the basin above me and then poured in a rich, divided mass of white into the lake; the rocky nooks at the side where the wild-flower dipped its chalice and the bush laved its leaves; the spray's silver; the dark pools where the dashing waters paused suddenly, gathering into stagnant quiet the floating plants and foam-bells.

We launched upon the lake once more, pulling toward our shanty of the spring. The twilight stole around us as we enjoyed our supper at the open front of our bark camp, inhaling the spicy odors of the woods and watching the melting colors of the water.

We were interrupted by a furious yelping which burst from the side of the shanty, and in a moment more, was ringing in the woods arousing a thousand echoes.

"Watch, by golly!" exclaimed Harvey, and he rushed with Phin around the corner of the shanty.

"Sure enough," said the former, reappearing, with a collar and chain, "Watch is off. He's seen a deer, I 'spose, and's after 'im."

"I chained 'im to a stump, round there," chimed in Phin, "and let the collar loose a leetle."

"And he's slipped it off," said Harvey. "I'm dreffle sorry. He's as valy'ble to me as the ball o' my thumb. Watch! Watch!"

The echo alone came back from the woods.

"It's no go," said Harvey. "But I guess we'd better wait a leetle, and then ef he don't turn up, we'll move torts camp, and mebbee he'll come in the mornin'."

The dusk gathered on the landscape, and the barred owl skimmed the bushes in his velvet flight, giving now and then his strange laugh.

The umber hues settled at length into the blacks of the forest and the clear darks of the slumbering lake. Mount Morris loomed up with an occasional flit of summer lightning around his brow; the Hawk's Nest bore a jewel in its hollow, and the Panther seemed watching with a starry eye over the raven woods of the wild river we had so lately tracked.

After vainly waiting an hour for the return of Watch, we embarked for Camp Cedar.

A divine quiet tranced the fragrant night. The measured dip of oar and paddle, and the low ripple at the bow, alone disturbed the silence. A starry realm was glittering on the water. Islands lay before us, each one mass of black; but as we glided by, the trees would part, letting out the stars. Crawling motions were perceptible along and beneath the banks, doubtless of the loon or mink, skulking into coverts.

Suddenly Harvey lifted his voice in a cry of "Watch!" The effect was magical. An echo started up. Far away it sped in dulcet boundings, and stopped. Again it sprang —away, away — far, far, far—and was lost. Again he shouted. Again the bell-like echo—pausing, sounding, stopping, sounding—on, on, fainter, fainter, fainter—seeming to pierce illimitable depths; waxing more ethereal, more transparent, till it melted so deliciously, the tingling ear could scarcely tell the delicate sound had ceased.

Two hours passed on, the shores and islands loosening from their massed blackness as we neared them, with the same ethereal melting of the magical echo waked by the frequent shout of Harvey.

We had now reached the farther end of the east Brother Island, when Harvey exclaimed,

"I don't see no signs of the camp. There aint a spark, o' fire! I guess they've pulled up stakes!"

Sure enough, no tent glimmered from the gloom, and the sounds of nature, generally hushed in the close presence of man, were in full career. Among them was an occasional chest-note rolled out by a wakeful frog; the silvery chirp of the cricket sounded about the space, and a fir seemed tolling a little bell in its dark steeple.

"That's the grey owl, I telled ye about on the Racket, makin' the noise in the fir there," said Harvey as we struck the shore. "They're all gone sure," continued he, stepping out and hauling the bow up the margin. "Here Phin, light the jack, and hand me some o' them pine knots from the box, and we'll hev a fire a-burnin', that'll make this dark hole laugh."

Kindling the knots and the jack from his matches, Phin

planted the first among the stumps and logs around, and then threw the jack's half-circle of light upon a charred log, which told where had been the camp fire. Soon another fire blazed there, pouring the dark scene full of ruddy, merry light.

Immediately a stick, bearing in its split head a piece of silver birch bark, and inserted in an old log, sprang to sight. On the bark were pencil marks (the most villanous scratches imaginable, the words sprawling into each other as if for a general fight), which ran thus, "gwontewsetnpolraped."

"What in the name of common sense is this rigmarole, Harvey?" said I, after trying it upside down, backwards, and all ways at once.

"I thought they'd go there," said Harvey, taking his pipe from his mouth, and glancing at the scrawl. "It's jest as I consated."

"Go where?" enquired I.

"Why, the bark tells ye! to Settin' Pole Rapids."

"Oh!" said I. "Well, we'd better join them in the morning!"

"Sarten," returned Harvey. "'Twont take more 'n two or three hours. They're unly a mile below Racket Pond, and that's scurce three miles from here. But what say yer, Mr. Smith, to a moose-steak afore turnin' in?"

"It wouldn't be amiss. But who is the writer of this, Harvey?"

"I kinder consate it's Mart's handwrite. He's the best at readin' and writin', and all that kind o' trash, of all the guides round. But come, Phin, let's hev supper."

The odors of broiling meats soon vanquished the balsamic night-scents of the wilderness. After a pleasant meal by the genial blaze of the camp-fire, which had long since chased away the chill of the night, we wrapped ourselves in our blankets and sought repose on the boughs left by the party, with the gabble of a couple of loons, answered by the scornful hoots of half-a-dozen owls echoing in our ears.

Beautiful and bright dawned the day, suffusing the lake and forest with a cheery beauty.

The morning sunlight has a jocund splendor, not shared by the sunset. The former, fresh from heaven, seems gladdened in obeying the behest of the Creator, while a sadness mingles in the latter's brightness, as though it grieved over what it had witnessed in its course; a sadness that would darken all its lustre, were it not for joy that its bidden ministry for the time was ended, and it was leaving, if but for a season, a world it had illumed only to behold follies, calamities and crimes.

As I left the shanty, I found Harvey and Phin roaming about the deserted camp.

"There's an orful sight o' used-up bottles round here," said the former; "all hands must a bin more dry than common, the last two or three days. There's enough to set up a small chany shop. Goll, but here's a bottle filled with" (uncorking and tasting) "rum, by golly! and rael old hunderd, too. Well now, this doos beat me, how they could a left this 'ere. Wa-a-l! there's no 'countin' for ennything in this world. Here's luck, Mr. Smith. Oh, but aint this fust best!" glueing his lips to the bottle again, and withdrawing it with a sigh. "Here, Phin, try some!, a leetle, though—a leetle! it'll bite young folks!"

We lingered until noon, and then bade adieu to Camp Cedar. We crossed to the outlet, the whole water-scene etherealized in the dreamy haze of the noontide. We turned into the narrow channel, and the lovely lake of the island-pathways was hidden from our view.

With the Indian Park at our left, we entered the basin into which the river broadens in its downward course. We had proceeded some little distance, when clearing a bend, we found ourselves in a scene of excitement. A couple of bark canoes, in each of which was an Indian, were darting forward a little in advance of us, while twenty or thirty rods ahead was a deer swimming gallantly down the river.

The sight fired Harvey and Phin.

Down sped all three of the boats in line, the Indians gabbling their gutturals, their wild faces gleaming with ardour.

On went the deer, turning toward a point at the right.

"Row, row, row, Phin!" exclaimed Harvey, bending low to his paddle, "he's 'most to the shallers, and we must be nigher than this, or he's off."

As he spoke, the deer struck the shallows and bounded on in a shower of foam.

Harvey sprang to his feet.

"A leetle nigher!" exclaimed he, twitching up one leg after the other, "a leetle—a leetle!" presenting his piece; but as he did so, one of the Indians fired; and the next moment the deer vaulted upon the bank and vanished into the forest.

"Well," said Harvey, lowering his piece, "I don't bear no malice agin that buck; he fit like a man for his life. But, goll, ef here aint old Leo agin!"

"Yese, yese," said one of the Indians; "how do, how do?"

"Fust best, fur an old man," returned Harvey; "how is't, yourself?"

"Good, good, where nindunhe—aha!"

"Here!" uncovering the quarters from the blanket. "Eh! aigh! uh, uh! oh hang! where git? uh, uh! up dere, down dere, over dere—eh?"

"Sarten!"

"Oh hang! Onyarhe—he go up de—uh, uh—de—Ahonogeh Keech-honde—dat ees de"—

"Bog River, I spose you mean?"

"Yese, yese! Boog Rivaire—up dere—squaut"—

"Oh, ef you're a goin' to squat agin, I'm off!"

"Ticknee"—

"Goin' to camp, Leo?"

"Shagh day"—

"What a derned old fool"—

"Yese, yese," said Leo, smiling and bowing, as Harvey, in the energy of his vexation, motioned toward him. "Yese, Onyarhe fool of uh, uh, o-kah" (placing his finger on his eye), "fool of, uh, uh, ooh-tah" (touching his ear), "fool of, uh, uh, owyngawshaw" (placing his hand on his heart), "g-r-e-a-t beeg Achshanuane" (lifting his form), "de chief de Senekee!"

"Well, Leo, we go to wigwam now," said Harvey.

"Oh yese — nindunhe — uh, hah! — you git moose! Onyarhe beeg chief! he no git no moose up dere"—

"Come 'long, Leo!"

"Oh yese, you git moose. O-h hang! yese!"

In a little cove to the left, canoes were moored, and thither the Indians led the way. As we struck the bank, I saw through the open trees a long tent or shanty on the brow of the ridge. Two of the canoes were of birch-bark, beautifully made, sewed with deer's sinews, and shaped in a crescent, with pointed tips, swelling gradually to the waist or middle. They were without seats, and of a rich yellow hue. Moose hair was braided into their sides, with bright beads and bits of red and purple cloth. The paddles were smooth; and altogether the canoes seemed admirably fitted for the streams and lakes of the wilderness.

The two other craft were mere dug-outs, birch logs, hollowed, and as Harvey expressed it, "consid'ble tottlish."

A peculiar jack for night-hunting leaned against a tree. It was of tin, shaped like a little cask, with the handle in the middle, and a leather blind, so as either to cover the light, or, by an aperture the size of a buckshot, to diminish it to a speck.

A slight track led me up the ridge to the wigwam. It was merely of blankets over a skeleton of poles, and stood in a small space cut from the forest, with large peeled logs before the entrance, evidently the out-door settees.

Two Indian women, one a crone, and the other a large-framed girl of twenty, were in the shanty, seated on their knees, embroidering a pair of deerskin moccasins.

An Indian lad of sixteen was on one of the logs fastening hooks to fish-lines.

They were a family of the St. Regis Tribe, living by the Lake of the Two Mountains, an expansion of the Ottawa River in Canada. Every summer, for the last year or two, they had ascended the Racket, and while the men foraged the waters and forests for trout and venison, the women tanned deerskins and worked them into purses and moccasins.

The girl, I found, was the wife of the Indian I had seen among the lumber people at Cold River.

Although Leo had joined the Tribe of the Two Mountains, he was in fact a Seneca.

"Talk Iroquois?" said the girl to me, after I had bought a pair of moccasins. "St. Regis?"

I shook my head.

"Senekee?"

Again a negative shake.

In a low, musical voice, she then began: "Hah-wen-ne-yo (her broken English I discard) loved His children the Iroquois. They lived scattered, till To-gan-a-we-ta joined them in the League, making the branches one tree. Then they grew mighty. Their tomahawks turned red among the snowbanks of the Hurons and the flowers of the Cherokees. One end of their Long House looked upon the great River, where tumbles the Thunder-Water, the other on the stream that crawls from Ta-ha-wus to roll into the Salt Lake that has no shore. How strong and happy they were! But two large birds with white wings came—one up the stream of Ta-ha-wus, the other up the River of the Thunder-Water. They bore the white man. Where are the Iroquois now?" in a wailing accent, clasping her hands and bowing her head in an attitude of intense grief.

"Gone!" here broke in the crone. "Ho-de-no-sonne gone! white man here—red man no here no more!"

"Well, Mr. Smith, we'd better be agoin', hadn't we?" said Harvey, coming up with Leo and the other Indian. "I've bin lookin' at a wolf's paw that the critter 'ad gnawed off after he'd got inter Leo's trap out there. What a farse critter a wolf is, after all! though I don't mind 'm in the woods a bit more'n a dog. But good-bye, Leo, and all the rest on ye!"

"Goo-bye, goo-bye," returned Leo. "You kill moose—me no kill no moose"——

"Good-bye, good-bye!"

"Up dere, over dere—Boog Rivaire! oh hang! goo-bye! hang!"

"I'd ruther talk to a beaver, enny day, than old Leo," said Harvey, after we were afloat again. "He raally don't 'pear to onderstand nothin'."

We wound along the banks, the water green with the floss silk of the rich, swaying eel-grass which the boat drew into the most graceful and plume-like shapes.

"The deer's very fond of the roots of that aire grass," said Harvey, "as much a'most as the yaller lily-stems. The white lily they never take to, when they kin git the other. The stem's tougher. They're very fond too, in the spring, of the lily-pots."

"Lily-pots?"

"Yes. They're a plant that grows on the bottom of the water, the fust thing in spring. They look a good deal like a collyflower."

The white and yellow water-lilies also grow from an immense, rough stem, several feet in length, embedded in the bottom. This throws out fibres which, lengthening, lets up the bud to blossom on the surface.

May crowns the yellow lily with her gold diadem, but the white receives her perfumed chalice from the hands of more beautiful June. As before observed, the chalice shuts at sunset to re-open at the morn.

The white lily delights in the empire of the ponds and lakes, as if her loveliness demanded a broad domain, wherein to smile upon island and headland, ripple of breeze, wake of loon and shadow of eagle; but the sister finds more congenial reign in the narrow kingdom of stream and river.

The following is a St. Regis legend concerning the origin of the lily, yellow and white.

"The eagle is screaming, hark! Soaring and screaming on high! See! the red war-path is bright! See! the great warrior comes! He, the Brave of his people, Wa-yo-tah the Chief of the Saranacs! He The Blazing Sun. He comes from the trembling Ta-ha-wi—kooh! the quaking Ta-ha-wi. The Blazing Sun has changed them to women! Hooh, hooh, The Blazing Sun! Wa-yo-tah, the Chief of his Tribe! Wa-yo-tah, The Blazing Sun!"

Such were the sounds that pealed from the Isle of the Eagle in the Lake of the Clustered Stars. Beautiful Lake of islands, that are strewed on its bosom of crystal as spots on the back of the loon!

Wa-yo-tah, Chief of the Lower Saranacs, has come from the war-path laden with scalps of the wild Ta-ha-wi—the foes of his people and race. Therefore the song goes up in the sunset from a hundred voices; from the boy whose plume is the red rose of the dingle to the sire on whose head fourscore winters have frozen. And the matrons and maidens of the Tribe, they, too, raise the song.

And as all sing, all dance the dance of victory. The warriors circle the war-post, whirling their hatchets and knives that glance round their forms as lightnings glance round the trees. And the women in their ring apart, sing their sweet-voiced songs and toss their arms in triumph.

But who is that pale and silent maiden hovering near the ring of the women? Pale is she as the first little flower that Spring opens with her timid touch, save when the red tints glance across her face, as sunset glances on rippling waters.

Now her eyes flash in triumph and now their sparkle is quenched in tears. Who is this lovely maid of the Saranacs? Why does she stand apart, changeful in her mood as the month of the dawning blossoms—the month of the sun and rain? Ah, O-see-tah, sweet Bird of the Tribe! she loves and she suffers! She loves the Chief of her people, Wa-yo-tah The Blazing Sun. She loves and she suffers. Hah-wen-ne-yo has given a mate to the lodge of the Sun; not O-see-tah the Bird; but To-seen-do the Morning. Still, Wa-yo-tah is young and has seen that O-see-tah loves him, and his own heart is wild with love for O-see-tah. And therefore has he whispered in her ear, "Let the beautiful Bird of the Saranacs warble to The Sun her melody of love!" And she has answered, "Go! Wa-yo-tah does not well! Hah-wen-ne-yo has said, 'Let the glance of The Sun shine only on the cheek of The Morning!' Go, leave the Bird of the Saranacs to pour her note in loneliness!"

But Wa-yo-tah has despaired not; he has trusted that the music of The Bird might still be waked to the kindling glance of The Sun. And now in this hour of his triumph, he has watched her as she smiled and wept, blushed and grew pale, to his praises from the Tribe.

And at last the sorrowful maid, she, the lonely O-see-tah—pure as the fountain under the rock—has unbound her fleet canoe and fled through the starry darkness to an island of the lake—fled to moan her sorrow to the water and the wind.

Wa-yo-tah has watched her and followed. "Bird of the Saranacs, let thy warble cheer the heart of Wa-yo-tah. Behold, he has come from the trail of the proud Ta-ha-wi, and his belt is heavy with the scalps of the foe! 'Hooh, the Brave of his people! Hooh, The Blazing Sun!' These are the songs that pealed in the ear of O-see-tah and Wa-yo-tah, but all would Wa-yo-tah give for one note of love from the bright Bird of his Tribe."

"Away! Sun of the Saranacs! Shall the Blaze that scorched the fierce Ta-ha-wi burn the little Bird that has piped to her harm to the Fiery Light? Away! O-see-tah's heart is weak, but her ear shall not listen to the words of Wa-yo-tah!"

"O-see-tah must listen!"

"Away!"

"The Bird must fold her wing to the warmth of the loving Sun!"

"Away!"

"O-see-tah shall listen to the Chief of her people!"

He darted forward and she bounded away. Away her light form flew, to a rock overhanging the lake. She stood upon the edge and waved him back.

But he came onward.

She balanced on the edge and waved him back.

But he came onward.

She waved her arms upward to Hah-wen-ne-yo and sprang. Wa-yo-tah darted to the brink and sprang also. He rose—the water was black in a crossing cloud; the black water alone met his yearning sight. "O-see-tah! O-see-tah!" as with maddened strength he cleaved the wave, "where art thou? Bird of the Saranacs! ah, beautiful Bird of my Tribe, speak! let Wa-yo-tah rescue thee and no more will he molest thee with his love. O-see-tah! O-see-tah!" but no voice answered.

And the East opened her eye over the Lake of the Clustered Stars, but where was the Bird of the Saranacs? "Where is my little Bird, the little sad warbler of my lodge?" asked the old father—a Brave of many battles. "Oh, where is my Bird, my Bird?" moaned the mother—she the most honored of all the matrons that bore the totem of the Panther. "Where is O-see-tah?" asked the young warriors, and "Alas, where is O-see-tah?" asked the blooming maidens.

The Chief heard, and as he heard, his head sank lower and lower. The day passed and the night, and again the East opened her brightness, and his head drooped lower still, and his step was slow, for his heart was heavy. And the sorrowful To-scen-do told her sire that Wa-yo-tah moaned in his sleep like the pine in the low breeze of the evening.

Well might Wa-yo-tah moan, and name himself Ne-so. Truly had the Sun become the Night; Night with the wail of the whippoorwill, instead of the Sun with the scream of the eagle. Night with eternal wail; wail for the love that

Hah-wen-ne-yo frowned on; wail for the love that should have been all To-scen-do's; wail for the love that had destroyed The Bird; wail, wail for the fate of the beautiful Bird of the Saranacs!

And the Night sought in his sorrow the lonely lodge of the Great Medicine of the Tribe.

As noon gleamed on the village, a fisherman came with tidings of a strange sight. In a hidden cove of the Isle of Elms, was a robe of flowers on the breast of the water, some white as the feathers of winter and others yellow as the lake at sunset. The Tribe all hurried to the scene, and there indeed was the sheet of blossom.

And "See!" said the old Medicine, the pine ringed with a hundred winters, "there lives O-see-tah! the white her purity, the yellow her burning love! And see!" said he, after they had gazed again and again, on the beautiful blossoms, "holy in her purity, the love still sways her. She closes her bright heart in sorrow at the going of the sun, to open it in joy at his coming."

"And," continued the old Indian, the narrator, "Hah-wen-ne-yo, to mark between the love and the purity, placed a moon between the blossoming of the two, and made the broad lake cherish the purity, and the narrow stream the love."

We turned a thicket, and a light, brisk, sipping sound, or whistling chirp, came from the bank.

"There's a mink on shore there somewheres," said Harvey. "I see 'im! He's nosin' up suthin' fur dinner."

The little animal was bounding between the thickets with its head grazing the earth, like a hound's. It stopped a moment, and Harvey raised his rifle.

"Ah, it's gone!" exclaimed he, "yusp, yusp—'twill be out in a minute agin though."

"Let's see what it will do, Harvey!" Harvey nodded, and we glided behind a bush.

He repeated his chirp, and the mink reappeared, this time pricking its short ears and rearing its white-starred throat, apparently at some object. The next moment a frog, with a flying leap, plumped into the water, and the little shore-haunter vanished.

"Where do they have their burrow, Harvey?"

"They don't have none of their own, as a gin'ral thing. They're squatters like, in mushrat holes. They're a farse little critter. They'll take a mushrat by the throat in the water, for all he's the biggest, and kill 'im 'most as quick as a dog. But here's Racket Pond."

This pond, or Lough Neak (its Indian name is Tsi-kan-i-on-wa-res-ko-wa), has an average width of half a mile, and is three miles in length.

"'Sposin' we call at MacLaughlin's a moment," said Harvey, pointing at a large log hut which stood with outhouses on the north bank of the pond, "and hear what news there is."

As he spoke a succession of yelps burst from the direction pointed out, sounding as if in the insanity of canine joy.

"Why, that's Watch, sarten," said Harvey, "and here he comes."

Sure enough, the hound at seeing his master, had taken to the water, and whimpering, with his head up, was rapidly approaching. We pushed to meet him, and in a few minutes he was drawn into the boat by Harvey, shaking a shower of spray around him, and the next moment was thrusting his nose all over his master, whining, and twisting his lithe frame almost double.

"Poor dog, poor pup, good Watch! where has Watch bin, hey?" said Harvey, patting his head and smoothing back his ears, while Watch broke every moment out from his whine into a shrill bark of delight.

"You've got your dog, I see, Harve," said a man on the shore as the boat touched it.

"Where did you pick 'im up, Mac?" returned Harvey.

"B'low Settin' Pole Rapids. I see 'im swimmin' crost the river, from about the lay o' Gull Pond."

"I hev it. He left us last night at the head of Tupper's Lake, after a deer I'm sarten, and druv it inter Gull Pond. That's it. How is't, Mac, about the deer here? Plenty?"

"I see two yisterday at the Irish Clearin', and an almighty sight o' tracks jest opp'site Captain Peter's Rocks."

"Did ye see a party at the Rapids?"

"Oh yes. There's four on 'm with Cort, Mart, Will, and Corey, without reck'nin' little Jess."

"Hev they had enny luck?"

"Lots o' trout, and three deer."

"How long had they bin there?"

"About two days, I b'leeve. They're hevin' all sorts o' fun there."

"There's one feller there," said a rough-looking black-bearded woodman, who had joined us from the house, "a tall chap, wot seems determined on claimin' two of the three deer as his shots. And Cort, he backs 'im up. The three others, smart bright chaps they are too, do nothin' but laugh when the tall feller (I forgit what they called 'im, but I call 'im Legs, and dreffle long ones they are), goes on to explain matters, as he says. 'Why gen'l'ums,' he'll say, 'there's no mistake about it. How could I help kill 'm? I wasn't ten rods off from both on 'm.' And then they'll laugh agin. He's consid'ble techy, I've an idee, on the p'int o' killin' deer, though he seems etarnally runnin' the others on every other p'int. Oh, they're heving a high old time there."

"Well, we must be a goin'. We're on the way to jine this party. We b'long to 'm."

"So I onderstand," said the woodman. "Legs was a-shoutin' and a-preachin' about Smith (I b'leeve that was the name) gittin' up Bog River there, and never findin' his way out. 'Fur you see, gen'l'ums,' he'd say, 'ef there's a wrong way, Smith's al'ys sure to take it, and ef Harvey should lose sight on 'im a minute, he'd stray off, and ef he found his way out 't all, which I've no idee he would, he'd come out torts St. Lorrence; kind o' burrer out like a mole."

"Push off, Harvey," said I, "or we wont get down there to-day."

"Good bye!" said Harvey, with a chuckle, and, dipping his paddle while Phin, grinning, bent to his oars, we stretched out into the pond.

"In them rushes out there," remarked Harvey, after a little while, and dipping his head to the north, where a broad surface of those plants extended, "it's fust best for floatin', and 'long in Wolf Brook, that comes in out there. But look at the eagle's nest on that dead pine," pointing out the object on the same side of the bank. "You kin see the young 'un lookin' over the edge o' the nest for its daddy or mammy to come home, with suthin' to eat, I 'spose."

True; there was a small head pointing from the grey nest, and I fancied the gleam of the young tawny eyes, as the fierce dam swooped down with the partridge or rabbit for the expected feast.

We now glided along a shore (also on the north side), which presented that same soft and rural look, with its single trees, shrubbery-like bushes, and smooth, green-sward I had so often admired throughout the forest. At the left rose the top of Gull Pond Mountain, and the higher summit of Mount Morris; and all around, with the exception of MacLaughlin's uplands, and the beautiful park just noticed, swept as usual the wilderness.

We landed, for a moment, on a beautiful island full of elms, where, as Harvey said, "There might be suthin' of a chance o' seein' a deer," and where he pointed out a tree, in the fork of which "he'd time and agin sot hours watchin' fur deer on the shores and round;" and then, finding his "suthin' of a chance" nothing, we continued on our way.

The old guide also showed me the Irish Clearing, or the "Paddy's Choppin'," a steep clearing on the south bank, "made by a little stumpy Paddy who'd cleared the country;" adding, "there wa'n't no better place fur deer about."

In a mile or two more, the banks approached each other.

"Cap'n Peter's Rocks, and we're through the pond," said Harvey, glancing at several immense grey masses standing in the water and separating it into alleys. "Old Cap'n Peter was an Injin and used to hide his game there. Mitchell Sabatis, the Injin guide up in Newcomb, is his son."

A mile more of the stream was passed, and we came to a broad bend, the gleam of a fire breaking out from among the trees.

"There's the camp," said Harvey, "and a nice, high, dry spot they hev, too. It's at the head o' the rapids. Don't ye hear 'm rattle?"

We struck the bank at our right, where a beautiful cove rounded into the shore. Here we found the boats of our party moored to the logs, and drawn half-way into the wild grass. A light path wound up the bluff or headland, and, ascending, I found myself at the camp.

A large pine, with a hollow in its heart from decay and fire, was at my left; and flanking it, with a background of thicket parallel to the rapids below and with an open space before, stood the two tents. A large camp-fire blazed in front. A buck's head was looking from the hollowed pine on a pole, and the usual quarters of venison and piles of trout were hanging and lying around. Supper was now preparing. Cort was toasting slices of bread, fastened by wooden pins to a large maple block; Mart was cooking rows of trout, pinned in the same manner, one row over the other, with shreds of salt pork, to a concave flake of birch bark curled at the bottom to receive the drippings; and Will was giving the "ramrod toast" to cuts of venison, *i.e.* roasting them on sticks which he held before the fire. Corey was bending over the camp-kettle, ladling out smoking hot potatoes on a leaf of spruce bark. The table was at one side, with Little Jess arranging the pewter dishes upon it, while, seated on a log, were my three comrades.

Wandering sunset lights put their kindling touch upon

various points of this picture, chequering tents, comrades and guides; and showered into the forest so that a sprout, a mossy stone, a bit of cedar fringe, a tassel of tamarack, or the round of a hemlock stem glowed seemingly in golden fire.

"Hurrah!" exclaimed Bingham, standing up and striking an attitude. "Art thou a goblin damned!—sent to torment us before our time!—come, let me clutch thee"— mixing his quotations and gestures most energetically. "Gentlemen," taking an oratorical position, "behold a wonder! Smith has returned! Chance or Harvey Moody has favored him, not himself! He never would alone have returned to bless his friends. Why, I made up my mind to begin to-night to mourn the dead. Well, we're awful glad to see you, Smith! But where's your moose?"

"In the boat!" said I, after exchanging warm greetings with Ralph and Gaylor.

"Umph!" said Bingham, "as much as I am in Elysium, among the gods. How this world is given to—what shall I add, gentlemen?"

"Add, bragging about deer one never shoots," said Gaylor.

"Confound it!" returned Bingham in a heat, "I tell you, I've no more doubt I shot those deer·than—but here comes Harvey and Phin! Well, Harvey, is it a fact you've got a moose among ye?"

"It's a rael old hunderd truth, Mr. Bingham! you kin go down to the boat and look at the quarters!"

"Lord!" said Bingham, "what luck some folks have. Still, two deer are equal to one moose, eh, Harvey?"

"Why, yes; that is about, ef so be Mr. Bingham has shot two."

"If! if!" said Bingham. "Well, I'll say no more," waving his hand. "Cort, bring me my rifle, I want to examine it a moment."

Here Sport appeared around a thicket, trotting rapidly sidewise, steering by his perpendicular tail, while Drive cleared a bush with a flying bound, both darting toward Watch. The three in a moment made one revolving braid, then galloped away, the two lavishing caressing bites on Watch, until, gurgling and yelping, all disappeared down the bank. Meanwhile, Pup, knowing he would receive in the hubbub more cuffs than caresses, had stood apart, jerking himself off his feet with his barks. As the three vanished, however, he set off after them with legs that seemed split up into a centipede's.

Right pleasantly passed our meal, all together once more, and after it I strolled about, marking the localities. From the overhanging corner of the bluff, where the rapids begin, I looked at the bold sweeping bend, the quiet cove, the high banks; and caught glimpses of the dashing, foaming waters, now crimsoned by the sunset. An evening in camp succeeded, the hours passing quickly away in smoking, talking and dipping moderately into Harvey's fragrant punches, with the monotone of the rapids filling the pauses (to say nothing of the needle-points of the infernal mus-quitoes sprinkling us all over as with fire-dust) till the stars of midnight warned us to repose.

CHAPTER XXI.

Fish-Hawk Rapids.—Perciefield Falls.—Death of Sabele.—Beaver Trip agreed upon.—Floating.—The Dark Woods.—The Foot-Tread.—The Indian Jack-Light.

RENNING and Gaylor started down the river, as the sun rose, to fish Dead Creek. Coburn and Bingham went with Cort to the Irish Clearing for a drive, while Harvey and I left for Perciefield Falls, three miles down the Racket.

Shrouding his head and the greater part of his back in the shell of his reversed boat, Harvey strode over the carry round the rapids like some paleozoic lizard on two legs, speckled with the light trickling through the leaves, while I followed. Embarking at the foot of the swift water, we glided two miles down between the wooded islets and grassy spaces of the broad river which expands from Tupper's Lake downward to double its size above.

"Here's a boom o' the river-drivers," said Harvey at length, as we skirted a long piece of timber stretched upon the surface of the river; "and over there," nodding to the east, "is Gull Pond Brook. And here's Fish-Hawk Rapids! What a rattle they keep up! They're called so from a fish-hawk's nest that used ter onst be on the top of a pine at the head on 'm. Jess so, Settin' Pole Rapids is called from the Injins in old times, when they used ter come up the Racket from St. Lorrence, leavin' their settin' poles stuck in the bank at the head o' the rapids. But there's a carry here to the falls."

We left our boat, and after a half-mile's tramp down the west bank, along a narrow path, we heard the rumble of the water-fall.

We again struck the river at the foot of the rapids, where a short space of smooth water intervened between them and the falls. Skirting then the bank and scrambling over fallen trunks which bridged chasms, through prostrate trees bristling with sharp points, among brambles and blinding thickets, we emerged upon the broad, smooth granite ledges, at the head of the falls and forming a stairway to their foot. Descending, we stood on a projecting rock, whence we gained an upward view. Down three terraces the torrent sprang, almost directly at us, white and wild with fury; then, flinging upward its mane of spray, it plunged into the tranquil Racket.

As I stood where the surges boiled like a witch's cauldron, over a rock, and gazed at the river hidden away in the wilderness's heart, here bursting into foamy lightnings and jarring thunders, the reverie into which I was gliding was broken by Harvey.

"One o' the guides hed a tight squeeze of his life above these falls," he remarked. "He took the idee to shoot Fish-Hawk Rapids, and went through safe, but he got kind a foolhardy in the smooth water, and the fust he knowed he was goin' it fast torts the falls. D'ye see that dam o' timber up there at the head? It's called a wing dam, and was made by the river-drivers to hev it easier fur the logs to shoot over. Well, when he—what was that feller's name?—I disremember now, but he went by the name o' Paddlin' Pete, 'caze of the nice paddle he drawed, night-huntin'. Well, when he found that he was likely to go down over the falls, he throwed himself out o' the boat and ketched by chance a hold o' the bushes on the side o' the dam, and away went the boat. It shot agin the timber and then, whang, down it tumbled and rolled; and by the time it got to where we are, there was some sticks and splinters a-whirlin' and a-floatin' round, but nothin' else. Didn't that guide quake when he stood safe on the bank? 'Twas touch and go with him, and more likely the go, unly it jeest wa'n't."

As we returned, Harvey related in detail the fate of the old Indian Chief Sabele, as told him by an eye-witness, a hunter, who was shantying for the time on the spot, trapping sable.

Left alone of all his tribe and borne down by his many sorrows, feeling, too, the near approaches of old age, the Chief launched his canoe, after bearing it over the carries of the two rapids, on the calm water at the torrent's head. Arrayed in the full costume of a Chief and warrior, glaring in black and crimson paint, his wolfskin round his loins, the scalplock erect on his head, knife in his wampum belt, and gun and tomahawk slung at his back, the aged savage stood singing his death-song as he glided toward the verge. Nearer and nearer slid his canoe; higher and higher swelled the death-chaunt. The frail bark trembles at the edge; it bends; down like an arrow it shoots, down over the terraces of foam. The hunter, quivering with horror, gazes on the dark water below the falls; he sees nothing but a few splinters floating along the quiet river.

I had a pleasant sail and stroll in the afternoon light, and at Camp Tamarack found Ralph and Gaylor with two fine baskets of trout, and Bingham and Coburn with—loud assertions from the former, that "he must have killed him! why, he couldn't have been more than ten rods off," but I regret to say again, with nothing else.

Hearing that Mart and Will talked of a hunt by jacklight in the evening, I determined to join them in this fascinating sport.

At dusk, while they were preparing, Harvey joined me with his rod at the rock by the cove, where I was watching the fading colors of the scene.

" Well, Harvey, you know, I suppose, we break up camp to-morrow."

" I hed an idee so from the talk at supper," answered he, whipping up a trout, " and as I went by the tent jest now, I heerd Mr. Bingham sayin' that he was tuckered out with Settin' Pole Rapids; that there wa'n't no deer here, and that he for one was a goin' to move his settin' poles rapid torts Baker's as sun as poss'ble—ha! ha! ho!"

"You remember our talk about the beaver up in the St. Regis woods, Harvey?"

"Sarten."

"My friends return to Baker's by way of the Racket. Suppose we separate from them, and take the jaunt we agreed upon."

"I'm with ye, Mr. Smith."

"What will be our course to reach the St. Regis Ponds?"

"Go up Wolf Brook out of Racket Pond to Little and Big Wolf Ponds, and then through a passle o' ponds, west and north o' Upper S'nac, to Hoel's Pond."

"How many carries?"

"Eight to Hoel's: two a mile long, and one half a mile, and the rest from four to twenty rods."

"After we get to Hoel's, what then?"

"We leave the boat and steer into the woods, five or six mile, till we come to the waters where the beaver is. Onderstand now, Mr. Smith! I won't promise to show ye the beaver, and I wont not to, nuther. But I'll show ye plenty o' beaver sign and fresh too; and beaver housen good as ef made to-day. Many and many's the time I've trapped beaver on them waters, and last October I trapped two."

"Enough, Harvey, we go; and as the route must be a pretty hard one, take Phin with you."

"All right! and we'll hev an airly start to-morrer mornin'."

"How long will it take to make the trip?"

"About four days."

At this moment Mart and Will informed me all was ready, and we pushed off, Mart rowing and Will at the stern with the paddle. The jack was not yet lighted.

"This is the lucky boat, Mr. Smith," said Mart; "one deer, as Harve says, is as good as dead, and mebby two; hey, Will?"

"Oh yes!" said taciturn Will.

"The other fellers goes out," resumed Mart, "and ef so be as how they don't git no deer, there's a'lys a reason for't, a'lys. They didn't see right or the deer was too fur off, or the rifle wasn't good, or"——

He broke off, looked keenly a moment, grasped his rifle, and fired. We were just abreast of a wild meadow, and I caught a dissolving view of a deer bounding away between two bushes.

"He's gone, Mart," said Will, looking at him. Mart looked at his rifle.

"He wan't mor'n ten rods off, Mart," said Will.

"Hey?" ejaculated Mart, still eyeing his rifle.

"Jeest about ten rods!" responded Will.

"Twenty, by hookey! Will. I jest got sight on 'im, that's all. This aiht my rifle, Will. It's Harvey's, as sure as preachin'. I didn't look at it when we left camp, and thought as much as could be, 'twas mine, they're so cluss alike. I kin hardly tell 'm apart any way, but I see it's his rifle. Well, I snum!"

"Zactly!" said Will.

"Twenty rods, Will!"

"Jess so!" said Will, with a gurgling sound in his throat.

"And then the rifle! Will. Unly think," looking up and down and all round the weapon. "I don't b'leeve (lengthening out his words as if in deep thought), I raally don't b'leeve I ever shot this rifle afore in my life. There's everything in a rifle that you've a'lys shot with, hey, Will?"

"Jess so," said Will, turning his face aside with a broad grin on it.

"Ah, it's old hunderd, as Harve says, to shoot a rifle you know all about. By the way, I didn't see enny thing but the tail, Will. 'Twas dreffle quick work to see 't all," and Mart essayed to sing. He couldn't; so he whistled.

The gold light faded into grey, as we reached Captain Peter's Rocks and skirted the shore of Racket Pond to the left, and when we had arrived opposite the Irish Clearing, the trees were mingling in the umber dusk.

While listening to the pleasant ripples of our darkening course, I saw Mart thrust forward his head and aim his rifle like lightning. A shoot of red light, a crack, and a dart of the boat toward the shore followed. As we entered the shallow, rustling through a belt of lily-pads, I caught sight of a large object glancing in the dark water, and the next moment Mart had grasped the antlers of a buck.

"Dead enough, Will," chuckled he.

"How on earth could you see to shoot, Mart," remarked I, "in this light?"

"I see 'im and heerd 'im too," said Mart, laughing. "I heerd his drip, drip, in the water, and then I see suthin' dark, that I had a notion might be the head or forequarters of a deer, and blazed away. He was feedin' on the pads."

It was really an extraordinary shot, and fully redeemed the first failure.

Indeed I have been frequently struck with the keenness of both ear and eye possessed by these guides, seeming, in many instances, almost intuition, and rivalling that of the native Indian.

Mart now kindled the jack, and I was noting the flitting effects of the light upon the bank, when I heard the quick click of Mart's locks, succeeded by another report of his rifle.

"He's off!" said Will, urging the boat ashore with a powerful sweep of his paddle.

"Not fur, though, I guess," returned Mart, springing from the boat.

He lighted a match, and making a little lantern with his hollowed hand, lowered it to the shrubs around, kindling them with a fire-fly radiance.

"There's blood," said Mart; "one drop here, and one on this brake. Bring on the jack, Will; I've peppered 'im. See," lighting another match, and sprinkling more light from his sweeping hand upon the herbage, "he's bled some, I tell ye."

Will now came up with the jack, which cast a broad, steady radiance.

"Here's the track," said Mart, holding the jack close to the bushes; "and here's more blood and hair. We'll find 'im lyin' down furder on;" and we entered the forest.

We had gone on a little in the black woods, Mart and Will bending low, scrutinizing the weedy growth at our feet, when the former, turning to me, said:

"Will you please stay here a leetle, Mr. Smith, and Will and I'll go furder in. When we whoop, ef you'll whoop too, we kin find the boat agin. It's so dark, we'll lose it ef we don't do so."

I assented, and the two pushed on, the light, low voices, and slight crackling of even their careful footsteps, becoming fainter and fainter, until all ceased.

I was now in almost impenetrable darkness, or rather blackness, only two or three outlines around and above betraying the trees.

Presently the hissing whine of an owl commenced close to me; but it soon ceased, and a breathless silence again reigned. Suddenly I heard in the sable depths a low rustling, as of a slow, stealthy tread—sounding, ceasing, sounding again—coming closer and closer. It approached to within a few rods, stopped, advanced, stopped again; then came nearer, nearer, till within several feet of me; and then once more it stopped. A slight scratching sound succeeded; but at this moment a clear whoop rang in front. I answered it; a touch of light showed upon a bush, and a glow lighted upon a trunk. At the same time, I heard a loud and now hurried rustling, with boundings, in the direction of the former sounds and lessening, until lost in a course the farthest from the light.

The latter brightened momentarily; voices again sounded, and Mart and Will approached.

"We hevn't hed no luck, Mr. Smith," said the former,

18

as we returned toward where we supposed the boat lay. "The deer's bin 'cute enough to git off so fur; but I raythur guess we'll try it agin in the mornin'."

And such disappointment has been generally my experience in following wounded deer, the animal's endurance being so great, and its haunts so secret. Now and then the hunter, tracking by signs, finds the victim where he has lain down to die; but the success is the exception, not the rule.

We found our boat, and pushed off.

"Spos'n we try Wolf Brook now, Will?" said Mart.

Will nodded, and we continued upward.

As we turned a curve of the bank, a light like a star appeared ahead, just over the water, rapidly enlarging, and coming down the pond obliquely.

"A jack makin' for the Brook," said Mart, in a whisper. "I shouldn't wonder ef 'twas the Injins. Quick, Will, quick, or they'll be ahead on us, sure as a gun!"

Onward skimmed the light, like a will-o'-the-wisp, toward the shore at our left, and onward we darted at the same point. The race became animating, Mart having betaken himself to the oars. Both lights were within the broad rushes that cover the shallows of the pond in this direction; and it seemed at one moment as if we should win the entrance; but the red spot glanced through a cluster of thicket and vanished.

"Gaul hang!" exclaimed Mart, "they're in the Brook. But spos'n we go up past where the Injins is camped. I don't bleeve they've floated up there to-night, and we might stand a good chance o' findin' another deer afore we git to the Injin Park."

We accordingly floated to the basin before the Park, and back again to within a short distance of Racket Pond, but without success. Suddenly a light appeared from around a bend of the river. It was zigzagging along toward us, pausing a moment, then advancing as before. As it glanced in and out, gliding in a half-circle around, lost for an instant, then sparkling out and skimming on, I almost fancied it the eye of some swimming animal searching the banks for prey.

Suddenly it stopped; dwindled, until it glimmered a mere grain of light, and then vanished. In a few minutes more, a black object skulked close along the bank. Mart turned the jack upon it, and a canoe with two Indians gleamed forth.

"Old Leo and t'other Injin," said Mart. "They've either got a deer up Wolf Brook and don't want us to know 't, or they hevn't and don't want us to know their bad luck. But spos'n, as it's so late, and the deer don't seem very plenty, we don't hunt no more, but git back to camp as sun as we kin; and, Will, let's hev a song as we go! and let it be what we've bin on to-night, 'Floatin' fur Deer.'"

Will accordingly, as Mart bent to the oars and he to the paddle, struck up the following song (altered from the original), Mart tugging along by his side in gutturals more loud than musical:—

> The woods are all sleeping, the midnight is dark;
> We launch on the still wave our bubble-like bark;
> The rifle all ready, the jack burning clear,
> And we brush through the lily-pads, floating for deer,
>   Floating for deer.
> And we glide o'er the shallow, boys, floating for deer.
>
> We turn the low meadow;—now breathless we skim;
> That eye! no, the phosphor! yon head! no, a limb!
> This step in the stream! no, a spring dripping near!
> Thus we brush through the lily-pads, floating for deer,
>   Floating for deer.
> Thus we glide o'er the shallow, boys, floating for deer.
>
> Yon nook! spring the locks! the deer's eyeballs of fire
> Still, still as a shadow! hush! nigher, yet nigher!
> He falls! draw him in! now away in good cheer,
> Through the lily-pads blithely from floating for deer,
>   Floating for deer.
> Back to camp, through the shallow, from floating for deer.

At length the light of the camp-fire saluted us, and leaving the two guides busy with the boat, I ascended the bank.

Suffused with the social radiance of the flame, my four comrades were seated on the log which served for a camp-sofa, each with a glass of what I took, from the fragrance, to be punch.

"Ha, ha, ha; he, he, he; ho, ho, ho!"

"What's the joke, boys?"

"Ha, ha, ha; he, he, he; ho, ho, ho!"

"Can't you tell a fellow? I want to laugh too! We've had pretty good luck, but I'm very cold."

"Ha, ha, ha; he, he, he; ho, ho, ho!"

What the joke was, I have never learned to this day.

CHAPTER XXII.

Setting Pole Rapids left.—Wolf Brook.—Little Wolf and Big Wolf Ponds. —Lumber-Road in the Rain.—Picture Pond.—Beaver Meadow.—Maine Shanty.

AT dawn we broke up Camp Tamarack. While the boats were being prepared for our departure, I wandered a short way into the forest by a path that had been bushed out to the spring, for a last draught of the delicious water. Beyond, I came upon another decayed log-hut. The bark roof had fallen away; the broken and prostrate door was nearly buried in herbage, while the area was choked with bushes. It had once, doubtless, been the home of some hunter or trapper who, with characteristic restlessness, had abandoned even this remote spot to plunge into lonelier wilds.

A low whoop from Harvey recalled me to the bank; we all embarked, Corey and Jess leading the way with the tent, baggage, and what remained of the stores.

At the head of Racket Pond we separated; my comrades with their guides turning to the right, up the Racket, on their way to Baker's, while I, Harvey and Phin, with Watch chained at the bow (Harvey no more went without his hound than his rifle), sought Wolf Brook at the left. Henceforth we were to travel rapidly, passing through a wilderness, a portion of which was but little known, even to the guides, pushing on by day and sleeping on the ground at night. We were encumbered therefore with no luggage or stores we could possibly dispense with, the trip being limited to a week, to enable me to rejoin my comrades at Baker's previous to their (if not my) departure for home

Passing through an alley in the rushes, we struck the mouth of the brook, and were soon threading the sharp windings of the stream. Openings scattered with alders and swamp willows lined the banks, yielding soon to the usual close forest. Through the green light, the water dotted as with golden beetles, with gnats whirling their speckled wheels in front, dragon-flies shooting like sapphire darts cast right and left by elves, and now and then a bird whirring athwart, we went, with oar and paddle. The channel grew shallower and more winding, so that only Phin's paddle could be used, Harvey and I aiding by pulling on the branches, like sailors at the ropes.

At length, the water growing so shallow, Harvey said, "We'd better git out at the sand-bank, Mr. Smith, and let Phin paddle up to Little Wolf. We kin go on foot through the woods. It's unly half a mile from the bank through, but it's more'n a mile and a half by the brook."

We accordingly landed on a broad space of sand, at our right, where a huge wolf-track had been freshly stamped, and entering a cleft in the bushes, we found ourselves in a winding deer-path. A labyrinth of stems was round, below was a dense undergrowth and above a web of branches. Through them fell the scattered light, here in rich spots like myriads of yellow butterflies, there in broad patches kindling the pine cones, dead leaves, sprouts and ferns into lambent flame. Now and then a tree dropped an arch so low as to make us dip our heads to pass, or thrust forth a green hand as if to tap our breast; and under the chequered light, the forest floor was radiant with the differing hues of the lichens, mosses and creeping vines, that velveted every rock and log, and threaded every patch of earth not covered by the undergrowth.

After a half hour's walk, we came to an old deserted chopping, with black logs, cushioned in blackberry brambles. We regaled ourselves upon the fruit, and struck soon a bend of the brook, crossing it by a little log bridge.

Again we entered the forest, and shortly emerged upon

Little Wolf Pond, the first of the chain in our road. Resting a moment on a fallen tree at the margin, we started for the head, along the sandy edges, printed over with deer tracks. Here we sat down and gazed over the expanse, which is nearly round and a mile in diameter. Nothing appeared on the surface but the brush of a breeze, and nothing above but a sailing fish-hawk. The silver sunshine, for the sky was thickening, fell pleasantly upon us as we lay upon the warm earth, and the scents of the forest were delicious.

At length a boat, with its bow in the air, a hat at its stern, and flashes at either side, appeared from the forest rim opposite, all which turned out to be Phin, skimming rapidly towards us.

We struck our first carry, and passing a deserted sawmill upon the brook-link between the two ponds, came soon upon Big Wolf, where a little bark shanty was crouching in the bushes, with "Ring's Camp" scrawled upon its front. We drank from a clear spring, at the base of a grassy point, which was bare of trees, except a large pine at the tip; and turning the point, we enjoyed a bath in the little bay which, rimmed with white sand and clear from the usual lilies, rounded into the shore. We then crossed a portion of the pond (which is a third larger than Little Wolf), and, passing a group of islands, struck the bank, where a lumber road had been bushed out for drawing logs through the woods. At the edge of the water was another deserted camp, a large cedar slanting almost horizontally, the sides closed with lopped maple branches, whose wilted leaves emitted a pleasant perfume.

Here began, as Harvey remarked, a mile carry, to a small pond without a name, hidden away in the woods, but in our direct path. Leaving the two guides to follow with the boat, I went on before; the "dudods," as Harvey called the luggage, being placed, with the oars, paddle, and neck-yoke, in the boat. Sinking ankle deep in the green morass that spread from the margin, and seesawing over the logs, or corduroy which spanned the deepest parts, we entered the forest. Now I stumbled over a great root, coiled in and in like a knot of sleeping black snakes, now threshed through a barricade of bushes, and now scaled some enormous pine fallen athwart. Stumps studded the margin, and chopped logs lay parallel, embedded in ferny and shrubby leafage, and pointing from the sumacs and hopple bushes like cannon-muzzles; while a dense carpet of various wood-sprouts, intermingled with dead leaves, evergreen cones, and dry pine-needles covered the dark forest mould. Suddenly there sounded a slow, measured dropping, which quickened, until a steady hum in the green depths told the rain. At first, its coolness in the close forest air was delightful, but it soon fell so dense that I looked round for shelter. The thatch of a slanting cedar offered its protection, but I soon discovered, that if in old times

"Such tents the patriarchs loved,"

they must have loved the tents better than the contents, for I soon found mine decidedly leaky.

A large hollow hemlock, no doubt the winter nest of a bear, promised more comfort, and thrusting myself within, I looked out protected, upon the scene, and listened to the forest roof rumbling in the rain.

The maple trembled all over as the rapid shot of the drops pelted its broad leaves, the pine shook its loose tassels as if to repel the rainy attack, but the hemlock only twitched his sturdy branches as a dog beset with flies twitches his skin.

Suddenly the sounds ceased, and stepping out, I resumed my way amid a throng of loosened odors in the damp, bland air. By and by, Harvey and Phin, bearing the boat upright, under a layer of spruce, overtook me. Then came another shower, more heavy than the first. Dislodging the boat of its load, which they covered with more boughs, the guides propped it on a brace of stout sticks, and lo! an off-hand shanty, under which we crouched, bidding defiance to the torrents. The rounded roof echoed to the batterings upon it, splintering the streams into spray. Through a narrow front I could only see a breadth of quaking undergrowth, with one green log that absorbed the rain like a sponge, and a cushion of ferns between two roots that slaked itself in it like a duck.

At length the shower expired of its own violence, and another half-hour brought us to the nameless pond.

A most beautiful liquid gem it was. Opposite rose an acclivity of cedars, with a smooth, green headland. At the right, and forming a little winding bay, stood a small, bare, pyramidal island. The scene was lonely as beautiful. We crossed, cutting through the sunset colors, and entered the bay, which was roofed with foliage. Here and there a drop of carmine or a spangle of gold had fallen, or a little arrow of light had shot through the woven canopy upon the dark water. We returned and skirted the island, Harvey pointing out a turtle-bed on its summit.

We traversed the rich, beamy polish of the pond, which I named Picture Pond, with the dabble of Phin's oars (Harvey sat idle at the stern) wakening the profound stillness, and landed.

"I guess we'll leave the boat here," said Harvey. "There's a Maine shanty a little ways above here, where we kin spend the night. We'll leave the Bluebird here. I'll stand bail there's nobody round to be off with her. Phin, you're young, you take up the dudods."

Ascending a ridge, we found ourselves in front of the shanty, which was a low, comfortable log cabin. Below, at our left, lay a large beaver-meadow, long, narrow, irregular, with little points of wood jutting into it, and tamaracks streaking the edges or grouped like islets in its cove-like nooks, and ground cedars planting their dark tents picturesquely around.

In one of these nooks stood two stacks of hay, under a low pencil of light, while in the farthest distance a quick glitter told of water.

For the hundredth time I asked myself, where was the farm-house, with the grazing cows, the dotted sheep, the yoked oxen dozing in the lane, and the sturdy steeds cross-necked in the shade.

Instead of this rural picture, I saw a deer under a lurching tamarack, now feeding, then stopping to look, then dropping its head again to the grass. At the same time, I caught sight of Harvey, with his rifle, creeping from bush to bush, toward it, stealthy as a wild-cat. The next, the deer lifted its pointed face; then, with a gentle trot, glided between some cedar thickets, and vanished.

We now crossed the meadow, to see the remains of an old beaver-dam at its head. We passed the little pond whose winking eye I had seen, and whose margin was a picture-writing of deer-tracks. Ascending a hill spotted with thickets, we came upon a low, gently-sloping wall of wild grass, which Harvey pronounced the dam. We then retraced our steps toward the shanty, turning on the bank to gaze at the meadow glowing like green velvet in the last rays of the sun, with long black shadows printing its surface. The soft look of culture was stronger than ever, but all resemblance to civilization there ceased. Instead of the crow of chanticleer, the wild cry of a hawk circling a dry pine startled the echoes. A grey fox was skulking between the golden-tanned haystacks, instead of the house-dog, roaming around with his protecting tread; and in place of the laden honey-bee seeking the sunset hive, the hungry deer-fly threaded the tangle of the wild beaver-grass.

Twilight now rested on the rough clearing before the shanty. I sat at the rude porch while Harvey and Phin began the night-fire. The evening was close and sultry after the rain, and of course it was holiday among the musquitoes. Their premonitory symptoms were discernible in the actions of Harvey, who was in the clearing, gathering chips (left by the lumbermen) for the fire. From that staid soberness, not only natural to him, but quite becoming in one of his age and experience, I saw him suddenly transformed into a dancing-Jack. At the same time, a sting on my forehead, another on the throat, and a most diabolical one inside my pantaloons, showed in earnest my time was come. Bred from the beaver meadow, and this generation probably never before tasting human blood, the musquitoes poured a living torrent.

At first I pounded myself as much as the little mocking fiends could wish, but at length encased myself in the mail of philosophic don't-care-ativeness, and "took it" like a hero. In fact, I began rather to enjoy the thing, and at last took notes. One fellow, I particularly remarked. First, he darted across my forehead, then down the cheek, then glanced into my eye with an "Aha!" Next, he sent a twang into my ear like the first nip of a fiddle-string, then gave a sounding flourish, intensifying it into a fine hum, which rang like the buzz of a sharp bell, warning me plainly to look out. At last, down pounced the little grey-coated, globe-eyed sapper delicately on his elastic, long-angled legs, and planted his slender sucking-pump on a pore of my hand. I endured the tickling, and watched the enormous pouch and transparent, black-ribbed needle of a body expanding ruddily, till the elfin marauder, gorged to repletion, lifted with difficulty his pump and floated sluggishly away.

Glancing upward as it flew, I saw with a thrill the new moon beaming timidly on the edge of the warm, red west, a silver barque upon a ruby sea.

The dark night now came, blending all objects in one general gloom, except within the crimson ring of the camp-fire.

We enjoyed our supper of dried trout and venison, and then went into the cabin for rest. There was but one room; the board floor was partly broken, showing the dark earth below. The shaft of the chimney of stones and clay ran up from the centre, and a large, flat, upright stone, blackened by fire, with two stone jambs, made the hearth.

"Them lumber fellows had rousin' times here in the winter, fur all they was clearn away from folks," said Harvey, as he entered, after lighting his pipe at the fire.

"They must have had some cold, stormy times in this wild spot," remarked I.

"Yes, the winds blowed and the snow flew, sometimes, but, bless ye, they didn't mind it a bit. I've lumbered it myself among 'm. They're jest as tough as a pine-knot, them fellers!"

"Did they cut the hay stacked in the meadow?"

"Sarten! to fodder their oxen with. But they left the next winter fur Big Square Pond, nigh Upper S'nac. But as we must be out o' here afore sunrise, what say ye fur sleep? Good night!"

So saying, he and Phin threw themselves on a bed of hay, which the latter had found in a little log barn, back of the shanty, and I followed, falling into slumber, while fancying a wild winter storm thundering through the woods and raving round the shanty for entrance.

CHAPTER XXIII.

Path Resumed.—The Medal.—Musquito Pond.—Rawlins Pond.—Floodwood Pond.—The Sable.—A Network of Ponds.—Long Pond.—The Cranes.—Slang Pond.—Turtle Pond.—Hoel's Pond.—Boat Left.—Through the Woods.—Beaver Meadows.—Beaver Signs.—Beaver Pond.—Beaver Houses.—A Beaver.—The Bivouac.

THE grey of the early daybreak was struggling in the air, as I was aroused by Harvey, who, with Phin, had already brought the boat from the pond. My first plunge into the atmosphere was like a cold bath; I was refreshed in an instant. The stars were fading, and the confused woods becoming momentarily clearer, as we resumed our road, which shortly brought us to another pond, smaller than the last and almost perfectly round, which I named :" The Medal." Crossing it, the next water in our chain was Musquito Pond, with a mile carry, the least known of any in our path. No signs of a track met our eyes, and the guides decided to leave the Bluebird and push on with me to the pond, over the best path to be found, then return and transport the boat. Long and toilsome was our way through the tangled and trackless woods, but at last the shining level of the pond broke through the trees; and leaving me in a little green dingle on the margin, with Watch for company, my guides went back.

The scene, after they had left, was as utterly lonely and wild as could be imagined. The shores, unlike those of the other lakes and ponds in this alpine region, were low, belted with swamp and disfigured with dead, ghastly trees.

Although I am a lonely man by nature, habit and choice, shrinking from mankind instinctively as from a blow, yet as this profoundly desolate scene smote my sight, I felt a weight deeper than I had ever experienced in the forest.

Watch looked up into my face; cocked his ear inquiringly, as if to say, "What d'ye think of it round here?" Then he dropped his jaw and panted the pantomime for "Rather hot!" snapping this way and that to suggest, "Flies plaguy thick!" A short, rapid laugh, under his breath, probably at my woe-begone looks, followed, till at length he fixed his head between his paws and winked himself to sleep.

On the pond a couple of copperhead ducks, their brown necks shining in the light, were steering out, and soon vanished in the dazzling glare midway. Then a raven slowly flapped over, and then a kingfisher, settling on a dry limb, threw a bit of rich color on the mirror below.

At last I fell into a day-dream, only broken by a whimper from Watch, and looking in the direction his nose pointed, I saw at my distant right Harvey and Phin emerging from the forest with the boat. They skimmed rapidly to where I stood and took in myself and the hound. Crossing the length of the dismal sheet, we then passed over a dry open ridge of a few rods, and embarked upon Rawlins' Pond at the head of a long narrow bay with an arm penetrating the woods at our right.

"This pond's the head waters, through Fish Creek, of the three S'nac Lakes and S'nac River," said Harvey while passing an island he named to me as Camp Island. "Fish Creek," continued he, "is a string o' ponds, and throws an all-fired big batch o' water in Upper S'nac, about three quarters of a mile from its head."

Passing three other islands, and crossing northerly a distance three times the extent of Musquito Pond, we landed on the left, at the foot of the pond, where the swift, rocky outlet brawled forth into the forest. Here, surmounting another ridge of six or seven rods, we launched into Floodwood Pond, linked to Rawlins by the outlet.

It was about the same size as the latter, and lay in a general easterly direction. Pointing north-easterly we passed a small island, and leaving at our left another and larger (called by Harvey, Beaver Island), we glided along a third one still larger. We had passed midway, when, suddenly, Watch, who had been all along curled up at Harvey's feet, rose on his haunches, and jerking his ears, looked narrowly at a small maple on the bank.

"Down, Watch! what are ye pointin' that nose o' yourn out there fur? Down with ye or I'll"——

Watch melted away. In a moment after, however, he sprang, this time to his feet, with a yelp, still gazing at the same place.

"What's he seein', Phin?" asked Harvey.

"I dunno as I kin tell," commenced Phin, settling his oars in the water.

"I do though!" broke in the former, throwing his paddle into the boat, dropping a sounding knock as he did so on poor Watch's skull (who complained by a dismal howl), then catching his rifle to his shoulder and firing. "Saples aint so mighty plenty that I kin afford to let one go, even if 't aint in season." Then driving the boat to the margin, he stepped on shore, and soon returned, bringing a dead animal with a white head and coat of light tawny fur, large hind quarters and bushy tail; which he handed me for inspection. It was the sable, rare even here.

"The nicest and most valyble fur in the woods," continued he. "I've telled ye afore how we ketch 'm. I drive sometimes a fust trade best in this fur, as well as what I git from fisher and mink, to say nothin' o' rats. But about these ere ponds we're crossin'. The whull region is as full o' ponds as the ponds is o' lily-pads a'most. Now, a leetle south o' here, p'intin' from Rawlins torts Big Square Pond to the east, there's Whey Pond, and a leetle one that hasn't no name. Furder from here, torts Fish Creek waters, is Otter Pond and Buttermilk Pond. Then up west and north, a mile or two, is two or three more ponds, and north o' Long Pond is Rainbow Pond. You can't go amiss scurce, and reck'nin' in the lakes and streams, may go ennywheres a'most in your boat, with a few carries. But here we are at the end of the pond, with a carry of half a mile afore us inter Long Pond."

Day was creeping low as we crossed the carry, and he had thrown a golden path over the pond as we struck it midway its winding three-mile length.

We had gone nearly through when, turning a point, a deafening clamor and a novel sight saluted us.

In a low marshy spot, hundreds of cranes were running, walking, hovering, darting through the air, and cleaving spirally upward until almost invisible, and then swooping downward on their broad sails, their plumage flashing white in the sunset. The voices were prodigious, and quite peculiar. One who seemed the stump orator to the crowd, standing some four feet on his pins, was, at the moment of our arrival, making a speech at the top of his harsh voice and stamping his foot as if to emphasize it.

As we passed, the whole flock, seemingly unable longer to restrain their fire, broke in upon the harangue, with, as it were, three cheers and a tiger. Even as far off as the carry, the echoes were in a flutter, from the tall orator's eloquence. The name of the next pond struck me as appropriate in the highest degree to stump speeches in general.

"Slang Pond," said Harvey, as the inlet, in the form of a bow, received our boat. Through its half mile channel we went, in the golden glow succeeding the sundown, the rustle of our way amid the continuous lily-pads of the upper end, sounding like a shower in the woods.

"The next is Turtle Pond," remarked he, as we entered a little, swift, gravelly stream, "and the outlet here, after about three rods, brings us inter it. It lays straight along about a mile, has a waist jest like a woman, and hasn't no lily-pads 't all to speak of."

I found the comparison just. We traversed the sheet in the "gloaming;" and as we crossed the last carry, between us and Hoel's Pond, Harvey and Phin bearing the boat on the same shoulder they had from the beginning, so that I thought the spot must, by this time, be grooved, the woods began to grow dusky.

The night had quite settled down, with the crescent moon too faint for light, as the guides woke with oar and paddle the breathing silence of Hoel's. Gliding for some distance in the ambrosial dark of the air, and over the star-sprinkled ebony of the water, we landed on what appeared a point, penetrating far into the pond.

Soon the blaze, kindled by my guides, stripped the darkness from the scene, showing our camping spot to be indeed a long tongue of the mainland. The light threw a scarlet over the backs of the old logs at the margin, blushed on the bushes covering the point, and reddened the stars from out the sable water.

Our simple supper ended, overcome by fatigue we stretched ourselves in our blankets on the grass, with our feet to the camp-fire; and under the cool stars, and lulled by the natural sounds of our wild bivouac, the gentle talk of the ripples to the sand, the murmur of the night wind through the leaves and the fitful chirping of some wakeful bird, we resigned ourselves to slumber.

Day was just breaking as I awoke. A chill, misty air was flowing through the woods and curdling the water.

My guides had already dragged the boat over the point to the eastern of the pond's two divisions and we shortly struck the opposite shore. Here we were to leave the Bluebird and take up our line of march through the forest to the beaver waters, several miles to the east. We accordingly hid the boat in one hollow log, and to prevent the use of it, if found, hid the oars and paddle in another. Harvey shouldered his rifle which supported a coarse check sack with half our stores, and a small camp-kettle, while his left hand grasped his axe.

Phin carried a knapsack of leather, containing the rest of the stores, and his rifle, with Watch buckled to his waist by a long strap. I avoided all encumbrance, anticipating truly a toilsome tramp.

We then started, Harvey leading the way, Phin following close in his footsteps, and I bringing up the rear.

An aisle between a colonnade of trunks, invited us through its grassy length. We then ascended a somewhat open ridge, or "hog's-back," continued upon it for a considerable distance, and then descended. The woods grew darker and wilder. The underbrush deepened. Decayed logs more thickly blocked the way. Harvey began to hack the trees on either side, making what in woodcraft is known as a "blazed line."

At every step, I could see we were piercing deeper and deeper into the wildest, loneliest recesses of this wild and lonely wilderness. The great trees stood round in myriads upon myriads, with smaller ones between, bewildering the eyesight; the ground entangled with the densest growth, which almost buried the fallen trunks, patriarchs of the forest, that had been undermined by age or hurled flat by storms. Now and then a broad tract of laurels over which rose dead tamaracks and cedars, warning the foot not to enter its blinding and treacherous depths, or an immense labyrinth of prostrate trees, all twisted and interlaced, showing where some tornado had whirled, sent us widely from our course. Wilder and wilder grew our way. Here and there a broken sunbeam lay athwart the higher branches of a pine or hemlock, or a long spear-like ray reached to a bush, or its splintered point sprinkled the innumerable woodsprouts, but the general tone of light was grey and sombre. The leaves of the forest's summit frequently fluttered in passing currents, but below was a stagnant quiet. No sound could be heard, save the sharp hack of Harvey's axe, or the "uggle-uggle" of the crossing raven, that might well be deemed some flying ghoul of the sepulchral recesses.

Nature showed herself, not in the fresh loveliness of her sylvan haunts, but as if borne down by the weight of centuries; and was mouldering silently and sullenly away, under a mantle of moss that clothed rock, log, bank, and hollow, clung in great patches on the trees and was so intermingled with the dank, rotten leaves upon the earth, as to nearly overlay their umber hues. The sunken streams, crawling under logs and between rocky crevices, burrowed at times underneath this mossy screen, flashing out here and there like a deer's eye from ambush.

Threshing through bushes, scaling enormous logs, slipping and tumbling over roots, tripping among tough creeping plants, plunging headlong into thickets and falling to the waist in mossy cavities, on we went. Now and then, a bear-path showing punctures of the huge creature's claws, or a light deer trail, was seen, but it was quickly lost, and all became trackless as before. The inequalities of the ground too, heightened my fatigue. Now a ridge forced us to cling to the branches, in laboring up; the steep descent proving more toilsome still. We paused, however, frequently, to drink at some lurking spring, bared by scooping out the dead leaves, thus resting my tired limbs a moment; but soon forward again was the word, for my guides seemed men of iron.

" 'Tisn't like floatin' down the Racket, is't, Mr. Smith?" said Harvey, as trembling with fatigue, I grasped a bough to keep from sinking to the earth. "But take some o' this," cutting a portion of gum from a spruce with his axe; " 'twill make yer stronger, and keep yer from being so dreffle dry. This drinkin' at all the springs, on a tramp like this, isn't the best thing in the world. It makes yer, after all, unly more tired."

"Look a' here!" said he, a little farther, pointing at some gashes in several stems. "See where the confounded bears 've stuck their teeth inter the bark and wood, and here they've scratched with their sharp claws, and here they've twisted off the limbs with them paws o' their'n. They're a plaguy wild brute, them bears, as bad as a mad moose a'most, when they're ugly."

We crossed one more ridge, and turning another ledge, saw water glancing brokenly through the trees.

"The fust o' the St. Regis Ponds," said Harvey, and in a few moments a most lovely pond gleamed in the sunshine before us. Sheer to the edge came its circle of forest, save where one small headland, green as an emerald, rounded into the water. Once more did I notice with delight, the shrubbery-like grouping of the thickets. Streaks of cedars also wound along as if the hand of taste had guided them. I stepped on the back of a log, lying, like a gigantic lizard, far into the water, and drank in the beautiful picture.

In the middle was a loon, drawing a track of silver, and sounding incessantly his bugle note, awaking a thousand echoes.

"What is the name of this pond, Harvey?"

Receiving no answer, I turned to the old guide, and repeated the question. I was struck with the expression of his face. It was blank and puzzled. He exchanged glances with Phin; both retired a little, and conversed in low tones. Harvey pointed in several directions, and swept his arm round with a keen, but doubtful look. At length they returned; Harvey looking up and down the pond, and glancing back the way we came.

"Confess, now, Harvey," said I. "You don't know where you are."

"Well, I must say, Mr. Smith—that is, I b'leeve—I kinder think—I dunno but that—that—hem."

"In other words, you're lost."

"Well, I vow, things does look a leetle queer to me, around here. I can't 'zactly git straight. Strannge too. I've ketched fur and killed ven'son on the St. Regis waters year after year, and yit, somehow, I—a—a—I don't"——

"Know where you are," added I.

"Well—a—I dunno—as I ever—see this pond afore."

"Why, Harvey! what shall we do? How many miles have we travelled, and how long will it take us to get out of these terrible woods, supposing we are lost," said I, breaking into a heat with my apprehensions.

"Well, ef we kept right straight along, I rayther guess we could scratch out after about—I say about—forty miles travel."

"Forty miles!" exclaimed I, starting; "forty miles—the Lord deliver us!"

"W-a-a-l, mebby a leetle less; mebby not more'n thirty-five or six—that is, ef we go ahead. But we might turn back, that is, ef I knowed 'zactly where back is. I b'leeve I'm kinder turned round. It's very queer! I've not unly trapped here, but I've bin guide all through these woods some years ago to a pairty o' surveyors, when they run the line o' Township Twenty. Well, I am beat! an old woodsman like me, too. What kin this pond be!"

"Heavens! that I should ever have been such a fool to come out here after beaver!" groaned I, sinking on a log.

"Don't give up so, Mr. Smith," said Harvey, who had started down the pond to a curve, and returned. "I aint dead yit. And somehow or other—jest let's go down the pond a leetle. Down there, torts the outlet."

"Ef it turns out there as I expect," continued he as we went down, "I'm all right. I think I've trapped on that outlet; but as fur this pond!—it's strannge I shouldn't a come upon't. But we'll see—we'll see."

With many misgivings I tramped along with him, and arrived at last beyond the curve, at a sharp oxbow, where the pond was completely hidden.

"All right," said Harvey. "I'm as right as a book. Here's the very place I footed a fisher three year ago next October. After that, I started straight fur hum, and never see the pond. Yes, yes, it's all right now!"

I need not say I felt relieved, and with a lighter step I again followed my guides.

A mile farther, and we came upon a small beaver-meadow, with grass waist deep, and shortly after a second, through which we also waded. At the edges of this we noticed the first beaver signs. Saplings, and even considerable trees were cut asunder by the teeth of the animal. The edges were black with age, and chiselled irregularly to a point. Again we entered the forest; and in a little while a third meadow, with borders full also of chiselled signs, immersed us.

We now ascended a comparatively open pine-ridge, whence at either hand shone glimpses of water.

"There's ponds on all sides," said Harvey, "and all on 'm used to be great places fur beaver; but they're sich a shy, timorsome thing, they're most on 'em cleared out. Some's left, though; and ef we don't see them, we'll see their housen, as I said afore, and 'twont be a very long time nuther. There's otter sign, too, here! See the slides o' the critters!" pointing to discernible paths down the declivities, which were slippery with the dead pine foliage.

Descending the farther point of the ridge, we struck off at our left, and soon came to the sloping border of a beautiful little pond, where a narrow stream flowed out through a natural meadow.

"The pond that the beaver housen is on is jest back o' this," said Harvey, pointing diagonally with his left hand, "and after we've had a bite o' suthin' we'll go there. It isn't over half-an-hour's walk," opening his knapsack in the grass of the little dingle where we had halted.

And here let me whisper that cold pork and baked beans, although homely and possibly vulgar in some eyes, are two of the standing dishes of the forest. The former is particularly grateful to the palate, after being cloyed with trout and venison, and the latter is like solidified cream, crumbling in the mouth in brittle and mellow richness.

These, with dried deer's flesh (we saw the last of our smoked trout at Hoel's) and biscuit, strewed on the wild grass of the spot, formed our meal.

"I've trapped beaver in these ponds fur thirty year, off and on," said Harvey, "but the unly fam'ly left now is on that pond out there torts Catamount Mountain (pointing to a near, dark summit among a group of hill-tops rising above the woods), where the housen is. I've kinder nussed 'm along, and never take more'n two at a time. There isn't another feller in the whull S'nac region that knows about this pond but me. Phin, here, don't know it, nur Will, nor Mart, nur enny on 'm. I've al'ys gone alone, and kept my own secrets. But you'll know it sun, and"—

Here he broke short off, glanced his keen eye. toward the outlet, snatched his rifle from the grass with one hand, and stopped a yelp from Watch by a blow with the other, and swiftly, but cautiously, descended the slope leading to the water. As Phin grasped Watch round the nose, thus effectually sealing another yelp, I glanced in the direction indicated by the eyes of both, and saw a deer gliding between the thickets of the wild meadow, toward the outlet. Crawling like a snake from bush to bush, Harvey went nearer and nearer. At last he fired. The deer, however, did not fall, neither did it swerve from its course toward the stream. It probably had never before heard the report of a gun, and took this for one of the natural sounds to which it was accustomed. But a second crack from Harvey's double-barrel came, and the animal, who had just stooped his graceful neck to drink, fell in his tracks. Phin and I, followed by Watch, who poured out a torrent of cries, overtook Harvey as he was wading the outlet, and we all reached in a twinkling the spot of long grass where the deer had fallen. He was a two-year-old buck, and in excellent condition. My guides shouldered him, and all returned to our dingle, merry with our luck.

"We'll let 'im lay there," said Harvey, after he and Phin had deposited the animal on a bank of moss, " till we come back from the beaver housen. I don't bleeve enny painter or wolf 'll git 'im the short time we're away."

We rounded the pond, and after the toilsome ascent and descent of a ridge, reached at last a small sheet of water lurking among acclivities, and sleeping so dark and still in their shadows, Nature seemed to have forgotten it as soon as formed. Plunging through the dense underbrush, which not only heaped the margin, but tangled for some distance the water, we came at length to a little opening in the foliage.

"Here's the fust of the two housen," said Harvey, pausing before an object standing on the very edge of the water, "but the ruff's all to pieces. You kin see though how 'twas made inside."

It was a fractured mound of smooth clay, about two feet high, and six across, inside which were layers of water-lily leaves. A roof had been over it, made of broken sticks that lay around, smeared with dried mud.

"Them pads is where the beavers lay," said Harvey, "and unly a few days ago too. You see they're fresh! Some bear or other has come along and made the house fly with his tearin' big paws. They're apt to do it to git at the beaver, and they've skeered 'm clearn away. I hope they've left t'other house alone. It's much bigger 'an this. Beaver, Mr. Smith, is like the rich folks in the big settlements, sich as York is, I spose. I've never seen any place bigger 'n Burlin'ton, and Plattsburgh and Keeseville, and Liz'bethtown, and so on, but onst, and that was when I straggled down to Troy with a load o' fur, and nice fur they was too. There was fisher, and saple, and mink, to say nothin' o' rats in fust best order. Well, I went there and come back too, mighty quick. I thought I'd choke to death, the housen was so cluss t'gether, and the air so kinder thickened up. And then the people a-flyin' about! 'Twas some great day or other—a p'litical meetin' I bleeve —and some feller was a-goin' to tell what his idees was on matters in gin'ral, the Gov'nor or some other big bug! what was that chap's name! well, no matter, I heerd it too at the time. But there was sich a pressin' and pullin' and haulin', and so many folks jammed up t'gether, that I went to the tavern, settled with the landlord right off, and started a-foot out o' the confounded hole, and tramped on till night come, when I camped in a piece o' woods jest outside a village till mornin' and then made tracks torts old Champlain fur the steamboat to Keeseville. Wasn't I glad to git back to S'nac agin? I tell ye! But where was I? oh—the beavers has their city house and their country house, one fam'ly gin'rally to a pond. This was their country house. But s'posen' we move torts t'other.

"Here's more sign," continued he, pointing to a quantity of saplings gnawed asunder like those we first saw, "and a good part on 'm fresh. The beavers is here, but where, at this partic'lar p'int o' time, is more'n I kin say."

We struggled along the pond's edge once more, until at last Harvey ascended a fallen tree, and stepping downwards, said—

"Here's t'other hut, and all right and tight too, thank fortin'."

I scrambled across the barricade, and saw what I first took to be a collection of driftwood, partly on the bank and partly over the water. I stepped upon it. It was a rounded fabric, fifteen or twenty feet in diameter, wrought of dry saplings and water-grass, welded together smoothly with dried mud. An extra roof of long loose poles was placed upon the top, making the projection over the shallow.

The fabric itself rested on the bank, and before it, heaping the bottom of the shallow, were stems of small trees.

"The beaver lays round the sides, inside o' this Dutch oven, on sep'rit beds," said Harvey. "They don't gin'rally stay in their housen in summer though, but roam about. The wood in the water's what they feed on. A good deal on't 's moose-missee that they're most fond of, with birch, willer, and water-maple mixed in. They haul the stuff down with their teeth, and then stick it to the bank someway. I've never seen 'm make their housen but I've hearn tell how. They gnaw the trees down, haul 'm to the water, and plaster mud over 'm with their forepaws, and some say they smooth it over with their flat tails."

"Well," continued the old woodman, after I had lingered over the localities some little time, "we've seen all here, and I guess we may as well be movin'. A ven'son steak wouldn't be bad to take after we git back, would it? Ef I could unly put a beaver's tail now by it, 'twould be rael old hunderd. But, goll, look at that!" suddenly pointing to the pond.

Upon it I saw part of a dark head, a mere dot, skimming rapidly along, and approaching a small grassy point.

"There's a beaver by golly! and I mean to hev't too," continued the old guide, raising his rifle, but at the very instant the head vanished behind the point.

"Ah, it's gone!" added he in a disappointed tone. "So we might as well trudge on fur all the beaver's tail we'll git, this time enny how."

The west was on fire with the sunset, and the woods were sounding with the flute of the Saranac Nightingale as we re-entered our dingle. The guides prepared our supper of toasted venison, and after we had taken it they built a framework of poles over the fire to dry the remainder of the deer.

The trees crept into the night; the pond winked and glimmered into a dark-grey dimness, save where a portion glowed softly to the young moon, which had filled with silver her fairy shell over Catamount mountain. Seated on a root, I watched the dark forms of my guides flitting athwart the fire as they superintended the drying of their venison, and listened to the low tones of their talk. No other sound disturbed the silence.

At length the guides left their venison to harden in the smoke throughout the night, levelled a small hemlock, made a bed of its fringes, and close, as usual, to the camp-fire we lay down side by side, wrapped in our blankets, I for one soon passing into the shadowy realm of dreams.

CHAPTER XXIV.

Return Path.—Clamshell Pond.—Song-birds.—Beaver-dam.—Beaver-talk.—Absence of Serpents.—Hoel's Pond.—Carry.—Green Pond.—UPPER SARANAC.—Eagle.—Water-thatch.—Tommy's Rock.—Goose Island.—Harvey's Opinion of Neighbors.—Phin's Idea of Subordination.—The Loons.—Loon Talk.

DAWN was peeping with his ashen face through the trees, as I awoke. I sat upon the half-burned log of the blinking camp-fire, watching my guides completing their arrangements to start, and, from my yesterday's fatigue, dreading the signal. At length, Harvey and Phin had shouldered their knapsacks and rifles, and hung all their articles around them, and "All's right, Mr. Smith!" came from the former. I rose, and our return line of march was taken up. As I turned a thicket, I cast a last look at the dingle. There was the framework, there the green couch of hemlock branches. I caught a farewell flash from the pond, and then left the camp-fire to blink itself to death, and silence and solitude to settle on the spot, as profound as when we first invaded it.

We had not gone far before Harvey paused at a pine tree.

"Here was one o' my fisher traps," said he, pointing at a pole slanting upward from the ground at the root. "I ketched two on 'm the week I was here last fall."

Again over ridge and hollow, plunging into mossy clefts, dashing aside low branches, wading through underbrush, with short stoppages for rest. Again, stooping to drink at some streak of a runnel nearly choked in fern, picking the blisters of gum from the spruce to refresh the lips, stumbling among sharp hidden rocks, and vaulting over prostrate trees. Here, a cedar colonnade received us, smooth to the foot, balsamic to the scent; there, a miry bog, shaking like quicksilver as we crossed.

Again Harvey paused, this time before a decayed stump.

"Here I had a wolf-trap, chained round. It had a snap like a gunlock. I come one mornin', and found old clawtooth had the biggest kind o' wolf in the tightest kind o' place. Massy, how he grinned, and clicked his jaws! You could a heerd it a quarter of a mile. He was farse for fight, his neck and back a bristlin' like a porkypine. I wonder he hadn't gnawed his paw off. Didn't I send a ball straight through that skull o' his'n, right 'twixt his eyes? His skin and sculp fetched me five dollars!"

We now turned a little off from our course, on both sides of which I recognised Harvey's blazes of the day before, to visit Clamshell Pond, where were the remains, as the old guide said, of a large beaver-dam. The water-gleam soon shot between the trees, and we made our way to the margin. The surface, on which a little breeze was dancing, spread blue and cool to the sunny morning sky, the waterlilies glittered, the rushes trembled, the forest leaves sparkled as with stars, and a general gladness brightened the scene.

There is a prevalent idea that songsters in these woods are wanting. This to an extent is true. Still many of our rural birds are here. Their colors flash in the broken sunlight, and their notes pierce the sweeping verdure, but the restless eye and the open ear of the lovers of nature alone detect them. To others, their shapes are unseen in the dim vastness, and their tones are unnoticed amid the voices of the larger and more infrequent of the feathered race here found.

The Saranac Nightingale is, however, an exception. The loud, clear, triumphal music of this lonely bird claims the ear, amid the shriek of the eagle, the croak of the raven, the whoop of the crane, the boom of the bittern, and shouting of the loon.

In the moist sand of the margin I noticed a swarm of deer prints, with here and there the broad track of the bear and panther. Presently the guides, who had left me to turn a bend of the pond, reappeared with a quantity of beautifully tinted shells, which give the water its name.

The beaver dam was a rod or two from the pond. It was a long, low mound of earth, broad at bottom and narrow at top, overgrown with grass and shrubs, with the usual meadow before it.

We seated ourselves upon the dam. The green round of the meadow looked pleasant and soft in the circle of the forest; insects were chirping, and the warm air was full of fragrance.

"D'ye see them alleyways?" said Harvey; "you kin jest spy 'em now! They was the roads the beaver had 'twixt the pond that stood where this meader is now, and the big pond there. They used 'm to travel 'twixt the two, and to haul the wood they fed on to the housen here. They're an awful knowin' critter. When they want to change a place for another where there's more o' the sort o' wood they like to feed on, or when some on 'm want 'er to go off—pull up stakes as 'twere, jest like the b'ys of a fam'ly goin' off to Californy, or out West, to seek their fortins like—one on 'm goes ahead and marks out the p'ints o' compass he goes, by leavin' heaps o' mud along, scented up with castor or bark-stone, as we call it; so there's the track all marked out like a blazed line o' trees, with these castor beds.

"There's another kind o' these queer fish, called bank beaver. They don't make no housen, but burrow in the banks o' the ponds, like mushrats. But we must be goin'."

I picked a beautiful wild flower from the grassy dam, and we all then pressed onward. After another hour's struggle, I found, to my dismay, that my strength was failing. Lagging behind, my guides were frequently lost sight of, but as I checked my footsteps in doubt where to go, the direction was given by a low whoop from Harvey, or a clink of his rifle against the camp-kettle. In these pauses, I was more and more impressed with the utter savageness of the scene, and my entire helplessness should I be left alone. The few paths, if not of deer, could only be of bear, wolf, or panther, and tended doubtless toward their fearful haunts. The deep marks on the trees, cutting into the wood, were more frequent than those of yesterday, and I shuddered at the thought of the merciless fangs that made them.

There was one thought, however, from which I derived comfort, assured of its truth by all the guides: I could plant my feet anywhere in the wilderness—in the deep grass, the crumbling trunk, or the rocky cavity—without fear of noxious serpents.

"Ef them infarnal critters—copperheads and rattle-snakes, and sich like—was about in these 'ere woods," said Harvey, once, in conversing on the subject, "a feller about my size, for one, would be scurce there. A man mought as well die at onst as be skeered to death. But the long, cold winters does the business up fur them divils."

My every step was at last more and more painful. I tottered with weakness, and was obliged, at times, to pull myself forward by the branches, and even by the trees themselves. On every ridge I looked for the expected sparkle of Hoel's Pond, but was disappointed. In fact, I began almost to fancy the pond gifted with a fiendish trick of receding as I advanced. At last, on the brow of an acclivity, I caught a watery twinkle, and heard, with a flash of delight, from Harvey,

"There's Hoel's!"

We found the boat, oars, and paddle, safe in the hollow logs, and very shortly we were afloat. It was with more pleasure than I care to acknowledge that I felt the smooth glide of the little Bluebird in exchange for the toilsome tramping of the woods. We passed the tip of the tongue near the base of which we had camped before our plunge into the beaver recesses, and after a delightful sail we landed on the southern bank, where a huge root grasped the smooth bank like a gigantic claw.

"The carry 'twixt this and Green Pond, the next water in our way," said Harvey, "is rayther long—half a mile, mebby—but it's a nice, dry, open one, as good a'most as the Injin Carry."

Inflamed by this flattering contrast to the roughness of my late path, and considerably renovated by the passage over the pond, I insisted upon bearing the camp-kettle, and at least one of the oars, across the carry. Harvey, complaining of a touch of "rheumatiz in the small o' the back," directed Phin to shoulder the boat while he loaded himself with the "dudods."

We then started, the latter loping ahead with blankets, overcoats, two knapsacks, two rifles, and a basket, with Phin lurching just behind, in a haze of musquitoes, his head and shoulders extinguished in the huge chapeau of his upturned boat, and threatening to run into his sire's back at every stagger.

At first I stepped with considerable elasticity; but toward the end, such was my weakened strength from my tramp, that my oar had the weight of a pine-tree, and the kettle bore down, as if to drag me not only to, but into, the earth at every tread.

Lovely Green Pond, with waters that seemed distilled from the foliage around them, next received us, and crossing its half mile extent, we came to the last carry between us and the Upper Saranac.

This was brief, a few minutes bringing us to a little clearing of logs and raspberry bushes, in which stood a deserted Maine shanty, with a cloud of swallows twittering around its caves. Winding down the bank, through tall wood-plants, we pushed our boat into Spring Pond, and rippled through a water so clear, I could trace the lithe ribbons of the numberless white water-lilies down to the large, rough stems at the bottom.

The reds of the upturned white lily-pads, glowing like

live coals in the slanted sun, spoke vociferously of deer-feasts, eliciting loud laments from both Harvey and Phin, that the moon would rob them of a night hunt. One cove in particular, at the right, was pointed out by the former as " old hunderd fur floatin'."

We emerged into Spring Pond Bay, and at length the noble expanse of the Upper Saranac opened before us.

It lay more than a league in breadth, with three islands —one a mere speck of rock—alone in sight.

As we glided along, a splendid black eagle caught my eye, flying over the lake.

Now he skimmed onward, dipping his stately wings on either side; then he poised himself, remaining motionless a moment, and then up, up he mounted—a speck, a dot, a pin-point, and was gone.

Such, I thought, is the flight of genius. In its proud disdain, its conscious power, onward it directs its kingly flight, onward and upward, high above mortal ken, to its cloudy pinnacle.

"The water-thatch out there makes pipe-stems that's parfect inkstand to smoke with," said Harvey, bringing my heroics flat, and pointing to a space of tall rushes. Pushing among them, we gathered a quantity of the long, jointed tubes, which I afterwards found fully equal to the eulogy of the old boatman.

We landed upon the farthest isle. It sloped steeply up from the water, covered with grass and whortleberry-bushes, and scattered thickly with trees.

Westward rose the rocky islet, and gleaming in the sun, it looked, as Harvey once said, like a turtle on the water.

"Tommy's Rock," said Harvey, in answer to my look; "and this we're on is Goose Island."

"Goose Island!" I exclaimed. "No, no! Wild Goose, at any rate, if there must be a goose in the name!"

"Alter it as you like, Mr. Smith. There's one thing that's a fact! 'Twould puzzle the smartest l'yer in York or Albany to find a tame goose about! How of'en I've camped here," he continued, as we ascended the acclivity, "ketchin' fur along these waters. It's so nice and lonesome, I al'ays try to git here when night comes, 'cause I'm pretty sarten there's no one to trouble me."

"Do you like to be away from people, Harvey?"

"Well, I like, as a gin'ral thing, to be alone, 'specially when I'm huntin' or trappin'. When I'm fishin', it's no great matter."

"I shouldn't think you'd be troubled with neighbors anywhere in these woods."

"There's no tellin'! Sometimes you may be campin' in sight a'most o' somebody without you're knowin' it, the woods is so al-mighty thick, and then the fellers come snoopin' about, talkin' and askin' questions, when you'd a good deal ruther be a fixin' up your traps or rifle, or snellin' your hooks or what not. I'm never better off when I go out fur business, than when me and Watch hes the campin' spot to ourselves. I kin talk a little to the dog, and think over what I've got to do next day; where to set my traps, or where it's more likely to roust a deer. There's plenty o' things to think on when a body's alone so, that he can't do when folks's a-dingin' into his ears suthin' or other all the time. But how would you like to take a swim? There's a nice place out there, where you kin dive and kerlikew round consid'able."

I found the bath delicious, the cool delicate lymph lapping me in elysium after my tramp. With the blood tingling in every invigorated vein, I re-entered the boat, and once more we pushed out into the lake.

The broad surface was now kindling to the level sun. Down we rapidly went, Tommy's Rock and Wild Goose Island lessening in light purple haze,

As the wild freedom I was enjoying glanced for the hundredth time through my mind, I spoke to Phin.

"This life of yours, Phin, must be very pleasant!--going when and where you please, asking no one!"

"Well," said Phin, feathering his oar, "y-e-s—I dunno

but 'tis. But I al'ys hed a notion I might do better workin' in some big settlement, and lay up more money than in killin' ven'son and ketchin' fur, and guidin', and so on."

" You have no one to ask as to your movements about this region, have you?"

" No, sir-ee," giving a sweep to his oar. " Now, I'm of age, even father there don't never tell me nothin' when to go, and which way to go, and so on."

" Well, now, suppose you were working in one of these settlements and the boss should reprima—blow you up, for one thing or another, what then?"

"Blow me up!" said Phin, stopping his rowing, "blow me up!"

" Yes!"

" I'd like to see the man that 'ud blow me up!" hitching down his hat.

" Well! what would you do?"

"I'd see plaguey quick who was the best man! I'd lick him or he'd lick me!" and Phin plunged his oar so deep he caught a crab.

" Them big bugs in the settlements 's mighty sassy when they've got a leetle money," said Harvey, his cracked voice more cracked than ever. " They think, I do bleeve, that a poor man haint got no right to live, no how. But sich kind o' chaps 'ad best keep out o' the woods, fur they'd git more sass 'an gravy."

Down we still went, and gliding along near a large island in mid-channel, with no object save enjoying the beautiful sunset hour with its wooing airs and streaming golds and purples before selecting our camping spot for the night, suddenly we heard a wild shout ringing over the water.

"It come from Fish Hawk Bay, over west there," said Harvey. " S'posen, Mr. Smith, as we've got nothin' else to do, we hev some fun with the loon? I see't there, in a line with that elm slantin' out from Buck Island here. Goll, there's two on 'm! We'll make chase."

Oars and paddle plunged deep and brought us swiftly to the bay.

"It's a mother and her young 'un; you see how grey the second one is," continued Harvey. "'Twould be a pity to shoot her, though loons is the tantenest and most aggravatin' critters next to black flies and mitchets I knows on. But I won't shoot her! 'twould be too much like shootin' a doe with her fa'n. We'll skeer her though!"

The birds had evidently caught sight of us the moment we left Buck Island, for they buried their bodies almost under. As we came near, the mother gave a deep shout, breaking up into a shrill scream, and dived, followed by her young.

Some little time passed, and then both necks suddenly emerged a long distance upon our right.

The boat flew over the water, approaching so near to them that their hand-breadths of back became visible as they wallowed swiftly onward.

Again came the cry from the mother, the warning cry, and both pitched under again, quick as thought. This time they shot up so near, I caught the wild, red gleam of the mother's eyeball. With a frightened "phibb," down again she went with her young, and once more the dark necks of the two came above the surface. It was touching to see the anxious care with which the old bird endeavored to guard the other, keeping in front of the boat, which was all the while doubling upon them like a hound upon a deer.

Suddenly a clarion sound pealed over the water, and a superb loon came sailing down the lake, lifting its trumpet tone as it moved.

"The old man," said Phin, "comin' down to see about his fam'ly, and what all this carryin'-on's up to!"

"And, massy, how mad he is, and so full o' consekens too! You'd think he owned all cr'ation, lettin' alone my blacksmith shop," added Harvey.

Up came the magnificent creature, riding high upon the

water, and swept past us, so intent upon the two birds before him that he did not seem to fear, or even notice us.

Reaching the others, he made a circle as if to enfold them in a protecting ring, while shrill cries echoed from the three. Pushing then to the front he led the way downward, all in file, he frequently turning completely round as if to see whether danger menaced the rear.

We ceased following, in pure admiration of the sight, and far down the lake the three sailed, lessening into specks, until they vanished in a rosy gleam of water.

"S'posen we drop into Buck Island Bay, there to the east," said Harvey, after we had turned our course, and doubled the lower end of the large island. "We might as well be lookin' out for our campin' place. I've sometimes camped on Wind Island, in the bay here—but durn me, ef that loon aint a comin' agin!" as the well-known peal once more shook upon our ears.

"It's the same one, I consate, that is, the old he feller. 'Tisn't of'en you see two sich big ones cluss together. Now, ef he comes nigh enough, I'll fix 'im. They're the sassiest, provokinest critter"——

"That's so," chimed in Phin. "Ef ye git sight on a deer, jest as yer paddlin' up still like, or mebby about to fire, the fust you know, a dod-blamed loon'll set up his sass, hoo-oo-in' away, and the deer'll look up; and then the loon'll sass up agin, and, hokey! the deer's off like lightnin'."

"It's jest as if it said," continued Harvey, "at fust, 'Look out there,' and next, 'Be off;' and off 'tis. On top o' that, ef you should be ketched out on the lake in a spit o' rain, the loon'll al'ys hoot out jest afore it, as ef 'twas laughin' at ye. Or ef so be there comes up a smart blow, we'll say in the Narrers down there, you'll hev the confounded loon a-yellin' and a-bowwowin' and a-tantin', as ef it raally enj'yed itself in seein' you a-bobbin' up and down. I hate 'm. There he comes!" handling his rifle.

Up again swept the bird, riding high as before, and carrying his neck proudly, sounding at intervals his ringing, triumphal, defiant note.

"Don't be sassin' us too much," said Harvey, as a bold flourish burst from the bird. "I'll give ye Hail Columbee"——

"Don't shoot him, Harvey," interposed I; "he's a brave bird, and has done bravely."

"Ef you'd lost as many deer as I hev," returned Harvey, squinting over his barrel, "you wouldn't be so tender-hearted about the divils."

"I tell ye, it cuts cluss," added Phin, steadying the boat with his oars, "to lose a nice fat buck from the yellin's and catterwaulin's of these 'ere good-fur-nothin's."

"Zactly," said Harvey, and he fired.

Down plunged the loon; but immediately after there was a flutter near the surface, and then a glance of white.

"He's got it this time," said Phin, grinning, and pulling at his oars. "No more hoo-hooin' from that critter."

"He's got a hole in his neck that isn't his mouth," said Harvey, as he lifted the lifeless bird, and placed him in the boat; "and now, s'posen we go inter Saganaw Bay, instid o' Buck Island, and find a campin' spot. In the mornin', ef you say so, Mr. Smith, we'll go up the Fish Creek waters inter Big Square Pond, and then about a mile in the woods, nigh Rawlins Pond, where I'll show ye the biggest beaver-dam and meader you've seen yit."

As the boat glided downward, I looked again and again at the dark purple-green of the loon's neck; the two white collars below; his back and wings of ebony, inlaid with pearl; the pure snow of his undershape; the black dagger of his beak; his fierce red eye; and his short, straight, jointless leg, so adapted to propel the buoyant barque of his body. His structure was wild, almost grotesque, and, like his Indian whoop, in harmony with the secluded and savage waters which he alone makes his home.

"They're an odd fish," said Harvey, as he watched my interest in the bird. "In the spring, jest as soon as tho ice is out o' the lakes, you'll see 'm start up, as 'twere, out o' the water. In the evenin' there won't be none on 'm seen, p'raps; and the next mornin', mebby in a snow-squall, the fust thing you'll hear'll be their hoo-o-o, looddle, loddle loddle, by some island or other. And jest so it is, late in the fall. At night you'll hear 'm in full blast, and at mornin' they aint nowheres. They're the queerest critter to get out o' the water, too. Fur all they swim so fast, they're an awk'ard thing to rise, their wings is so short and their body's so heavy. They'll mebby go on a-strugglin' a rod or two, beatin' the water with their wings, and at last they'll make out to git clear. The best way they find to raise up is agin the swells; they git a cant-up then quick. Onst up, they fly like the mischief high in the air, so that you kin jest see 'm, and they keep up a terr'ble hootin' and squallin' as they go, the same as in the water."

"They have nests, of course?"

"Sarten. They build 'm along the edges o' the islands, and on the p'ints, and in the lonesomest coves. Very of'en they build on floatin' bogs, which is tied by threads of grass to the bottom, like the water-lilies. I've seen 'm a half a mile from shore, sometimes, on these bogs. The nests is made of wet mud, and they lay two or three big-sized, green-lookin' eggs, speckled with brown spots. In the spring, and along airly in the summer, the male bird 'll go with his mate. After that, the mother 'll go with her young, and the old loon goes sailin' about alone by himself. It takes a quick hand to shoot 'm, they dive so at the flash o' the gun."

"They can't be eaten, can they?"

"Oh massy, no! I'd as lieve eat a raven. They're so full of ile, that their feathers, as ye see, is as dry as a pine-board as sun as they come out o' the water."

"What do they feed on?"

"Fish and frogs and plants and grass, and sich like, that they find round the water. They dive after the fish, and gulp 'm down while they're under water. They're weather-wise, too. Such a howlin', and catterwaulin', and bow-wowing as they'll set up afore a rain-storm or a gale o' wind! Hark!" as a succession of faint cries came from behind a point. "The loons in Gilpin Bay, down there to the west, is sayin' that rain's now makin' fur us. There's the deer, too. They kin tell three days aforehand when a long storm's a-comin'. No matter how clear the weather is, they'll go off from where they've bin in the habit o' feedin', to the thickest woods and swamps, a-housin' themselves agin the storm. The truth is, Mr. Smith, I'm in a wonder like, how much all the dumb critters in the woods knows. They kin take keer o' themselves a good deal better than most folks. I've watched a common mushrat, afore now, seein' 'm dodge about after his food, keepin' a good look-out all the time for dannger, till I raaly didn't know what to think, except that all this preached up, jest as clear as the sun, that there was suthin' directin' all this. Even ef there was no sich thing as a Bible, all what I see in the woods tells me there's a God."

We turned a long point, and directed our course toward a bay on the east side of the lake.

. "Markham P'int," said Harvey, " the biggest p'int on the lake. The bay here is Saganaw Bay, where we'd better camp for the night. The island is Trout Island."

We landed upon a beautiful beach of smooth white sand, in a little green nook. The broad print of a panther's paw was stamped in the sand near the water, where he had probably paused to drink.

The sun had now set. As I watched him sinking below the tree-tops, I felt, with the wide lonely lake in front and the overwhelming forests around, more profoundly than ever before, as if some protecting power had departed.

Rosy clouds were scattered over the zenith. On the rim of the west was a cloudy terrace of violet, pink, and lustrous grey; the lake displayed a rich burnish, and the island began thickening in golden umber.

We selected our sleeping-room beneath an old iron-like trunk, glued to the ledge out of which it twisted, the whole looking as if the rock had shot out into a tree. Here we spread our mattresses of boughs, built our camp-fire, and ate our evening meal. The dusk crept on, and the night breeze came in delicious breaths of coolness. Above, the moon was shining, yielding to the water a dim, tremulous lustre, and painting the forest with silver lights and deep, sweeping shadows.

After a while, father and son commenced a song, which I give in "corrected form."

>Oh, give me a home where the far winds roam
> Through the forest, as over the sea!
>Where the waters wide are flashing and the torrents bold are dashing,
> And the eagle waves his pinion far and free!
>Where the trout is glad up-leaping and the lily-cup is sleeping,
> And the deer is skimming onward like a dart;
>In this home of simple pleasures, which in sooth are greatest treasures,
> In this home, this free home of the heart!
>
>Oh, why should we stay, where our toilsome way
> Is beset by the pitfall and thorn!
>Where we call each other brother, but to prey on one another,
> And we better, never, never have been born!
>Yes, why should we so sorrow, when here the day and morrow
> Are made of vanished Paradise a part!
>In this home of leaf and fountain! in this realm of lake and mountain!
> In this home, this free home of the heart!

CHAPTER XXV.

Up Fish-Creek Waters.—Old Dam at Floodwood Pond.—Big Square Pond.—
Maine Shanty.—Beaver-dam.—Wind on Upper Saranac.—Bear Point.—
The Narrows.—Deer in Lake.—Camping on Point.—Moonlight Scene.—
Dawn.—Trail in the Woods.—Down Lake to Bartlett's.—Moonlight Sail
through Lower Saranac.—Baker's.

DAYBREAK saw us afloat, our dips alone disturbing the crystal of the lake. Little wheels of dead leaves revolved occasionally athwart the open dingles of the woods, along the bay; the nervous aspens shook their round leaves in quick, glancing motions, like the play of water, while the wan tinge of the sky was momentarily darkening the blue into brown, threatening to drive away the sunshine. All betokened rain, like the loons in Gilpin Bay the day before. We decided, however, to visit Big Square Pond, as contemplated, and accordingly we crossed the lake to Fish Creek Bay, directly opposite where we had encamped. Passing through the bay, we entered Fish Creek northwestwardly, and went through its first three ponds, from the third of which Big Square Pond opens to the west.

"Shell we go up as far as Floodwood Pond, Mr. Smith?" said Harvey; "I'd like to show yer the old dam at the outlet of this creek, where I net white fish in the fall. I start from hum so as to be on the ground airly in the mornin', fill my barr'l and git to hum agin afore night."

We pushed accordingly through the other expanses of the Creek, silvered over with the white lily-blossoms, and glanced at Little Square Pond, lying also to the west and looking sombre under the fast darkening colors of the sky. A mile farther of the Creek brought us to the dam.

An immense log lay athwart the mouth of the outlet,

resting on beds of gravel. At the left were the blackened timbers of the old dilapidated dam, while the broken, precipitous banks were bristling with cedars, the lighter green of the hard or deciduous trees mingling with their dark hues. Beyond, spread the waters of the pond, dim under the leaden sky, which was fast thickening into mist.

The quick drops were beating merrily upon the lily-pad surface of Duck Pond, as we passed downward, and when we turned into Big Square Pond, the whole scene was roaring with the rain.

"Thank fortin' for the Maine Shanty up ahead," said Harvey; "it looks to me 'twould rain all day."

The shanty was at the extreme western end of the pond, and proved tight and comfortable.

"The lumber fellers has left a good stove, I see," continued the old woodman, "and," picking up a fragment of spruce board, "here's a part o' the deacon-seat, that'll be old hunderd fur kindlin'."

The stove, after puffing a little in smoky anger, supplied farther by the dry billets of wood lying in a little closet, diffused a ruddy glow through the room and a grateful warmth over our chilled frames. All the afternoon we heard the monotonous song of the rain upon the roof, only varied by the gusty strike of the sheets against the sides of the cabin, as if they wished to make us a visit bodily. The open door let our vision out upon the white, bubbling surface of the water, and the dark, wet woods.

There was a second story, of one room, littered with straw, in which I found a dingy pack of cards. The hollow bass of the rain alone awoke the silence, and I listened to it with the pleasure yielded by my security from the "pitiless" peltings without.

At sunset there was a change. The storm struggled heavily against the charging winds and the spears of sunshine, marshalling its sullen columns and rolling and weltering over the battle-ground of the concave, but at last piled its black masses in retreat at the east, leaving a bare zenith and a west glowing in ruby.

At midnight I was awakened by a wild shout. I started to my feet, for I thought some wretch was drowning in the lake, or perishing in the woods. A second cry came, and I found it was that of a loon. I looked from the little window of the loft. It was repeated, and, in the dead darkness of the hour and blackness of the water, the cry seemed the wail of some demon mocking, while it despaired.

Morning arose with a high wind. We crossed the pond to another lumber shanty, and then followed a faint trail through the woods for a mile, which brought us to the beaver meadow. It was larger than any I had found, with the usual grass and islands of wood and edges of tamarack. A stream coursed through, with two small ponds, one of which was skirted by the dam. This was much higher than those I had seen, having an altitude of six feet. Solitude and silence claimed the whole scene, and after enjoying the quiet beauty awhile, I returned with my guides to the boat.

"We shell hev a dancin' time on't, on S'nac," said Harvey, as we came in sight of Fish Creek Bay; "it's a south wind, and it has the whull rake o' the water."

The trees were waving on the borders of the Creek, and the leafy depths gave out a sullen sound, ominous of the truth of Harvey's words. No signs, however, were in the bay to verify them, the surface, though rolling, being by no means menacing. Nevertheless, as I looked into the main lake, I saw, with some misgiving, a black, stormy-looking water, with quick flits of white upon it.

Phin was at the oars and Harvey at the stern with his paddle. Watch was curled at my feet. Right toward the black water the old boatman steered, the swells, every moment, although we were still in the bay, growing more and more threatening. At length a dull, deep roaring met our ears.

"Old S'nac is rael mad to-day," said Harvey, quietly

looking at the black water in front. "This south wind plays the mischief with the lake. It rakes it all along and makes the edges jest as bad, if not wuss, than the middle. The swells 'ud pound a boat on the rocks and stuns o' the banks all to pieces in five minutes. We've got to take it in the deep water jest as we kin, and we will take it as sun as we git round Moose P'int there," nodding toward a point on the right, bounding the bay.

Higher and higher rose the swells, and at length, turning the point downward, we found ourselves amid rollers several feet high, flashing with foam and bursting with portentous roar. Up to the summit of the swells, and pitching into the hollows, on we went. Occasionally, as some roller higher than the rest hung over us, Harvey, with a gesture, would direct the course of Phin's oars, dipping a rapid paddle himself, and we would skirt the base of the threatening swell, like the darting swallow, until we could cross its lessened slope with safety.

For one mile we thus fought our way, Harvey smoking his pipe with great calmness, and Phin pulling with the same careless air he would have worn on the sheltered Racket.

At length Harvey spoke.

"You see that p'int out there to the right? That's Bear P'int, and there the wust part o' the Narrers begins. I don't want to be skeery, but I raaly think 'twont do to try to go through 'm in this blow. The rollers here's next to nothin' to them down there, and it's my jedgment we'd better land on the p'int and wait for the blow to die off, as I think 'twill about sundown. At all events we'll hev good dry campin' there ef we're obleeged to pass the night. Shell we do't?"

I gladly assented, and passing over several perilous rollers, we were at length enabled to moor our slight craft at the point, after a paroxysm of thumpings upon the rocks that threatened its destruction. Our spot was a small, treeless ledge rounding into the lake, with two or three little grassy hollows near the edge of the woods, and large blocks and points of splintered rocks at the water-margin, through and over which the angry swells dashed themselves into flying spray with hoarse sounds. Downward for half a mile rolled and foamed the black Narrows.

Harvey leveled a maple, and soon a blazing fire kindled the bleak point into comfort. We then partook of our frugal dinner, and passed the afternoon very pleasantly.

Although the gale swept furiously up the lake, whistling over the point and howling through the bordering trees, yet a little distance within, the branches, except at top, spread out in a silence and quiet as profound as in the most breathless atmosphere; so little did even this fierce wind affect the huge mass of the wilderness.

In front and on either hand, the dark, wrathful lake was tossing and bursting into white, while the roar of the swells was mingled with that of the wind. The upper clouds were almost motionless, but below, the ghastly scuds flew from south to north with almost the speed of lightning.

It was now near sunset, and the two guides had gone a rod or two into the forest for branches with which to supply the fire. Looking above the Narrows, I suddenly espied a small white object gliding over the rough water, which a second glance assured me was a deer.

The guides emerging upon the point at the instant, saw the deer also, and rushed to the boat, which had been drawn upon the rocks. Directly, they were tossing upon the surface in pursuit of the animal, which had caught sight of them, turned, and was now making back for the shore. Although the boat almost flew over the water, I saw the deer, which was swimming rapidly, still far in advance. At last he raised his light frame and shot up the bank. In a minute or two the Bluebird also touched the bank, and the two men disappeared.

After a half hour passed by me in watching the chasing swells, and listening to their tumult, I saw a black speck at the opposite shore, and then a flash of silver. It was the returning boat, bringing, however, no deer. Although shot by Harvey in the hind-quarter, it had managed to escape.

The wind, instead of lessening, grew wilder as the twilight thickened. The guides cut down a hemlock, and with its branches strewed our couches for the night, in one of the hollows nearest the woods. The fire was supplied generously. We hauled the boat up, propped it at the edge of the hollow, and then stretched ourselves for slumber under its roof, which curved half way over, thus protecting us mainly from the wind.

I raised myself on my elbow, before sleeping, to survey the scene. The jack had been kindled, and was burning under the stern of the boat; the fire suffused the point with yellow light, which caught upon our ribbed roof, and brought out in bold though unequal relief the background row of trees, leaving the depths beyond to murky blackness. The lake in front spread in lighter, but still uncertain hues, and the swells made a continual wash upon the point.

Suddenly the moon burst from a huge, black cloud, covering one-half the sky, and threw her soft smile upon the lake, in strong contrast to its rolling and foaming rage. The near picture of the point started out in clear outline; the paled fire, the phalanx of forest, the curved boat, the two sleepers, and the rocks at the edge of the water, now darkly glistening and now buried in the silver lashings of the spray.

The burst of moonlight seemed the sudden coming of a friend, and with a glow of pleasure from its guardian presence, I lay down beside my companions, and, to the moaning of the forest and splashing of the lake, fell asleep.

I woke. The fire had died away; the moon was filling the hollow of the boat with silver, showing, clear as day, my guides in the attitude of slumber; and the east was turning into amber with the coming of the sun.

The swells had ceased; the wind no longer moaned in the branches; all was peaceful and beautiful. An owl was whining in the yet murky depths, and a couple of loons were in a convulsion of howls and screams upon the lake.

. I again slept, and awoke this time at the summons of Harvey. The moon was in the west, blind and pale; the east was glowing with gold, and the scuds, which were driving like smoke before the again wakened, but now gentler wind, gleamed in flakes of flame.

The Narrows heaved, but were no longer swelling and bursting in anger.

We embarked; but previous to laying our course downward, crossed over to look up the wounded deer.

Harvey soon struck the trail among the herbage, where I saw nothing.

At none of the peculiarities of forest life have I been more astonished than at the quickness of sight and skill (I might almost say intuition) of the guides, in deciphering the little, delicate signs left by the wood animals, in token of their late presence. The tilting of a fern, the rent of a dead leaf, a dash of moss, a drop of rusty blood scarce distinguishable from a weather-stain, a crushed sprout, the edge-mark of a hoof, the puncture of a claw, even the cling of a hair on a shrub, etches the trail to the hunter's or trapper's eye, unerringly as the beaten deer-track winding through the woods.

The old guide wove the bits of his trail together for a mile, but in vain. He then decided to return, and resume our downward course, fearful the wind might again rise in its strength and imprison us another day.

As we passed through the Narrows, I asked Harvey some questions about the lake.

"It's ten miles long, and, as a gin'ral thing, three wide," he answered. "From the head, as you come out o' Spring Pond Bay, you can see clearn to the foot, where the Injin Carry is, lyin', as it does, about due north and south. From bay to bay—that is, through Fish Creek Bay to Saganaw Bay—it's, say, four miles; and it's four miles at the head, by Tommy's Rock and Goo—Wild Goose Island.

It's a grand sheet o' water, and has a shore line of mebby fifty miles, with nine bays, eleven p'ints, and twenty-five islands."

As we opened upon the broad part of the lake below the Narrows, the water grew rough again, and opposite a wild clearing at the west, belonging to Bartlett, we encountered a few rollers that reminded us of those of the day before; but we danced merrily over, making for the islands in front.

"There's smooth water agin, jest beyond Mink Island there," said Harvey; "and I smell the breakfast a'most from Bartlett's."

We threaded the islands and turned around a point into the bay or "Gut," from which dash the Saranac river-rapids.

Upon our right, at the foot of the beautiful lake, rose the woods of the Indian Carrying-Place; and I let my fancy wander through its leafy corridor to those wild realms beyond, I had so lately traversed with ever new delight.

We passed through the Gut to the carry around the rapids, and a short walk in the fresh morning air brought us to the dip in the road beneath which stood Bartlett's Inn.

Here I passed the day. I looked at the little garden; listened in the log-hut to the talk of two of Bartlett's guides; watched Bartlett himself, as in high good-humor he led his hounds by couples to the water for a plunge-bath, he shouting at the top of his shrill voice as they shrank and strove to escape; examined the dam; crossed the picturesque bridge, and wandered along the wooded acclivity opposite; re-crossed, and caught glimpses of the rapids from the carry; partook of a capital dinner of trout and venison; strolled in the gentle afternoon light through the whole grassy area of the little clearing; made the acquaintance of a party just setting out with their guides toward the Indian Carrying Place, over which a deep purple thunderstorm was lowering; opened another with a second party firing at the head of a dried loon-skin on a pine near the line of hound-kennels, the crack of the rifle and cough of the fowling-piece making the echoes rattle in the woods; and after the sun had closed his broad eye behind the western trees, listened to the song of the Saranac Nightingale, rising and sinking from the forest toward the Upper Lake.

How I love the music of this hermit bird! In the rudest recesses, it has caught my ear, as well as in the most beautiful. I have listened as it melted over the sunset mirror of the Lower Saranac, floated through the wild beaver-woods of the St. Regis, cheered the depressing loneliness of Dead Creek, spread a charm over the Bog River fastnesses, and pierced as with a silver arrow the roar of Perciefield.

> Oh the trill of the beautiful bluebird!
>   It sends a quick joy through the breast;
> For it tells us the blossoms are coming,
>   That Nature has waked from her rest!
> And witching the red robin's warble,
>   That floats the May sunset along;
> But the woods own a melody sweeter,
>   The Saranac Nightingale's song!
>
> And merry the lay of the bobolink,
>   Hither and thither so free,
> Till the bushes and stalks of the pasture-field
>   Tremble and sway in his glee!
> And the wren at her tiny wood-cottage,
>   What notes from her little bill throng!
> But both would I turn from to listen
>   The Saranac Nightingale's song.
>
> When saddened, how low sinks the melody!
>   Lower and tenderer still;
> Till a fountain, distilled from true happiness,
>   Softly the heart seems to fill!
> When blithe, oh how loud and how bell-like
>   The strain she then seems to prolong!
> Yes, the spirit of rapture is ringing!
>   The Saranac Nightingale's song.

I have heard it when day-break was blushing,
  When evening was gleaming in gold,
When sunshine was sparkling around me,
  When storm robed the sky with its fold;
And to each of the summer-day changes
  Her song seemed in turn to belong.
Oh, faithfullest echo to Nature!
  The Saranac Nightingale's song.

And now when fond memory pictures
  The far-away wilderness scene,
Where I wandered, unchained as the eagle,
  Among the rich splendor of green;
Though the pine sounds its deep-hearted harmony,
  Ripple the waters along,
Far dearer one strain to remembrance,
  The Saranac Nightingale's song!

Twilight had shown its last tint in the brightening moon as we crossed Round Lake, which was one glow of ruby. We entered the narrow channel of the Saranac River, and the close woods threw a darkness over the scene, save where a reaching moonbeam kindled the silver birch or flashed upon a reach of the river.

We made the short portage of the Middle Falls, and at length, emerging from the gloom of the river, saw before us the superb moonlight picture of the Lower Saranac.

So quiet was the water, we seemed floating through air, with the shadowy islands like clouds around us. Now we glided over a broad space of splendor, and now blended ourselves in the gloom of some aisle of foliage or rock. The quiet was perfect, for Harvey had shipped the oars, and Phin was drawing the paddle noiseless as in the night hunt. Not a leaf rustled, not a ripple murmured. Never did the world appear so far away, with its childish pomp, its hollow conventionalities, its follies and its crimes. Nature seemed to whisper rest to the weary heart, to throw her arms around it and say, "Come! find on my bosom the solace of thy sorrows and thy cares." And never had my whole being been so spell-bound in the witchery of the moon. I have since seen her glowing above the awful solitudes of the Indian Pass; on the slope of Mount Seward, I have marked her silver pouring upon the terrific wilderness that stretches southward from his base, the mysterious region of "The Chain Lakes"—the lone eleven; I have gazed upon her, a pearly pendent on the sublime brow of Tahawus, and thought her loveliness enhanced by the stern contrast. But now all was in harmony; all one blended scene of almost heavenly beauty.

At length we glided between the Two Sisters, leaving Eagle Island to our right one ridge of pearl, crossed the molten silver of the intervening basin, and stopped at Martin's.

Here we refreshed ourselves on some of the host's excellent wildwood viands, and then, leaving the guides to care for the faithful Bluebird, which had so long borne me in my wanderings, I took up my solitary midnight, moonlight way to the Lake House.

The tops of the woods were illumined; splashes of white light lay on the bushes, chequered the prostrate logs, and turned the twisted roots into slumbering serpents. The rude houses of Harrietstown were painted into sharp-cut lights and shadows, and the dam was one sheet of silver. As I ascended the hill, I again noticed the picturesque river-bend more beautiful than ever in the delicate light. Another turn in the road brought in view the white, gabled tavern of Baker's.

How stifling was the air of my chamber after camping so long in the woods! It seemed at first I could hardly breathe, but the long usage of conventional life triumphed, and I fell asleep, the murmurings of the little rapid changing into the hum of the pine, and the lighter square of my open window into the parted drapery of the "breezy tent."

CHAPTER XXVI.

Whiteface.—Approach to Mountain.—Upward.—White Falls.—Chasm.— Little Slide.—Great Slide.—Summit.—Prospect.—Descent.—Baker's.— Backwoods' Dance.—Whiteface Notch.—Homeward.

THE next morning I started on the last of my excursions, the visit to the summit of Whiteface.

This mountain is the northern outpost of the Adirondacks. It is a detached summit, wearing near its brow a light grey appearance, which has given it its name; it is over five thousand feet in height, and owns but one superior, Mount Tahawus (a recent survey makes that doubtful) between the Connecticut and the Mississippi. Its south-western foot is bathed by Lake Placid, and along its southern and eastern sides flows the west branch of the Ausable River.

The great slide of the mountain is on its western flank— a steep channel of rock, like a torrent transformed into stone—and reaches from its brow half-way to its base. The mountain, with one exception—a rough, stony opening around its southern summit—is wrapped to its very peak in forest, is totally uninhabited, and is wild and savage to the last degree. It is seen in every direction for fifty miles, and might well be crowned the king of the region.

Our Club had already left the woods for their homes, and in the afternoon, through an air freshened by the showers of the morning, I started with a chance companion (a gentle- man who had just returned from an excursion up Bog River) for the ascent.

We took the road to Nash's, a ride of twelve miles

whence a half-mile on foot would carry us to Lake Placid, across whose four-mile length lay our course to the foot of the mountain.

I had a passing view of Harvey at the door of his cabin, with a sapling angle-rod leaning beside him and a rifle on his knee, the lock of which he seemed examining, and we exchanged a word of hearty greeting. Several hounds were gliding in and out, conspicuous among which were Watch and Pup.

We crossed "The Plains," noted for deer, passed the track to Ray Brook, famous for trout, and a few miles farther saw at our left, detached from the mountains that hitherto had formed our east horizon, the grand form of old Whiteface.

We emerged from the woods, that with intervals of rough clearing and wild meadow had crowded the wheel-track, and opened on the smooth fields of North Elba. Opposite the white dwelling of the blind Priest of the Adirondacks, we turned eastward, still finding a road.

At Thompson's we secured our guide—young Dauphin Thompson, since engaged in John Brown's famous raid at Harper's Ferry and there shot. Toward sunset, we reached Bennet's Pond, on the borders of which was Nash's clearing.

To the south stretched the superb Adirondacks, with Tahawus soaring above all.

Sunset came, flashing from his front the most imperial colors. The range turned into a haze of rose-violet, the little pond in front into a ruby, while to the extreme left of the mountain-picture gleamed the purple cone of White-face.

By and by the round moon rose, and the lovely landscape lay in the silver silence of the night.

Sunrise found us at Paradox Pond, which opens by a narrow channel into Lake Placid.

This beautiful lake lies in a northeast direction, two long islands and one smaller giving it the appearance of a series of lagoons. It is sheltered by lofty shores, and its quiet depths are of crystalline clearness. Not a trace of cultivation breaks the surrounding woods. Whiteface towers over its northeastern head. And here I may remark another peculiarity of this wilderness—scarce a mountain but owns its lake spread like a mirror to reflect its grand forests and beetling crags.

The outlet flows from its southwest border, and bends easterly to join the west branch of the Ausable River. Wild Chub River flows into the outlet from the southwest.

The whole scene is wrapped in loneliness. As we stood upon the edge of the Paradox Pond our presence seemed intrusion upon some enchanted region, and as if it might call up the awful Genius of Solitude in quick wrath upon us for breaking in upon his repose.

The guide drew a boat from a thicket, and we crossed the lake toward Whiteface, the mountain all the while lifting his proud cone higher and higher until the summit smote the blue of the morning.

But the dark mass seemed to cast a great sorrow over the brilliant sky and sparkling lake; for I was then full of trouble. To shun the haunting shadow, whither should I flee? In the sunshine, it was there, and in the quiet night; in the lonely musing; in the tumult of the storm and the music of birds and waters. Whence, oh heart! this sadness! Is hope indeed a mockery and love but a long-drawn sigh! Is life but another name for woe—its past a regretful memory, its present one dreary waste, its future lost in darkness?

Then I felt a voice sinking into the depths of my spirit, —as it were, the voice of the mountain.

"Cease, fool of thine own fantasies! cease thy vain repinings! Listen! Yesterday, storms beat upon my bosom; to-day, I rejoice in sunshine. But what if storms should return to-morrow? Still would I stand upon my solid base and brave the clouds that dashed upon my breast. Lightnings may shatter these crags and cut their pathway to my core, yet shall I keep my heart forever firm in the strength of peace."

I bowed to the teachings of the voice; I took the truth into my soul. If joy is transient, so, too, is sorrow; and sorrow nobly borne finds consolation in the very consciousness of the strength which it reveals.

It was seven in the morning when we commenced our three-mile ascent. Path there was none. Here and there, as in the beaver-woods, a trail of bear or deer meandered through the hollows and along the low ridges, and was often lost under prostrate trees and thickets.

The ascent at first was neither steep nor toilsome. Soon, however, it became obstructed by large rocks, which we clambered up, inserting our feet in the crevices, or resting them upon the mossy points and notches, and clinging to the knotted roots or branches of the firs and hemlocks.

A deep murmur at length filled the air, and, glancing to the left, we caught flashes of falling water. Descending, we reached the margin of a headlong brook. Above, a milk-white water-fall hurled itself over frowning ledges, and foamed past and down a wild ravine until lost in leafy gloom. It was the stream of the White Falls.

The ascent now became more and more precipitous. Dead trunks blocked our way, crumbling into brown, damp flakes almost at the touch of our climbing feet; immense masses of roots erect, with corresponding hollows, thickets almost impenetrable, mossy cavities in which we plunged waist-deep, underbrush that clung around our feet like serpents, and low boughs forcing us to stoop for passage, also interrupted our progress. As in the beaver-woods, again, the moss spread its piled velvet over almost every object—the coiling root, the mouldering log, the runnel cradled deep in the dingle, and the ledges on the levels of our way.

Although we were continually ascending I was unaware,

so dense twined the forest, of the height to which we had clambered. But suddenly the green gloom opened into broad sunlight, and, looking out and down in that direction, I instinctively recoiled, with thrilling nerves. There, its edge within three paces, frowned a terrific chasm, cloven thousands of feet down, down through the breast of the mountain. On the nearest side it sank almost sheer, while opposite, a wall slightly sloping rose hundreds of feet above. Half-way down this awful gorge, I saw a floating atom that I supposed an eagle tacking up the side. From a ledge, seeming but a hand's-breadth and near the moving speck, slanted what appeared a shrub, but was really one of those enormous pines which towered up into the sky opposite, and went dwindling rank below rank down the chasm.

Shuddering at the terror, and yet fascinated by the wild grandeur of the scene, I remained gazing, until a whoop from my guide recalled my thoughts, and turning, I once more bent my energies to clambering the mountain. This became harder and harder, from the increasing steepness and the density of the underbrush, as well as the barricades of branches through which we plunged, twisting aside and breaking off limbs for passage. Frequent halts were now made, generally beside some cool, clear spring, oozing from moist roots and mossy clefts, for deep and most delicious draughts.

Now and then a dead pine or hemlock, fallen from above, would bridge some deep ravine, offering an upward path along its broad breast and jagged points.

Struggling thus an hour longer, all at once, we broke through a dense thicket, and a startling sight met us. A slant plunge of rock, perfectly smooth and sloping steeply to a sheer precipice, lay directly in our path. A few spots of moss alone broke the smooth, glistening granite.

"This is the Little Slide," said Thompson, and to my amazement and no little dread, he planted his foot upon it with the evident intention of crossing.

"You don't mean to say that our course lies over that place!" said I.

"Sarten," returned he, "right crost."

"There's no right about it," returned I, "and hang me if I go!"

"No other way," responded the other coolly, and advancing toward the middle. "There aint no danngcr as I knows on. These spots o' moss is the dandy to git us crost."

"They are, eh! Suppose these spots of moss should slip, where would we go then? Down that precipice as sure as we're alive! There isn't a crack in that slide—and slide it is, sure enough!—as big as a knife-blade, to squeeze a finger in, and it's as smooth as a new-washed dinner-plate except the moss!"

"No dannger and no other way," returned the lad, treading over the shining surface unconcernedly as if on his cabin floor. "We can't go below it, that's sarten, and we can't git above it as I knows on; at least without tuggin' and scratchin' and scrabblin' wuss than a bear climbin' a tree with a twenty pound trap on his paw. Folly me, and we'll git crost, I'll be bound."

"Folly, sure enough!" thought I, "the greatest folly is in coming here at all! climbing this savage and nearly inaccessible mountain with a hare-brained boy! Why, that rock is like a steeple, and smooth as a looking-glass!"

"Come on Mister!" said the guide, who had crossed and was standing on the opposite edge.

Finding no help for it, I stepped upon the rock, and, with my frame tingling, moved cautiously along the slope, looking steadily before me, with my companion at my right. It was not more than two or three rods wide, and once over, I found myself inwardly vowing (forgetting that I must return) never again to commit such insanity.

Turning sharply to the right, we once more applied ourselves to our task. It was now doubly painful. The sides of the mountain became almost perpendicular. We made one continuous struggle of it; pulling ourselves up by branches, hanging to roots, scrambling through clefts and over ledges, until, bursting through a barrier of close underbrush, we found ourselves on the brink of a long, slanting pathway of granite. It was the Great Slide.

Down it pointed, and up, up, up it sloped, a stony ladder, grey and glistening, up to the very summit which now stood boldly out against the sky.

Although not nearly so steep nor so perilous, to all appearance, as the Little Slide, the thought of ascending it produced a new crawling of the nerves. I knew it must be four thousand feet in air, and that all around were tremendous chasms and dizzy precipices, over which, by one slip of the foot, I might be hurled. But the guide's figure, sharply relieved against the sky as he travelled upward, called me on, with my comrade by my side. The steepness hardly allowed us an upright position; huge boulders blocked our path; springs spread an oily, slippery ooze over the bare granite. My soles, too, from the polishing of the dead leaves and pine-needles, had become like glass, and my tread, consequently, was not sure.

But I persevered. The scene behind us was but a glimpse of a distant region, narrow and vague. On either side, the close forest stood up to the very edges.

We had been half an hour on the Slide, and still were toiling up, up—the grey path slippery and blocked with boulders as before, when we came to a bed of pebbles and broken rock, which often rolled from under our tread, and went rattling down the Slide. A little way above stood the summit—a high rampart of rock. Suddenly we turned from the Slide into a slight track winding upward, and went along a rocky platform or gallery, jutting from the sides of the rampart. Glancing to the left, I shuddered at the dizzy chasm below, and grasped a bush instinctively. A few more winding steps to the right, and I stood upon the summit.

A deliciously cool wind was flowing over the peak, as if the air was stirred by a mighty fan.

I threw myself beside my companion upon the ground; I drew in with delight the nectarean air; my heated pulses grew calm, and the dews of my long struggle with the mountain dried upon my forehead.

After a short repose, I turned to study the scene.

The summit was level, one or two hundred feet broad, with ledges of granite weather-stained and patched with lichen, cropping out of the thin, desolate soil. At the west, was a wall of serrated rock, the rampart as seen from below. I ascended by a step or two of jutting strata, and a most grand and enchanting prospect opened. Beyond the billows of verdure rolling down the mountain, lay, like a picture, Lake Placid, studded with emerald island-gems. To the utmost horizon, stretched the forest, surging into summits and sinking into valleys, holding the bright Saranac Lakes like a silver horse-shoe; while around and beyond, were other waters of their group, like shields of steel or meandering veins of light. A long gleam betrayed the course of the Racket, with Tupper's Lake, a glittering mirror, toward the south.

I descended from the rock and looked northward. At my feet, lay a cultivated region, meadows and grain-fields, the roofs of Wilmington, and the two villages of Jay; and afar, mountain-chains melted into the sky, with tracts of forest darkening between.

"Guide, what is that long, narrow gleam in the farthest distance north?"

"That's old Champlain," answered the lad, reclining on his elbow, and picking his teeth with a jack-knife.

"And that range of mountain?"

"The Green Mountains, in old Varmount."

I looked at the gleam and the misty summits, forty and fifty miles away, and realized the height on which I stood.

"The River St. Lorrence has bin seen from here, but it

must a bin on a clearer day than this," said the lad, again. "I never see't myself, but folks sez so. Still, folks don't say al'ys what they oughter!"

Southward rose the Adirondack range, breaking the sky with its pointed peaks. A single cloud stood over Tahawus like a plume—the only sign of human life between me and it, being the smooth, bright fields of North Elba; and I exulted in the feeling that I had conquered a height little inferior, if at all, to his imperial crest.

Turning from the prospect a moment, and while my companion and I were exchanging admiring expressions and sentiments inspired by the scene, I chanced to espy at my feet a little meek-eyed blossom, struggling through the ungenial moss.

Even so, thought I, are the feeblest natures lifted sometimes to positions fitted only to the sternest; and thus also do the hardest hearts wear the softest virtues.

My farther reflections were interrupted by the guide.

"Gaul darn!" said he, "how dry I am! as dry as a powder-horn! But here's some blueberries! Psha!" spitting them out in disgust, "they're as bitter as boneset. But say, some folks is great fools!"

"Indeed!" said I.

"Ef they aint, I'm darned. I've heerd a heap o' the fools say, and they bleeved it, too, that there was a pond right on top o' this 'ere mountain; and I must say I bleeved it too, before I come on top on't. Now, do you see any pond?"

"I must confess I do not."

"You'd hev to hev more eyes than you've got, to see one here on the top o' this all-fired big hill—so big, 'twould bung up, as a body may say, a crow to fly up't. But why can't you see no pond? 'Cause there aint no pond here fur to see. Consarn 'em!"

I once more turned to the prospect. For two hours I studied the splendid picture, stamping it upon my memory; and then observing that the shadows had wheeled eastward, and calling to mind that the wild mountain offered no hospitality for the coming night—that, in fact, the nearest shelter was Nash's, beyond Lake Placid—I suggested our return.

Bidding adieu to the stern summit, we wound down the rocky gallery and once more planted ourselves upon the Slide. Down we went, down among the loose pebbles, sending them spinning and bounding before us—down, scaling the boulders and sliding over the oily spots—down, until we reached the point where we had entered. We plunged into the forest, glad to change for trusty earth the slippery and treacherous rock. Then down again—down the ledges by the loops of roots and jutting crevices—down the abrupt, almost sheer declivities, steadying our descent by the pendent boughs, until we reached the Little Slide.

Once more, plucking up courage, I followed my guide safely across, my companion beside me as before. Down again, plunging down, vaulting over the prostrate trees, threshing through the thickets; down the ridges and through the hollows, pausing a moment at the silver springs, down, down we went, until once more we saw before us the welcome waters of Lake Placid, crimson now in the last lustre of sunset.

Our ascent took seven hours, our descent four.

Delightful was the skim of the boat, after my rough tramping. Some little distance on, I looked behind. Was it possible that I had trod the top of that tremendous cone, soaring so haughtily in the evening sky!

No doubt about it! Every bone in my body proclaimed it, "trumpet-tongued." Was it worth the toil? That was it, by the grandeur of the scenes beheld, and by the consciousness that, despite the monarch's frown, despite the "divinity" of dizzy terror that "doth hedge him in," I had planted my foot victorious on his brow. Sternly, old Whiteface! thou frownest back from thy throne of rock the mortal who approaches, but thou yieldest thy secret to endurance and energy, and rewardest graciously thy victor.

So with adverse fortune; stern in advance, but yielding to the will, it smiles on those who have the strength to vanquish it.

From the opposite margin, I again looked backward lingeringly.

The velvet softness, the dreamy haze in the twilight, was that the savage scene of such terrific chasms, such splintered crags, such dread acclivities? And was not another emblem of life offered by it, so smooth to hope, so stern to experience?

We reached Nash's, and there rested for the night. Passages of my tramp fashioned half my dreams. Now I was dragging myself up the ledges by the snaky roots, now swinging like a pendulum from a slanting tree over unfathomable chasms; now speeding on the wings of fear down the Great Slide from a huge rock that was bounding and thundering close behind me, striking fire as it flew. At last I was on the top of the rampart overlooking Lake Placid. Suddenly my head whirled, I fell, and in my wheel-like passage toward the lake, I awoke. A ray of moonlight through the little window shot athwart the entire length of the loft, kindling the rough beams and rafters All was quiet; and congratulating myself that I was not really circling five thousand feet into Lake Placid, I again slumbered.

With the returning light, in the glow of a beautiful morning, I returned to Baker's.

Here I remained two days; catching trout in the lovely windings of Ray and Mackenzie-Pond Brooks; chasing a deer of Cort's imagination on "The Plains," and finding fatigue and a ferocious appetite, with nothing there to satisfy it; achieving Baker's Peak and its radiant prospect; visiting Moose Pond, leafy and lone and beautiful, and gazing once more over the cool, blue expanse of the Lower Saranac, whence I again heard in the sunset the wild laugh of the loon.

Hark! the loon's laugh on the lake!
　Hark! the taunting, jeering sound!
Shore and wave in echoes wake;
　Mocking fiends seem revelling round.
What disdain on man it throws!
　"Heart, despair! in anguish, break!
Life is but a scene of woes,"
　Says the loon's laugh on the lake—
　　Laugh so scornful!
　Ah! the loon's laugh on the lake!

Fame! how gloriously it tears
　From unwilling Time the wreath!
Power! what haughty front it wears,
　Trampling all it meets, beneath!
Wealth—the monarch of its sphere,
　Breathing air that flatterers make!
Surely happiness is here!
　Hark! the loon's laugh on the lake—
　　Laugh so scornful!
　Ah! the loon's laugh on the lake!

Youth, that bright and bounding time,
　Treading paths knee-deep in flowers!
Manhood, in its towering prime,
　Heedless of the rushing hours!
Age, the sunset melting clear
　Hues that mellow lustre make!
Surely happiness is here!
　Hark! the loon's laugh on the lake—
　　Laugh so scornful!
　Ah! the loon's laugh on the lake!

The evening before I left, I stood on the rustic bridge below Baker's, and listened to the chiming of the little rapids. Gladly did they dash and glitter in the moonbeams, but sadly did my heart pulsate to their music. Oh, troubled heart!—but again? Remember the voice of the mountain, oh, troubled heart! and rest.

On returning to the tavern, I found three or four guides in the bar-room talking.

"Them two tame bear by the barn keeps up an all-fired pacin' back'ards and forreds," said one. "They'll sarten wear their paws out. And that puts me in mind, b'ys, of the almightiest big bear-track I see t'other day in Whiteface Notch. It"——

"Whiteface Notch!" interrupted I, "I've heard of that spot. What kind of place is it?"

"It's a tarnel big kind o' place. The rocks go up so high, it seems as ef they didn't want 'er stop at all."

"Aha!" said I. "And where is this Notch?"

"It's on the road to Jay. You go up the 'Lizbethtown road to North Elby, and then turn up the road, east by the O'Sobble river to Jay, and then by 'The Forks' to Keeseville."

"I wonder when the next dance 'll come off," said another a moment after. "I kinder feel as ef my legs want limb'rin."

"Less see, that last was at Bloomin'dale!" said a third.

"'Twan't nowheres else," responded the describer of the Notch, "and a good 'un it was, too, but nothin' like that we hed over Keene Mounting—less see—'twas last Washin'ton's Birthday."

"I heerd tell a leetle suthin' about that dance, Jake. Tell us about it!"

After the usual "drinks round," the narrator settled himself on a barrel, which shared a corner with two rifles, a pair of snowshoes and a bearskin.

"Well," commenced he, "I heerd the dance was a-comin' off, and so I went for Molly Keeler, a rael tip-top gal, with an eye like a fa'n's, and as fur dancin', there's no use a talkin'—the swells on Round Lake in a wind don't move no purtier. Molly was all prinked up in yaller, with a red ribbon round her little waist, and a pi'ny blow stuck in her hair as big as my fist. Well, we started. I hed a nice smart critter to go, and about the easiest buckboard that could be skeered up—why, Jim! you knows Bill Hoskin that made the slash last Spring jest t'other side o' Harrietstown, torts the pond! well, he hired me the buckboard, and I give 'im a mink skin fur the use on't. Well, as

I said afore, we started. Molly looked jeest as nice as a poppy-show, now I tell *you !* and her tongue was a-goin' and her eyes was a-dancin', the whull way—oh, orful! Well, we got to the tavern—Old Samson kept it, you all knows him! a purty clever old critter, but a hoss to drink —and the b'ys and gals o' the whull settlement was there. There was Jack Ketcham that shantied nigh Mount Seward last fall, ketchin' fur—he ketched an al-mighty sight o' fisher and saple that time—well, he was there with his gal, Betsey Parkins, and there was that Nelson feller—what was his fust name! you know, Josh! the feller that shot the big moose last October on Bog River—yes, that's it— Sim!—he was there with Faith Larkins. Then there was Pete Johnson, and—did ye ever go guidin' with Pete? He can take a bigger boat on a furder carry—well, I won't say no more. He hed Huldy Skinner with him. Well, I can't tell ye all on 'm! but there was as good a lot o' b'ys and gals as I've most ever seen. We hed good music too, what I call good music! Tom Stackpole was there with his fiddle! You all knows Tom, and you needn't fur to go tell me Tom can't handle a bow! Well, at it we went, rick-a-tick, rick-a-tick, rick-a-tick-a-ticky, hey, b'ys! Coats off after the fust breakdown and hankerchers tied round the waist, and didn't we go 't heel and toe! Oh, sha, there aint no use a-talkin'! And Tom, didn't he make that bow o' his'n fly! well, he did! and his foot it went tapity-tap, keepin' time, and he'd holler out, "All hands round! dance to pardners, down in the middle," as farse as a tadpole in a bog. And as fur Moll, I tell yer, b'ys, ef her leetle feet didn't go and her big eyes didn't snap, oh go 'way now! 'Hooray!' says Jack Ketcham, 'make way fur the bear down the middle!' Whiles Pete Sawyer's legs flew about so nimble, I consated he'd ontwist all the knots out o' his hankercher. Finally at last Jack Ketcham— well, I must say, b'ys, he was purty well swiped, ef he is old hunderd on trappin', as old Harve says—but as I was a-sayin'—finally at last Jack he kicks off his boots and goes

it in his stockin' feet, and he jumps up and down, and
'Whoop, h-o-o-r-a-y!' s'ze, 'fur the tiger,' s'ze, 'and the
rhinoceros,' s'ze, 'and all kind o' painters,' s'ze, 'lettin'
alone mushrats,' and kep' strikin' his hands agin his heels
every jump he made. Well, we kep' it up till about sunrise, and I hev an idee we'd a danced till after breakfast
time ef 'twant for one thing, and that is ef 't 'adn't bin that
all on us got a-fightin', that is, all the b'ys. And this was
the way on't. Every time twixt the breakdowns, all hands
went to the bar-room and we was all terr'ble dry, and you
needn't say 'twas buttermilk, nur 'lasses and water, nur
cider-ile and ginger, hey! Not by consid'ble! W-a-a-l,
'bout sunrise the whiskey begun to work. Jack Ketcham
was purty well loaded, and the last drink fired 'im off.
'I'll bet as much mink,' s'ze, 'as a leetle grasshopper like
me,' s'ze, 'kin put in his pocket,' s'ze (he was as big as a
two-acre clearin', Jack was) 'agin,' s'ze, 'a couple o' rats,
what this bull-moose,' s'ze—slappin' little Phil Campbell
on the back—'can't more'n carry on his shoulders,' s'ze,
'that this baby kin outdance,' s'ze, 'enny chap in this ere
breakdown,' s'ze, and 'whoop,' s'ze, and 'h-o-o-r-a-y,' s'ze,
and he jumped up three times, and hit his heels with his
hands every time agin. Now, b'ys, Phil was leetle, but
wa'n't he smart? wa'n't he? whew! He was the grittiest
critter! Well, Phil, he brustled up like a woodchuck in
his hole! 'What yer 'bout!' s'ze, 'slappin' folks on the
back,' s'ze. 'I aint a-goin' to stand no sich carryin's-on as
that,' s'ze; and with that he let drive r-r-r-ight agin Jack's
nose, and you may bleeve the fight was in. Nick Tanner
he sprung and Sam Libby and Chris Topple, and the fists
flew, and ye may s'pose, b'ys, that this chap wa'nt a-goin'
to be punched in the back and kicked round gin'rally without hevin' a hand in; and in the midst on't all, in come
Tom Stackpole fur his pay, and, 'b'ys,' s'ze, 'stop your
fightin' jest fur a minute,' s'ze, 'and gimme my pay! two
dollars,' s'ze, 'and what drink I wanted, and I've tuk the
drink,' s'ze, 'and now,' s'ze, 'fur the two dollars,' s'ze; and

as he said it, up went his heels, and down come his headpiece; and no wonder; fur I see Jack Tupper a-kinder swing his hands down, and Je-rusalem wa'n't Tom mad when he scrabbled up! But by this time, the landlurd 'ad hollored out that he'd stand treat ef they wouldn't fight no more! and all stopped right off and tuk a drink round, and was good frinds. But the gals, they wouldn't dance no more, fur they was mad at bein' left; 'fur,' says they, 'ef they like ter fight better 'n to dance with us, they may go on fightin', but we won't put up with no sich doin's;' and the whull upshot was, we all bruk up and tuk the gals to hum, and that was the eend on't. Ondrew! I'll take a leetle suthin'! B'ys, what 'll yer drink? It's my treat now!" and they all drank round again.

"Now, Josh," continued the narrator, "as I've give my story, you and Abe sing us one o' your songs."

And two of the group, taking seats side by side and clearing their throats, sang in a nasal drawl the following, which I have robbed of its vernacular—

> Gusty the day and the lake is wroth;
> Fearful its face with its flashing froth;
> Right in our teeth are the wind and foam,
> Down in the hollow, and up on the comb;
> Onward we dash and we sing in our glee,
> Things may take care of things, what care we!

> Sun of October! how soft its glow!
> Eager the hounds and away we go!
> Sorrow is working all over the earth;
> Wrong and injustice are treading on worth;
> Up springs the deer, and we sing in our glee,
> Things may take care of things, what care we!

> Starless the midnight and bitter the cold;
> Wild through the woods is the snow-storm rolled;
> Nought that is human breathes far or nigh,
> Hark how the fierce wolf is pealing his cry!
> Still round the camp-fire, we sing in our glee,
> Things may take care of things, what care we!

I left the bar-room and strolled for an hour through a
scene of silver, shaded with ebony, visiting many of the
localities, and then retired with the music of the rapid lulling
me to slumber.

The next morning, after a warm adieu to our good host
and his kind family, and shaking Harvey's honest hand
repeatedly, I left the Lake House and its forest luxuries,
with my companion of the Whiteface visit, in a conveyance
for Keeseville by way of "The Notch."

Again I took the Elizabethtown road, and hailed as an
old acquaintance the colossal pyramid of Whiteface looming
from the woods.

At North Elba, we crossed a bridge where the Ausable
came winding down, and then followed its bank towards
the north-east, over a good hard wheel-track, generally
descending, with the thick woods almost continually around
us, and the little river shooting darts of light at us through
the leaves.

At length a broad summit, rising to a taller one, broke
above the foliage at our right, and at the same time a
gigantic mass of rock and forest saluted us upon our left—
the giant portals of the Notch. We entered. The pass
suddenly shrank, pressing the rocky river and rough road
close together. It was a chasm cloven boldly through the
flank of Whiteface. On each side towered the mountains,
but at our left, the range rose in still sublimer altitude,
with grand precipices like a majestic wall, or a line of
palisades climbing sheer from the half-way forests upward.
The crowded row of pines along the broken and
wavy crest was diminished to a fringe. The whole prospect,
except the rocks, was dark with thickest, wildest woods.
As we rode slowly through the still-narrowing gorge, the
mountains soared higher and higher, as if to scale the
clouds, presenting truly a terrific majesty. I shrank within
myself; I seemed to dwindle beneath it. Something alike
to dread pervaded the scene. The mountains appeared
knitting their stern brows into one threatening frown at

our daring intrusion into their stately solitudes. Nothing seemed native to the awful landscape but the plunge of the torrent and the scream of the eagle. Even the wild, shy deer drinking at the stream would have been out of keeping. Below, at our left, the dark Ausable dashed onward with hoarse, foreboding murmurs, in harmony with the loneliness and wildness of the spot.

We passed two miles through this sublime avenue, which at mid-day was only partially lighted from the narrow roof of sky.

At length the peak of Whiteface itself appeared above the acclivity at our left, and once emerging kept in view in misty azure. There it stood, its crest—whence I had gazed a few days before—rising like some pedestal built up by Jove or Pan to overlook his realm. The pinnacles piled about it seemed but vast steps reared for its ascent. One dark, wooded summit, a mere bulwark of the mighty mass above, showed athwart its heart a broad pale streak, either the channel of a vanished torrent, or another but far less formidable slide. The Notch now broadened, and in a rapid descent of the road the Ausable came again in view, plunging and twisting down a gorge of rocks, with the foam flung at intervals through the skirting trees. At last the pass opened into cultivated fields; the acclivities at our right wheeled away sharply east, but Whiteface yet waved along the western horizon. On we still pushed, with the river brawling at our left, and soon reached the pretty little village of Jay, and soon again The Forks, with its busy Iron Works; and, keeping the beautiful Ausable valley upon our right, we arrived by twilight at Keeseville

The mellow moonlight found me in the fine steamer, The United States, gliding homeward over Lake Champlain, delighted with my month's excursion through the Woods and Waters of the Saranacs and Racket.

APPENDIX.

SOME OF THE PRINCIPAL ROUTES

INTO THE NORTHERN WILDERNESS.

FROM EASTERN, SOUTHERN, AND WESTERN NEW YORK.

I. INTO THE CHATEAUGAY WOODS.

1st. From Plattsburgh to Dannamora State Prison, and Chazy Lake, 25 or 30 miles, over a road.
2d. From Rouse's Point to Chateaugay Four Corners and Chateaugay Lakes.

II. INTO THE SARANAC REGION.

3d. By steamboat to Port Kent (or steamboat or railroad to Burlington opposite), on Lake Champlain. Thence by post-coach to Keeseville (Essex Co.) 4 miles. From Keeseville 46 miles to Baker's Saranac Lake House, 2 miles short of the Lower Saranac Lake; or to Martin's on the bank of the Lower Saranac; or to Bartlett's, between Round Lake and Upper Saranac Lake, 13 miles from Martin's.
The Keeseville road is a good, travelled road, planked from Keeseville to Franklin Falls, 30 miles from Keeseville.
At the village of Ausable Forks, 12 miles from Keeseville, the visitor can turn off into a road, through the village of Jay, intersecting the Elizabethtown road, about 12 miles from Baker's. This road leads through the famous Whiteface, or Wilmington Notch.
4th. By steamboat to Westport on Lake Champlain. Thence to

Elizabethtown, and thence to Baker's, or Martin's, or Bartlett's. This route is about the same distance as the Keeseville route, but the road is by no means so good.

III. INTO THE ADIRONDACK, RACKET, AND HUDSON RIVER REGIONS.

From Crown Point, on Lake Champlain, to Root's, about 20 miles. From Root's to the Adirondack Lower Works, 20 miles; thence to Long Lake, 20 miles. A stage runs from Root's to Long Lake usually once a week during the summer.

From the Lower Works to Adirondack village or Upper Works, by water (through Lake Sanford), 10 or 12 miles; by road, do.

From the Upper Works to Mount Tahawus (Mount Marcy), 4 miles, and 3 miles to top.

From the Upper Works to the famous Indian Pass (the most majestic natural wonder, next to Niagara, in the State), 4 miles.

From the Indian Pass to Scott's, on the Elizabethtown road (through the woods, with scarcely a path), 7 miles; thence to Baker's (over a road), 14 miles.

6th. From Glen's Falls to Root's, over a good road, 30 miles, viz.—

From Glen's Falls to Lake George, 9 miles; thence to Warrensburgh, 6 miles; thence to Chester, 8 or 10 miles; thence to Pottersville, 6 or 8 miles; thence to Root's, and thence to Long Lake, or the Lower or the Upper Works. Or, from Pottersville to the Boreas River, 15 miles.

7th. From Carthage, in Jefferson County (by way of the Beach road), to Long Lake, 40 or 50 miles; thence to Pendleton, 10 miles; thence to Hudson River Bridge, about 5 miles; thence to the Lower Works, about 5 miles. Can drive the whole distance from Carthage to the Lower Works.

8th. From Fort Edward to Glen's Falls and Lake George; thence to Johnsburgh; thence to North Creek; thence to Eagle Lake or Tallow Lake (the middle of the three Blue Mountain Lakes). From North Creek to Eagle Lake, 20 miles.

9th. By road from Saratoga Springs to Lakes Pleasant and Piseco.

IV. INTO THE JOHN BROWN TRACT REGION.

10th. From Utica by railroad to Boonville; thence to Lyonsdale and Port Leyden, 7 miles by stage road; thence to Deacon Abby's place,

APPENDIX. 345

5¼ miles, over a good road; thence to Arnold's (over rather a poor road, although passable by wagon), 14 miles.

11th. From Utica by railroad to Boonville; thence to Booth's Mills, 11 miles, over a good wagon road; thence to Arnold's by packhorses (sent by Arnold to Booth's Mills), 14½ miles, over a bad road.

12th. From Utica by railroad to Alder Creek; thence by road to the Reservoir Lakes.

13th. From the village of Prospect (Oneida County, and reached by railroad), through Herkimer County, to Morehouse, in Hamilton County.

14th. From Ogdensburgh to Potsdam, on the Racket River, by railroad; thence to Colton by stage, 10 miles; thence to foot of the Little Bog at McEwen's, on the Racket River, 12 miles, by private conveyance, over a good road; thence by boat, 1¼ miles, to Bog Falls; then a short carry on east side of river; thence to Harris' place, 4¼ miles, opposite the mouth of the Jordan River; thence 3¼ miles, by wagon road, to John Ferry's; thence 3 miles farther on, same road, to foot of Moose Head Still Water; thence through the latter, 6 miles; thence 9 miles to Racket Pond, and thence 5 miles to Big Tupper's Lake.

THE END.

www.ingramcontent.com/pod-product-compliance
Lightning Source LLC
Chambersburg PA
CBHW020237240426
43672CB00006B/560